Contents

Preface

Welcome to your new Study Pack.

For each subject you have to study, your Study Pack consists of three elements.

- A **Course Book** (the current volume). This provides detailed coverage of all topics specified in the unit content.

- A small-format volume of **Passnotes**. For each learning objective, these highlight and summarise the key points of knowledge and understanding that should underpin an exam answer. Use your Passnotes in the days and weeks leading up to the exam.

- An extensive range of **online resources**. These include a **Quick Start Guide** (a rapid 40-page overview of the subject), practice questions of exam standard (with full suggested solutions), notes on recent technical developments in the subject area, and recent news items (ideal for enhancing your solutions in the exam). These can all be downloaded from the study resources area at www.cips.org. You will need to log in with your membership details to access this information.

For a full explanation of how to use your new Study Pack, turn now to page xiii. And good luck in your exams!

A note on style

Throughout your Study Packs you will find that we use the masculine form of personal pronouns. This convention is adopted purely for the sake of stylistic convenience – we just don't like saying 'he/she' all the time. Please don't think this reflects any kind of bias or prejudice.

October 2010

The Exam

The format of the paper

The time allowed is three hours. The examination is in two sections.

Section A – case study scenario, with two role play application questions based on the case study, each worth 25 marks.

Section B – questions to test knowledge and understanding. Candidates will be required to answer two questions from a choice of four. As with Section A, questions will be worth 25 marks each.

The unit content

The unit content is reproduced below, together with reference to the chapter in this Course Book where each topic is covered.

Unit characteristics

This unit is designed to consolidate the learning from all four units in the CIPS Foundation Diploma. This unit is designed to enable students to apply the fundamental principles of purchasing and supply in a variety of different contexts, including a range of private sector organisations, including multinationals and small/medium-sized enterprises (SMEs), plus the public sector; national and local government; the NHS; and the third sector. Students will be able to consider the procurement cycle as it applies to a diverse range of purchased products and services including raw materials, commodities, components, utilities and services, both domestically and in an international context.

This unit will tackle the different challenges faced by a wide range of organisations and sectors as they strive to achieve value for money (VFM), quality, effectiveness and competitiveness within the broader supply chain. Successful students will be able to apply sound principles of purchasing and supply management to a diverse range of sectors and organisations utilising knowledge from across all of Level 4, and will be able to employ and develop transferable best practice where appropriate.

Statements of practice

On completion of this unit, students will be able to:

*   Identify the procurement cycle as it applies to a variety of different organisations and contexts
*   Recognise the transferability of the fundamental principles of purchase and supply management
*   Appraise the need for different approaches to purchasing in differing organisations and contexts
*   Recognise good practice procurement processes and consider how they can be adapted and transferred to other contexts
*   Compare the diverse legal and regulatory environments in which procurement activity takes place
*   Discuss the ethical implications of purchasing in different contexts
*   Evaluate centralised versus decentralised purchasing structures
*   Explain how to implement requisitioning and call-off to end users in decentralised value added electronic portals (VAEs)

Learning objectives and indicative content

1.0 Understanding diverse organisations, contexts and situations
(Weighting 50%)

Chapter

1.1 Evaluate the different objectives of public, private and third sector organisations and the different environments in which they operate.

• Ownership and control	1
• Sources of finance, financial structures and governance	1
• Resource issues	1
• Legal and regulatory environments	1
• Contrasting business objectives	1
• Importance of corporate social responsibility	1

1.2 Appraise the different types of private sector organisations and the differing demands that they place on those managing the provision of goods and services.

• Different forms, including limited companies, plcs and limited liability partnerships	2
• Formation and cessation of private sector firms	2
• Regulation of private sector and impact on purchasing	2
• Impact of profit motive on purchasing activities	2
• Transactional activity such as mergers and acquisitions (M&A) together with the role of the Competition Commission	2
• Specific types of private sector organisations and influences on purchasing function: manufacturing; engineering; fast moving consumer goods (FMCG); retail; technology; services	3

1.3 Review the different types of public sector organisations and explain the variety of approaches taken to the purchase and supply of goods and services.

• Different types of public sector organisations, such as central government, local government and government agencies	1
• Regulation of public sector and impact on purchasing	1
• Concept of best value, balancing conflicting objectives and priorities	1
• Multiple forms of stakeholder and their influences	1

1.4 Review the different types of third sector organisations.

• Different types of third sector organisations	3
• Regulation of voluntary and not-for-profit organisations and impact on purchasing	3
• Importance of corporate social responsibility (CSR)	3

How to Use Your Study Pack

Familiarisation

At this point you should begin to familiarise yourself with the package of benefits you have purchased.

- Go to www.cips.org and log on. Then go to Study and Qualify/Study Resources. Browse through the free content relating to this subject.

- Download the Quick Start Guide and print it out. Open up a ring binder and make the Quick Start Guide your first item in there.

- Now glance briefly through the Course Book (the text you're reading right now!) and the Passnotes.

Organising your study

'Organising' is the key word: unless you are a very exceptional student, you will find a haphazard approach is insufficient, particularly if you are having to combine study with the demands of a full-time job.

A good starting point is to timetable your studies, in broad terms, between now and the date of the examination. How many subjects are you attempting? How many chapters are there in the Course Book for each subject? Now do the sums: how many days/weeks do you have for each chapter to be studied?

Remember:

- Not every week can be regarded as a study week – you may be going on holiday, for example, or there may be weeks when the demands of your job are particularly heavy. If these can be foreseen, you should allow for them in your timetabling.

- You also need a period leading up to the exam in which you will revise and practise what you have learned.

Once you have done the calculations, make a week-by-week timetable for yourself for each paper, allowing for study and revision of the entire unit content between now and the date of the exams.

Getting started

Aim to find a quiet and undisturbed location for your study, and plan as far as possible to use the same period each day. Getting into a routine helps avoid wasting time. Make sure you have all the materials you need before you begin – keep interruptions to a minimum.

Begin by reading through your Quick Start Guide. This should take no more than a couple of hours, even reading slowly. By the time you have finished this you will have a reasonable grounding in the subject area. You will build on this by working through the Course Book.

Using the Course Book

You should refer to the Course Book to the extent that you need it.

- If you are a newcomer to the subject, you will probably need to read through the Course Book quite thoroughly. This will be the case for most students.

- If some areas are already familiar to you – either through earlier studies or through your practical work experience – you may choose to skip sections of the Course Book.

The content of the Course Book

This Course Book has been designed to give detailed coverage of every topic in the unit content. As you will see from pages vii–xi, each topic mentioned in the unit content is dealt with in a chapter of the Course Book. For the most part the order of the Course Book follows the order of the unit content closely, though departures from this principle have occasionally been made in the interest of a logical learning order.

Each chapter begins with a reference to the learning objectives and unit content to be covered in the chapter. Each chapter is divided into sections, listed in the introduction to the chapter, and for the most part being actual captions from the unit content.

All of this enables you to monitor your progress through the unit content very easily and provides reassurance that you are tackling every subject that is examinable.

Each chapter contains the following features.

- Introduction, setting out the main topics to be covered
- Clear coverage of each topic in a concise and approachable format
- A chapter summary
- Self-test questions

The study phase

For each chapter you should begin by glancing at the main headings (listed at the start of the chapter). Then read fairly rapidly through the body of the text to absorb the main points. If it's there in the text, you can be sure it's there for a reason, so try not to skip unless the topic is one you are familiar with already.

Then return to the beginning of the chapter to start a more careful reading. You may want to take brief notes as you go along, but bear in mind that you already have your Quick Start Guide and Passnotes – there is no point in duplicating what you can find there.

Test your recall and understanding of the material by attempting the self-test questions. These are accompanied by cross-references to paragraphs where you can check your answers and refresh your memory.

Practising what you have learned

Once you think you have learned enough about the subject, or about a particular topic within the overall subject area, it's good to practise. Access the study resources at www.cips.org, and download a practice question on the relevant area. Alternatively, download a past exam question. Attempt a solution yourself before looking at our suggested solution or the Senior Assessor's comments.

Make notes of any mistakes you made, or any areas where your answer could be improved. If there is anything you can't understand, you are welcome to email us for clarification (course.books@cips.org).

The revision phase

Your approach to revision should be methodical and you should aim to tackle each main area of the unit content in turn. Begin by re-reading your Quick Start Guide. This gives an overview that will help to focus your more detailed study. Then re-read your notes and/or the separate Passnotes accompanying this Course Book. Then return to question practice. Review your own solutions to the practice questions you have had time to attempt. If there are gaps, try to find time to attempt some more questions, or at least to review the suggested solutions.

Additional reading

Your Study Pack provides you with the key information needed for each module but CIPS strongly advocates reading as widely as possible to augment and reinforce your understanding. CIPS produces an official reading list of books, which can be downloaded from the bookshop area of the CIPS website.

To help you, we have identified one essential textbook for each subject. We recommend that you read this for additional information.

The essential textbook for this unit is *Procurement Principles and Management* by P Baily, D Farmer, D Jessop and D Jones, published by FT Prentice Hall (ISBN: 978–0–69438–1).

CHAPTER 1

Purchasing in Public Sector Organisations

Chapter learning objectives

1.1   Evaluate the different objectives of public, private and third sector organisations and the different environments in which they operate.

- Ownership and control
- Sources of finance, financial structures and governance
- Resource issues
- Legal and regulatory environments
- Contrasting business objectives
- Importance of corporate social responsibility

1.3   Review the different types of public sector organisations and explain the variety of approaches taken to the purchase and supply of goods and services.

- Different types of public sector organisations, such as central government, local government and government agencies
- Regulation of public sector and impact on purchasing
- Concept of best value, balancing conflicting objectives and priorities
- Multiple forms of stakeholder and their influences

Chapter headings

1   Private and public sector organisations

2   Central government, local government and government agencies

3   The legal and regulatory environment in the public sector

4   Stakeholders in the public sector

5   Corporate social responsibility

Introduction

This module, as its title suggests, is concerned with the different contexts in which buyers carry out their functions. One important distinction is between organisations in the private sector and those in the public sector. In this chapter we look at some of the practical differences that this gives rise to, and then focus on the particular circumstances of the public sector. In the following chapter we will turn our attention to private sector organisations.

1   *Private and public sector organisations*

Definition of 'organisation'

1.1   We come across 'organisations' many times every day, and the word is very commonly used in conversation and in printed text. But how can the term be defined? What features must be present before we can say 'Yes – that is an organisation'?

1.2   In some cases the absence of a clear definition might pose no problem. For example, few people would disagree with the following examples of organisations.

- A multinational company such as General Motors
- A government department such as the Department for Work and Pensions in Britain
- A charity such as Oxfam
- A university
- A professional body such as the Chartered Institute of Purchasing and Supply.

1.3   However, the need for a definition, or for a defining list of characteristics, becomes apparent in less clear-cut cases. Consider the following examples.

- A village cricket team
- A professional football club
- A school chess club
- A self-employed plumber selling his services as a 'one-man band'
- A family unit – say, a mother and father plus two young children
- A market stall run by a family – say, a mother and father plus their two teenage children

1.4   One standard text – *Organisational Behaviour* by Andrzej Huczynski and David Buchanan – offers a broad definition of organisations: '... social arrangements for the controlled performance of collective goals'.

1.5   Huczynski and Buchanan's definition suggests that the difference between organisations and other social groupings with collective goals (the family, for example) is:

- the pre-occupation with performance;
- the need for controls to ensure that performance goals are being met.

1.6   The collective goals of a business organisation might include a wide range of objectives such as: profitability, market standing or market share, productivity (efficient use of resources), innovation or social responsibility (compliance with law, ethical values and/or community expectations). Typically, senior managers will lay down strategic objectives to provide overall purpose and direction for the long term. These must then be translated into more detailed operational objectives, providing a framework within which teams and individuals can make their short-term decisions day to day.

1.7 As social arrangements, organisations are collections of individuals who experience common membership, occupy different roles, and share common goals – but also have goals and interests of their own. Organisations are, moreover, accountable in various ways to their owners and other interested parties (or 'stakeholders') for the achievement of their stated objectives and the use of their human, financial and material resources. These twin pressures of diversity and accountability create the need to control performance.

1.8 The need for controlled performance leads in turn to features of business organisations such as: a deliberately ordered environment; the allocation of tasks (division of labour); the setting of standards and targets (planning); and the measurement of results against them (control). This implies a structure of power and responsibility relationships (whereby some individuals determine and/or oversee the work of others) and a structure of communication channels (through which instructions, reports and feedback information flow).

1.9 All these elements are features of the **formal organisation structure**.

Informal organisation

1.10 Within – or underneath – every formal organisation, there is a complex informal organisation.

1.11 Formal organisation has a well-defined, fixed structure of task-focused roles and relationships which remains stable regardless of changes of membership. Informal organisation, in contrast, is a loosely structured, spontaneous, fluctuating network of interpersonal relationships.

1.12 When people work together, they establish:

- **Social networks and groups**, the boundaries of units established by the formal organisation.

- **Informal ways of getting things done**, often different from the formal rules and procedures of the organisation.

- **Informal communication networks**, often bypassing formal communication channels. This is sometimes called the 'grapevine' or 'bush telegraph'.

- **Informal authority structures**, often different from the formal position-based scalar chain of command. Non-managerial individuals may have informal influence over their colleagues (and even over their superiors).

1.13 These informal structures may support the objectives of the formal organisation. However, there is also potential for the informal organisation to work against the objectives of the formal organisation. When employees are dissatisfied with aspects of the formal organisation, they are likely to rely more heavily on the informal organisation for information, satisfying relationships and less frustrating ways of getting things done.

1.14 Formal communication systems, in particular, benefit from the support of a positive informal network – and suffer from undermining by a negative informal network!

Networks and the virtual organisation

1.15 The term 'network organisation' refers to a looser, dynamic, more informal affiliation of autonomous and broadly equal organisations, who exchange information and pursue ongoing (typically long-term) relationships for mutual benefit.

1.16 There are no direct contractual or financial obligations (eg investment by one company in another) shaping these relationships: they are purely based on collaboration, communication, trust and mutual advantage.

1.17 A special form of the network concept is the virtual organisation, where companies (or units of a single company) collaborate, coordinate their activities and share data, using information communications technology (ICT) as their main – or only – point of contact.

1.18 Operations can be geographically dispersed, global expertise drawn on, functions outsourced and 24-hour/seven-day communication maintained – while operating (to all intents and purposes) as a single organisational entity. Tasks are typically fragmented, performed by widely dispersed individuals, but integrated by communication and data-sharing, eg via the internet – online databases, interactive websites, e-mail contact, and web-/tele-/video-conferencing. Web retailer Amazon.com is perhaps the best known virtual organisation.

1.19 The virtual organisation model is gaining popularity as an organisational structure for several reasons. Virtual organisations:

- Are supported by ongoing developments in ICT which allow data-sharing and synchronisation, interactive communication and virtual meetings (eg by webcast), across barriers of time and geographical distance

- Allow a high degree of flexibility (numerical, temporal and functional). Membership is diverse and structurally fluid enough to respond flexibly to equally diverse and changing customer/client requirements.

- Enable information and other resources to be mobilised efficiently in widely dispersed regions and specialist sectors, while allowing central control, pooled information and consistency of service and image where required

- Offer cost savings in areas such as employment (no redundancy obligations, benefits), overheads and logistics, due to the physical dispersal of (and loose contractual relationship with) members

- Exploit an increasingly knowledge-based economy, where the prime commodities are knowledge, information and expertise

- Exploit international markets, as they enable members to take advantage of local knowledge, indigenous language speakers, indigenous trading partnerships, etc.

1.20 In the rest of this chapter we concentrate on **formal organisation structures**. To begin with, we classify such organisations as belonging either to the private sector or to the public sector.

Private sector firms

1.21   A major classification of buying environment distinguishes between private sector and public sector organisations. Somewhat strangely, most of the purchasing literature concentrates on private sector firms with the public sector often being treated as an add-on.

1.22   Although there are some understandable historical reasons for this, it would be wrong to see public sector operations as merely a trivial addition to the mainstream economic activity carried out by private sector providers. On the contrary, the spending power of public sector enterprises is enormous. The sheer range of public sector service provision is staggering: roads, law and order, education, health services, emergency services, and much more.

1.23   We begin by pointing out some of the main strategic factors that influence purchasing in the private sector context, with a view to contrasting the position in public sector organisations later.

1.24   To begin at the beginning, the main influence on strategic decisions in a private sector firm is the achievement of commercial objectives. In most cases, this can be simplified further: private sector firms are profit-maximisers, and managerial decisions are assessed on the extent to which they contribute to organisational profit.

1.25   Related to this is the very strong influence of competition. In nearly all cases, a private sector firm will be one of several, or many, firms offering goods or services of a particular type. Consumers are free to choose between the offerings of different firms, and their choices of course have a dramatic impact on the revenue and profits earned by the firms concerned. Securing competitive advantage is a large step towards realising the objective of profit maximisation.

1.26   The 'constituency' served by a private sector firm is limited in number – shareholders, customers, employees, all referred to collectively as 'stakeholders' in the modern phrase. This helps the firm to be focused in its strategy: it is usually clear which outcomes will benefit the stakeholders. Moreover, all members of the constituency are there by choice. They could have invested their money elsewhere, or in the case of employees they could have offered their labour and talents elsewhere.

Public sector organisations

1.27   In all these respects, and others, public sector organisations differ from their counterparts in the private sector. The differences are well analysed by Gary J Zenz (in an American context) in *Purchasing and the Management of Materials*. His analysis forms a starting point for Table 1.1 below.

1.28   The implication so far appears to be that purchasing in the private and public sectors are two completely different disciplines. However, this is far from the truth and the differences cited above should not mask many essential similarities between the work of the public sector buyer and his private sector counterpart.

Table 1.1 *Differences between public and private sector purchasing*

Area of difference	Private sector	Public sector
Objectives	Usually, to increase profit	Usually, to achieve defined service levels
Responsibility	Buyers are responsible to directors, who in turn are responsible to shareholders	Buyers are responsible ultimately to the general public
Stakeholders	Purchasing has a defined group of stakeholders to take into account.	Purchasing has to provide value to a wider range of primary and secondary stakeholders.
Activity/process	Organisational capabilities and resources used to produce goods/services	Add value through supply of outsourced or purchased products/services. (Tend not to purchase for manufacture.)
Legal restrictions	Activities are regulated by company law, employment law, product liability law etc	Most of this applies equally to public sector, but additional regulations are present too (eg EU procurement directives)
Competition	There is usually strong competition between many different firms	There is usually no competition
Value for money	Maintain lowest cost for competitive strategy, customer value and profit maximisation.	Maintain or improve service levels within value/cost parameters.
Diversity of items	Specialised stock list for defined product/service portfolio.	Wide diversity of items/resources required to provide diverse services (eg local government authority).
Publicity	Confidentiality applies in dealings between suppliers and buyers	Confidentiality is limited because of public interest in disclosure
Budgetary limits	Investment is constrained only by availability of attractive opportunities; funding can be found if prospects are good	Investment is constrained by externally imposed spending limits
Information exchange	Private sector buyers do not exchange information with other firms, because of confidentiality and competition	Public sector buyers are willing to exchange notes and use shared e-purchasing platforms, consolidate purchases etc.
Procurement policies procedures	Tend to be organisation-specific. Private sector buyers can cut red tape when speed of action is necessary	Tend to follow legislative directives. Public sector buyers are often constrained to follow established procedures
Supplier relationships	Emphasis on long-term partnership development where possible, to support value chain.	Compulsory competitive tendering: priority to cost minimisation and efficiency, at the expense of partnership development.

1.29   One reason for this is that differences in objectives, organisational constraints and so on may not necessarily lead to differences in procedure. For example, public sector buyers may not be seeking to maximise profit, but their concern to achieve value for money is stimulated by other influences, equally strong; in particular, the public sector buyer must achieve a defined level of service within a defined budget.

1.30   Similarly, the private sector buyer faced with a profit objective will identify customer satisfaction as a key criterion in meeting the objective. But equally, the public sector buyer will work in an environment where providing a quality service so as to delight 'customers' is an essential part of the organisational ethos. Often this commitment is evidenced by a customers' charter such as has been produced by such organisations as HM Revenue and Customs in the UK. Buyers in both environments will be concerned to a large extent with ensuring quality of output by influencing the quality of inputs.

1.31   Differences between public and private sector should not be overemphasised. An article in *Procurement Professional* recently noted that: 'key issues for the procurement profession… are as relevant for the public sector as they are for the private sector… Work is currently underway in public sectors around the world to address these issues, centred on:

- Developing standards for the assessment and ongoing development of public procurement professionals
- The greater application of strategic sourcing principles to public procurement
- The development and application of strategic procurement as a methodology that aligns strategic sourcing, supplier development and organisational strategic planning into a management mechanism and
- E-procurement systems.'

1.32   In addition, improving customer service and reducing cost inefficiencies to maximise value for money are now priorities in both sectors!

1.33   It is easy to see that many skills used by purchasing staff are as valuable in the public sector as in the private sector. Here are some examples.

- Knowledge of purchasing systems
- Methods of efficiently handling low-value orders
- IT skills
- Inventory management skills
- Knowledge of procurement management and structures
- Ability to negotiate on cost
- Experience of electronic trading
- Experience in drafting contracts
- Knowledge of risk management techniques
- Experience in competitive tendering
- Experience in supplier rationalisation
- Knowledge of ethical sourcing and corporate social responsibility

1.34   Even where differences between public and private sector did once exist they are much less apparent now than before. An important reason for this in the UK has been successive governments' strong commitment to introducing private sector disciplines into public sector organisations during the 1980s and 1990s, a policy which by and large continues today.

1.35   In some cases, the effects of this have been radical. Many previously public organisations have been privatised (for example the landline telecommunications industry). It is true that privatised monopolies remain subject to surveillance, but in all essential respects they function like any private sector organisation, and have to face up alone to competition from new technology.

1.36   In some cases, the political changes have led to public sector bodies becoming even more 'commercial' than private sector firms. This is the case for example in relation to competitive tendering. For a private sector concern the decision to use competitive tendering or not is exactly that: a decision. In most public sector contexts, no decision arises: use of competitive tendering is compulsory.

Areas of difference between public and private sector organisations

1.37   This last point gives rise to an important question concerning supplier relations. Modern approaches to supplier relations strongly emphasise the value of long-term partnerships between a buyer and a limited number of suppliers. Competitive tendering retains an important place in the buyer's portfolio of techniques, but is not generally suitable in relation to materials for which long-term partnerships are sought. The public sector buyer, constrained to use competitive tendering in all cases, therefore finds that the benefits of long-term partnership are unattainable.

1.38   Differences between public sector and private sector buying also arise from the question of **accountability**. As we have noted already, the stakeholders in a public service are more diverse than those of a private firm. Buyers in the public sector may be required to account for their actions to a wide constituency, most of whose members are entirely unknown quantities as far as managers in the public service are concerned. One effect of this is an insistence on detailed procedures and record keeping: it may be difficult later to justify a course of action which breaches defined procedures or which is poorly documented.

1.39   **Budgetary control** is another area where differences surface. The demand for funds in a private sector firm is limited, in that only some projects are commercially attractive. Other projects are not regarded as viable because, for example, they do not meet criteria for return on capital. In the public sector, by contrast, the demand for funds is limitless: no taxpayer ever complains that too much of a service is provided.

1.40   Another aspect of budgetary control concerns **cash limits**. A public sector buyer may enjoy less flexibility than his private sector counterpart. For example, a buyer in the private sector may weigh up the advantages and disadvantages of a bulk discount from a supplier. The public sector buyer probably has no option: if the bulk purchase would take him outside his budget he must forgo the discount.

1.41   Another difference is in the sheer **diversity** of items that may be purchased by a public sector organisation, which of course is related to the diversity of services it provides. Consider a local government authority in the UK: it may be a purchaser of construction materials for use in housing or road maintenance, of dustbin lorries for refuse collection, of sporting equipment for a community leisure centre, and much more. While large manufacturing organisations may purchase many thousands of different stock items, the diversity in their stock ranges will hardly compare with this.

1.42 Finally, difficult issues arise in connection with **specifications** in public sector buying. No matter how detailed a specification may be, there will always be areas of ambiguity, areas where slightly different approaches may be valid within the terms of the specification. Interpreting these 'grey areas' is a delicate matter, but in the private sector suppliers have a strong incentive to interpret them in a way that leads to perfect satisfaction on the part of the buyer. If they do not do so, the buyer will simply cross them off his list of possible suppliers for the future.

1.43 The considerations are different when a supplier acts in accordance with a public sector tender. Failure to provide complete satisfaction may lead to discontent on the part of the buyer, but he is not free simply to cross the supplier off his approved list. This is only possible if the supplier has demonstrably failed, but this will rarely be the case when any ambiguity was present in the specification.

Back to basics

1.44 We return briefly to the main reason for differences between public sector and private sector buying: the issue of overall organisational objectives. In the private sector, the objective of maximising profits is paramount, and means that there is a fairly simple guiding principle for managerial actions. Within reasonable limits (those imposed by ethical behaviour, for example) anything that improves profitability is good news; anything that reduces it is bad news.

1.45 In the public sector the situation is much more complicated. Andrew Cox has coined the term 'contested goals' to highlight the point that public sector organisations pursue many different objectives, which may not always be compatible with each other. For example, social objectives may include protection of property, law and order, equality of opportunity, improvements to education, and protection of the old and infirm. Economic objectives may include increasing overall financial wellbeing, redistribution of wealth, regional economic development, and so on. This diversity of objectives makes it much more difficult in the public sector to follow a single guiding principle.

1.46 Naturally, the existence of multiple objectives makes it impossible to satisfy every legitimate aspiration of the public sector's 'customers'. Managers therefore need to prioritise, and they must do so in line with policy decided upon by government. The government monitor the activities of public sector bodies to ensure that this is done. For example, the National Audit Office scrutinises public spending on behalf of Parliament, with a programme of regular reviews covering central government departments and a wide range of other public bodies. The Audit Commission performs a similar role in relation to local government authorities.

2 Central government, local government and government agencies

Central government

2.1 The UK is a constitutional monarchy, with the Crown (ie the reigning King or Queen) as head of state. All acts of government are carried out in the name of the Crown. However, although the reigning monarch has the right to advise, the right to encourage and the right to warn the government, there is no right to dictate government policy.

2.2   The main legislative body for the UK is Parliament, based at Westminster. Parliament is **bicameral**, that is to say it consists of two separate chambers: the House of Commons and the House of Lords. The country is divided into constituencies, each of which is represented by a member of parliament. The MP for each constituency is voted into office by those residents of the constituency who are eligible to vote. The MP then represents his constituents in the House of Commons.

2.3   A general election of MPs is held at intervals of, at most, five years. The party with most members elected to the House of Commons will form the government, and the leader of that party will be the Prime Minister. The Prime Minister will select other MPs of his own party to take responsibility for the major departments of state (defence, home affairs, foreign affairs, the Treasury, education, health, etc). These key individuals make up the Cabinet, which is the major policy-forming body in the country. The Cabinet meets regularly to discuss critical areas of policy.

2.4   Each minister is supported by a large staff of civil servants. These are non-political, and are not subject to election. They are charged with assisting government in the formulation and implementation of policy. They provide impartial advice to MPs of all parties, though in practice their main duties will be dictated by the party currently in power.

2.5   Membership of the House of Lords is not subject to election, and instead is mostly hereditary. The House of Lords plays a significant part in shaping policy and enacting legislation, but in the last resort it is the House of Commons that has supreme legislative power.

2.6   Although Parliament is a sovereign body, with overall power to enact legislation, in practice there are many bodies which have an interest in influencing this process. Often such bodies make concerted efforts (a process called **lobbying**) to ensure that their opinions are heard by MPs with power to assist them.

Local government in the UK

2.7   The machinery needed to run a modern democracy is not all concentrated in a single centre of power. Parliament devolves much authority to local councils. These comprise both elected officials, usually voted for by their constituents on party lines, and career bureaucrats (similar in principle to the MPs and civil servants of central government).

2.8   As with central government, much local policy is influenced by the activities of lobby groups.

2.9   In recent years, the Parliament at Westminster has also granted powers to parliamentary assemblies in Scotland, Wales and Northern Ireland. These assemblies have come into being largely to accommodate a desire for self-government among these communities. However, in crucial areas such as defence and foreign policy, the Parliament at Westminster has reserved all powers for itself.

Government agencies

2.10   In addition to the bodies already mentioned, there is a large number of organisations pursuing public work, with or without the guidance of the government. For example, the Child Support Agency was run as a private business, but with targets developed under government guidelines relating to parents who are failing to support their children. (In 2008 the CSA was replaced by the Child Maintenance and Enforcement Commission, CMEC.) And numerous advisory bodies (often referred to as 'quangos' – quasi-autonomous non-governmental organisations) work in areas such as National Health Service trusts.

Financing the public sector

2.11   To provide public sector services we naturally require finance. Where does this come from?

2.12   All sources of public sector income derive ultimately from the tax payer. Funds are collected in various different forms: direct taxes (ie taxes on income, such as the corporation tax paid by companies and the income tax paid by individuals); indirect taxes (ie taxes on expenditure, such as value added tax and excise duties); local taxes (such as council tax and business rates).

2.13   In the UK, most of this income is collected by central government (though some of it, such as council tax, is collected by local authorities). It is the task of government, and specifically the Treasury department, to then distribute the income for use on the purposes prioritised by government policy.

2.14   Government agencies too (such as the CMEC already mentioned) are provided with funds by central government for spending on their allotted responsibilities. In some cases, such agencies act as industry regulators, and when this happens, another source of their income comes from levies on the companies operating in that sector.

2.15   Where funds are collected locally (eg council tax) they are also spent locally on such services as law and order, waste disposal etc.

Purchasing in the public sector

2.16   Spending in the public sector must comply with detailed legal regulations (see next section of this chapter). All spending decisions are subject to detailed scrutiny. Invariably a distinction is made between capital expenditure (such as constructing a new public leisure centre) and current expenditure (such as the ongoing running costs of a leisure centre).

2.17   Setting budgets for public spending begins with the Chancellor of the Exchequer, who sets overall revenue-raising and spending priorities. The budgets of public sector organisations must be set within the framework that this provides.

2.18   As mentioned already, scrutiny of expenditure is carried out by the National Audit Office (who deal with central government departments) and the Audit Commission (who deal with local government authorities).

Public sector supply chain drivers

2.19 In contrast to the profit focus of private sector concerns, public sector organisations have a primary orientation to achieving defined service levels: providing efficient and effective services (education, transport, healthcare) and utilities (water, power) to the public, often within defined budgetary constraints and environmental/sustainability strategies. This less intensely competitive environment allows greater information exchange, best-practice sharing and collaborative/consolidated buying and supply arrangements, such as shared e-procurement platforms and buying groups.

2.20 The range of stakeholders in public sector organisations is more diverse, including funding and user groups. This creates a more complex network of stakeholder expectations, relationships and accountabilities to be managed. A much wider diversity of items/services may also be purchased and supplied: consider a local government authority in the UK, which may be a purchaser of construction materials for use in housing or road maintenance, of dustbin lorries for refuse collection, of sporting equipment for a community leisure centre, and much more.

2.21 Public sector procurement (and therefore the relationships within the supply chain) are governed by EU Directives in areas such as the compulsory use of competitive bidding, the use of e-auctions, ethical requirements (eg in regard to gifts and hospitality) and public interest disclosure of information (limiting the confidentiality of the dealings between buyers and suppliers).

2.22 **Compulsory competitive tendering**, in particular, has a strong influence on supply chain management. It is designed to ensure fair, non-discriminatory and competitive supplier selection, based on equality of access to tender information, selection of suppliers based on clear price (and non-price) criteria, and accountability for decisions (including feedback to unsuccessful bidders). It also supports public sector efficiency targets by maximising value-for-money purchasing. However, it also limits long-term supply chain collaborations, and the benefits that accrue from them. Particular efforts may have to be made to include relational compatibility (eg potential for EDI links) in tender criteria and to develop partnership during the period of the contract (eg for continuous improvement of quality).

Defence procurement

2.23 Defence procurement takes place in a very complicated environment, with multiple stakeholders and agencies, commercial organisations (as contractors and suppliers), a high degree of change and uncertainty (in regard to the nature and severity of threats to be faced), fast paced technological development, extremely high costs – and a range of political, social and economic pressures. In this environment, ineffective supply chains not only cost commercial or military advantage, but lives!

2.24 Following a major overhaul in the form of the Strategic Defence Review (SDR), the UK Ministry of Defence (MOD) has introduced a 'smart acquisition strategy', the key features of which are illustrated by *Baily et al* as follows: Figure 1.1.

Figure 1.1 *Smart defence acquisition strategy*

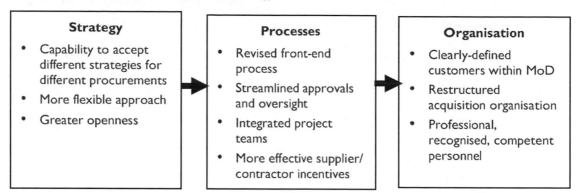

2.25 The old organisation of defence procurement frequently failed because it lacked clear customer focus and integration: the system was broken up into linked but separate phases, managed separately within the MOD. In order to facilitate a more efficient through-life management approach, the SDR created clear customer groups.

- Central Customer One: those concerned with the capability required of the armed forces (specification)

- Customer Two: the customer for the equipment when it is in service (support). This group ensures that equipment is supported with consumables, maintenance, transport and so on (the Defence Logistics Organisation)

These are serviced (and co-ordinated) by the Defence Procurement Agency, using integrated project teams (IPTs).

2.26 In addition, relationships with industry contractors and suppliers are more relaxed and open, 'based on principles of partnering and the identification of common goals and opportunities for gain-share that is underpinned by competitive contractor selection if this will provide value for money'.

Health services procurement

2.27 The UK National Health Service has similarly been through major reforms, the key effect of which has perhaps been to bring the provision of services more into line with the needs of customers (ultimately, the patients), by introducing a clearer separation between those who provide the services and those who purchase them. Specialists in District Health Authorities, and doctors in practices which have been granted fundholder status (with responsibility for their own budgets), have taken on responsibility for procurement. This also has the effect of introducing competition, purchasing disciplines and control over the use of resources.

2.28 The 'internal market' is regarded as a mechanism to apply pressure for greater effectiveness in meeting patient needs, and to increase efficiency and accountability in the use of limited resources (particularly since demand is growing on a year-by-year basis, partly because of demographic trends such as population ageing). With the introduction of competitive tendering and market testing, the internal 'direct service organisation' is treated as a contractor, separate from the 'client' for whom the service is provided, and in competition with alternative providers.

3 The legal and regulatory environment in the public sector

Regulatory bodies in the public sector

3.1 To ensure that taxpayers' money is well spent, there are a number of regulatory bodies operating in the public sector. As an example, we cite the work of Ofsted (The Office for Standards in Education).

3.2 Ofsted operates a system of inspection and regulation designed to ensure that schools and colleges in England provide a high standard of education and care. The organisation is a non-ministerial government department accountable to Parliament. This independence from the government in power is designed to ensure impartiality in the conduct of the department.

3.3 The activities of Ofsted include the following (which are typical of the work carried out by public sector regulators).

- Highlighting and advising on best practice
- Reviewing and evaluating government strategies
- Publication of evidence-based findings
- Helping parents to make informed choices about schools and colleges

The impact of regulation on public sector procurement

3.4 Public sector regulators are intended to ensure compliance with defined standards. For example, a buyer in the public sector must ensure that the goods he purchases match up to all public standards and specifications (as well as, obviously, matching up to the specification generated by the buyer himself). This includes compliance with relevant health and safety standards, not just in the products purchased, but in the entire purchase process (eg compliance with manual handling regulations in the delivery and handling of the goods).

3.5 The public sector buyer must also comply with relevant environmental standards.

3.6 The public sector buyer is subject to a high level of accountability. He must ensure that appropriate processes have been followed to acquire best value for the taxpayers' money he is responsible for, and must equally ensure that a full 'audit trail' exists so that his actions and decisions can be vetted.

3.7 The public sector buyer must ensure that appropriate service levels are achieved in the provision of services to members of the public.

The effects of European procurement directives

3.8 EU procurement directives are an important influence on the activities of buyers in the public sector. Their principal objective is to promote free, open and non-discriminatory competition within the EU.

3.9 Once a buyer has specified the product or service he requires, and has decided to use the tendering method, he must ensure that he complies with EU directives. These do not apply to private sector buying, but do cover purchases by public authorities unless their value is below a certain (low) threshold.

3.10 Subject to certain exceptions, the directives require public bodies to use open tendering procedures. They must advertise the invitation to tender according to defined rules designed to secure maximum publicity.

3.11 The contract notice advertising the requirement must be published in the Supplement to the European Journal before it may be published in any other media.

3.12 Contracting authorities have the choice of four contract award procedures: open, restricted, negotiated and competitive dialogue.

- For the **open procedure** there is no requirement for pre-qualification of suppliers. Tenders must be issued within six days of request by a prospective bidder. The contracting authority must set the closing date for receipt of tenders no less than 52 days from the publication of the contract notice.

- For the **restricted procedure**, pre-qualification of suppliers is permitted but the contracting authority must indicate in the contract notice a pre-determined range of suppliers to whom tenders will be sent. This must be not less than 5 and no more than 20. The contract notice must allow a minimum of 37 days for prospective bidders to register an interest and submit the required information for pre-qualification.

- Under the **negotiated procedure** where a contract notice is required, prospective bidders must be given a minimum of 37 days to register their interest to negotiate. Where there is a sufficient number of persons who are suitable to be selected to negotiate, the number selected must not be less than three.

- The **competitive dialogue** complements the existing open, restricted and negotiated procedures. It is intended to be used for large complex projects in circumstances where, currently, the use of the negotiated procedure might be considered.

3.13 In general, buyers are obliged to award the contract on the basis of the lowest quoted price, or on the basis of the economically most advantageous tender. If they choose the latter alternative, they must make the fact known to candidates, and must explain by what criteria they mean to assess 'economic advantage'. The purchaser is allowed to exclude firms if they fail to meet defined criteria relating to general suitability, financial and economic standing and technical competence.

3.14 The results of the tendering procedure must be notified to the Office of Official Publications of the European Communities, and will then be made public.

3.15 Unsuccessful bidders have the right to a **debrief**, if they so request. This must be undertaken within 48 days of the unsuccessful bidder's request.

3.16 The public sector buyer is subject to a high level of accountability. He must ensure that appropriate processes have been followed to acquire best value for the taxpayers' money he is responsible for, and must equally ensure that a full 'audit trail' exists so that his actions and decisions can be vetted. The public sector buyer must ensure that appropriate service levels are achieved in the provision of services to members of the public. These objectives are thought to be best achieved by an insistence on competitive tendering (unless the contracts are very small).

3.17   Other objectives of the directives include the following.

- To open up the choice of potential suppliers to public sector bodies, so reducing costs
- To open up new, non-discriminatory and competitive markets for suppliers
- To ensure free movement of goods and services within the EU
- To ensure that public sector bodies award contracts efficiently and without discrimination

3.18   The main means by which a breach of the directives may be remedied are by an action by an aggrieved supplier or contractor against a purchaser, or an action against them by a member state in the European Court of Justice.

3.19   The remedies include the following possibilities.

- Suspension of an incomplete contract award procedure
- Setting aside of a decision in an incomplete contract award procedure
- An award of damages (in cases where a contract has already been entered)

3.20   This regime of compulsory open tendering has certain disadvantages. All vendors are aware that a large number of bids are likely to be made, and this may deter some suitable applicants. Moreover, since very little prequalification of vendors is allowed under the directives, it is likely also that some will take risks in attempting to undercut potential rivals. The result may be a contract awarded at a price that gives no incentive to high quality performance. Finally, there is of course a great administrative burden on the purchaser who is faced with a large number of tenders to evaluate.

Buying consortia

3.21   One specialised aspect of public sector buying will be briefly mentioned here: the use of 'buying consortia' in local government authorities in the UK. (We say more about the general topic of consortium buying in Chapter 5.)

3.22   Many local authorities have centralised their purchasing activities, despite the very diverse range of materials and services that such an organisation requires. Usually this is accompanied by a centralised stores procedure under which the many different user departments order all or most of their requirements from a single source within the local authority.

3.23   Once such a centralised system is in place it is logical to ask whether it can serve more organisations than just one. This thinking has been pressed to its logical conclusion by certain groups of local authorities who have banded together to form buying consortia. The idea is that by combining their purchasing 'muscle' they can achieve more favourable terms from suppliers than would be available to any one of them singly.

4   *Stakeholders in the public sector*

Goal-setting

4.1   In comparison with the private sector, much less has been written about the application of strategic planning and goal-setting in the public sector and it is a great deal more difficult to define goals than for the private sector.

4.2   Probably the only generalisations that can be made are 'the provision of the best possible service at the least possible cost' or 'the maximisation of national welfare'. However, these generalisations are too sweeping to be of much practical use and the circumstances of the many different public sector organisations differ so widely that any more specific goals will also differ widely. In the Health Service, if more people become ill, more must be treated, but perhaps the very long-term goal should be a **reduction** in numbers, on the principle that 'prevention is better than cure'.

4.3   However goal setting processes are as appropriate for the public sector as the private. The problems experienced by many public sector organisations can be explained largely by conflicting goals. The goals of hospitals, schools and local government are often a mixture of service to the community, maintenance of standards, and minimising costs. The relative importance of each goal may differ depending on the interest group, and the extent to which their values differ.

Stakeholder theory

4.4   To discover the current goals, and appropriate future goals, of a public swimming pool (say) would require investigation of the needs, aspirations, values and expectations of different groups of people associated with the leisure/sports facility. The organisation is really a coalition of several groups, each giving and seeking different things from it. It is possible to think of such needs or expectations in terms of formally expressed objectives, and argue that these act as a focus for decision making in the organisation by providing a yardstick against which to measure performance or assess alternative proposals.

4.5   **Stakeholder theory** maintains that the objective of an organisation should be derived by balancing the often conflicting claims of the various stakeholders (or interest groups) in the organisation. The swimming pool providers have responsibilities to all these groups and need to formulate their strategic goals so as to give each a measure of satisfaction.

4.6   It is a balancing act between conflicting needs and priorities. For example, there might be conflict between meeting the swimming-pool needs of general users and specialist groups. If the strategy of the swimming pool providers is to reflect a correct balance of the interests of these stakeholders the planner will need to consider:

- the composition and significance of each group
- the legitimate claims that each group may have on the swimming pool
- the degree to which these claims are in conflict
- the extent to which the swimming pool is already satisfying claims
- the overall mission of the swimming pool.

4.7   Table 1.2 shows the separate groups who have stakes in the swimming pool, their reasons for interest and their different expectations. We assume that the pool is a municipal one run by Kenshire County Council. Notice that some of the stakeholders can be classified as 'internal' – eg the manager and staff – while others are 'external' – eg the county council.

Table 1.2 *Swimming pool stakeholders*

Stakeholder	Reason for interest	Expectations
Sports Council	Provide grant	Safety standards Customer mix Financial viability
Kenshire County Council	Provide funds 'Voice' of local community	Financial viability Breadth of appeal Customer mix Prestige
Manager	Management decisions	Number of customers Excess of income over expenditure
Staff	Employees	Remuneration Job security Job satisfaction
Education committee	Education	Education service
Clubs and associations	Special interest	Tailor-made services

4.8   Once the set of objectives are agreed on for the swimming pool, the managers of the facility would be ready to move on to the detailed work of strategy formulation and budgeting.

4.9   Stakeholder groups can apply pressure to influence organisations in different ways and to different degrees.

- Managers exercise direct influence (formal authority or power) over planning, organisation and control. They may also exercise informal power through leadership/charisma, influencing skills (eg in negotiation), or the exercise of discretion when implementing strategy.

- Staff members may have power through control over the labour resource or through specialist knowledge or skills (expert power) to influence human resource management policy and task performance.

- Customers are (in a 'marketing oriented' business) the focus of all organisational planning and activity.

- Supply chain partners have the ability to influence supply, quality, value addition, costs and pricing decisions, efficient flow-to-market, and therefore competitive advantage. They have power through control of strategic resources, expertise (eg subcontractors), influence on strategy implementation – and perhaps interpersonal influence with managers.

- Government has the power to constrain organisational activity by legislation and regulation – and so on.

4.10 All these influences may impact on the structure, systems, policies and values of the organisation – and individual functions such as purchasing and supply. The more influence a stakeholder has, the more likely it is that managers will have to take that stakeholder's needs and wants into account.

4.11 Note that stakeholders' influence is not just about power to get their needs met: stakeholders also make a contribution to the organisation's needs and objectives. (This is often what gives them influence: they have the power to give, or withhold, something the organisation wants.) Stakeholder management is effectively a mutual exchange of benefits: a marketing process. So for example, in an ideal situation:

- Regulators fulfil the organisation's need for reliable, cost-effective guidance – which enables the organisation to fulfil the regulator's need for safe, equitable, truthful, sustainable business.

- Suppliers fulfil the organisation's need for reliable, cost-effective goods/services – which enables the organisation to fulfil its suppliers' needs for ongoing business, profit and growth.

- Employees fulfil the organisation's need for skills, knowledge, commitment and labour hours – which enables the organisation to fulfil its employees' need for job security, livelihood, development and so on.

(You should be able to match needs/wants like this for each stakeholder group.) In practice, however, stakeholder and organisational objectives do not always coincide, and potential conflict must be managed.

4.12 In addition to 'organisational stakeholders' in general, each function, unit and project of an organisation may be said to have stakeholders, whose needs and influence must be taken into account. You should be able to identify the key stakeholders in the purchasing function, from each of the categories listed. The most obvious ones may be purchasing managers; employees; line managers on whose behalf purchases are made or to whom purchasing advice/policy is directed; suppliers; distributors; third-party service providers (eg logistics); and regulators (eg on public sector purchasing or health and safety).

4.13 Stakeholder management recognises the need to take stakeholders into account when formulating strategies and plans. For a purchasing manager, it may be helpful in several ways. It enables you to gain expert input from stakeholders at the planning stage of a project, to improve the quality of your decisions. Stakeholders are more likely to 'own' and support plans to which they have had input: this will make ongoing collaboration easier. Gaining the support of powerful stakeholders may, in turn, mobilise power and resources within the organisation in support of your plans. At the very least, sources of resistance to your plans (from stakeholders whose goals are different from or incompatible with yours) can be anticipated and planned for.

5 *Corporate social responsibility*

Social responsibilities of organisations

5.1   Ethical issues are increasingly a concern to organisations as public opinion emphasises the need for large enterprises to be good 'corporate citizens'. There are important issues which face an individual organisation as it formulates strategies and policies about how it interacts with its various stakeholders.

5.2   Some of these matters will be covered by legislative and regulatory requirements, and/or professional codes of practice.

- Legislative requirements include, for example, an employer's duty to provide a safe and healthy workplace (Health and Safety at Work Act) and the various legal protections afforded to employees by successive Employment Acts.
- Regulatory requirements include, for example, those laid down by specific industry regulators such as Ofcom for the communications industry, the Competition Commission (regulating merger and acquisition activity), and the Advertising Standards Authority (regulating media advertising).
- Professional codes of practice include, for example, the ethical codes published by such bodies as the Chartered Institute of Purchasing and Supply and the Institute of Chartered Accountants in England and Wales. Members of these bodies are obliged to comply with the rules they lay down.

5.3   Some organisations may have a 'compliance based' approach to ethics which strives merely to uphold these minimal requirements. However, the term 'corporate social responsibility' (CSR) covers policies which the organisation adopts for the good and wellbeing of stakeholders, taking a more proactive 'integrity based' approach.

5.4   Although corporate objectives may primarily be financial, many firms now also set social responsibility objectives, in relation to matters such as the following.

- Sustainability issues: the conservation and perpetuation of the world's limited natural resources (eg by limiting greenhouse gas emissions)
- Environmental issues: the reduction of environment pollution, waste management, the avoidance of environmental disfigurement, land reclamation, promoting recycling, energy conservation and so on
- Ethical trading, business relationships and development: consumer protection, improvement of working (and social) conditions for employees and subcontractors (particularly in developing nations), avoidance of exploitation, debt minimisation, contribution to local communities and so on.

Why should an organisation set CSR objectives?

5.5   Milton Friedman and Elaine Sternberg have argued the view that 'the social responsibility of business is profit maximisation': to give a return on shareholders' investment. Spending funds on objectives not related to shareholder expectations is irresponsible: regard for shareholder wealth is a healthy discipline for management, providing accountability for decisions. The public interest is served by profit maximisation, because the State levies taxes.

5.6   'Consequently,' argued Friedman, 'the only justification for social responsibility is enlightened self interest' on the part of a business organisation. So how does CSR serve the interest of the firm?

5.7   Law, regulation and Codes of Practice impose certain social responsibilities on organisations (eg in relation to health and safety, employment protection, consumer rights and environmental care). There are financial and operational penalties for failure to comply (eg 'polluter pays' taxes).

- Voluntary measures (which may in any case only pre-empt legal and regulatory requirements) may enhance corporate image and build a positive brand.

- Above-statutory provisions for employees and suppliers may be necessary to attract, retain and motivate them to provide quality service and commitment — particularly in competition with other employers/purchasers.

- Increasing consumer awareness of social responsibility issues creates a market demand for CSR (and the threat of boycott for irresponsible firms)

5.8   However, business also needs to remember the 'enlightened' part of the equation! Profit maximisation does not, by itself, always lead to ethical behaviour — as examples of environmental and human exploitation show. (High-profile past examples include: environmental degradation caused by Shell oil refineries in Nigeria; child labour used by Nike and other Western clothing manufacturers; fraudulent reporting by Enron...)

5.9   In addition, Henry Mintzberg notes that a business's relationship with society is not purely economic: a business is an open social system which makes a variety of non-economic exchanges with the society in which it operates (people, information/knowledge, image), and creates a variety of non-economic impacts. Social responsibility helps to create a social climate and infrastructure in which the business can prosper in the long term.

The CIPS commitment to corporate social responsibility (CSR)

5.10   The CIPS president for 2005, Ian Taylor, made CSR the theme of his year of office. The importance of the topic for CIPS members is underlined by the amount of material published by the Institute on its website. In particular, the Institute has published a comprehensive White Paper, *Corporate Social Responsibility*. The discussion below is a summarised version of the White Paper.

5.11   According to CIPS, CSR is important to all organisations for the following reasons.

- Enhancing stakeholder value
- Helping to increase reputation
- Ensuring increased knowledge of supply, enabling minimum risks from suppliers

5.12   The White Paper highlights concerns such as the use of child labour and sweatshops in the supply chains of many organisations. These are argued to have had an adverse impact on share prices, brand equity, staff morale and media profiles.

5.13   The Institute specifically encourages members to consider the long-term implications of their actions and to question objectives that may unintentionally have negative socioeconomic consequences.

Definitions of CSR

5.14   The White Paper cites a number of attempts to define or explain CSR.

*   CSR places a company's social and environmental impacts in the context of its obligations to society. It promotes the integration of stakeholder issues into business operations. CSR makes company values come alive (values such as accountability, transparency, ethics, respect, integrity and humanity).

*   CSR is concerned with treating the stakeholders of the firm ethically or in a responsible manner.

*   CSR is about how companies manage the business processes to produce an overall positive impact on society.

*   The commitment of business to contribute to sustainable economic development, working with their employees, the local community and society at large to improve their quality of life, in ways that are good for business and good for development.

Key areas of CSR for purchasing professionals

5.15   The White Paper identifies the following key areas of CSR.

*   Environmental responsibility
*   Human rights
*   Equal opportunities
*   Diversity
*   Corporate governance
*   Sustainability
*   Impact on society
*   Ethics and ethical trading
*   Biodiversity

5.16   **Environmental responsibility** is not just desirable for moral and ethical reasons, but is also increasingly addressed by legal regulations (for example, the EU Environment Liability Directive).

5.17   **Human rights** refers to such issues as child labour, working conditions, wages and exploitation. Organisations are increasingly aware that they can influence such issues, not just in their home countries but also in areas of the world from which they source supplies.

5.18   **Equal opportunities** have been the subject of legislation in the UK since at least 1976, and the Race Relations (Amendment) Act 2000 outlaws discrimination in all business functions. Purchasing professionals must be aware of the need for equal opportunities both in terms of the products and services produced, and in terms of the supply base (the issue of diversity, see next paragraph).

5.19   **Diversity** of suppliers means the structuring of the supply base in such a way as not to discriminate against minorities. Many organisations in both the public and private sectors are adopting supplier diversity programmes, which foster economic growth.

5.20   **Corporate governance** has come to prominence in the wake of some well publicised company failures. Terms and conditions agreed with suppliers may cover such areas as limiting the organisation's exposure to unnecessary risk, putting in place measures to control the circumstances under which risk will be borne, and positioning the organisation with regard to ethical matters such as CSR.

5.21 **Sustainability** means living in ways that do not compromise the wellbeing of future generations. Purchasing professionals can help in this area by ensuring appropriate policies both within their own organisations, and by encouraging similar practices among their suppliers.

5.22 **Impact on society** is an increasingly important area of concern for purchasing professionals and for top corporate management. The White Paper distinguishes between the forward linkages and backward linkages that can affect an organisation's impact on society.

- In its backward linkages an organisation should be concerned about the conditions and wages provided by their suppliers, particularly those in third world countries.

- In its forward linkages an organisation should be concerned about how, further down the supply chain, their products are disposed of or recycled.

5.23 **Ethical trading** has increasingly come into prominence in recent years. How can organisations reconcile their obligations to shareholders – above all, their obligation to achieve the maximum possible profit and capital growth – with broader standards of ethical behaviour? For example, is it permissible for an organisation to keep labour costs down by exploiting poorly paid workers in third-world countries?

5.24 The overwhelming opinion in most modern organisations is that the answer to this question is 'No'. Responsible companies believe that their obligations to maximise profits should not be fulfilled at the price of unfair exploitation. It is interesting to look at why this opinion has become the prevalent one.

5.25 One reason is simply the increasing thought that has gone into the issue. When companies were locally based, such problems were either non-existent or at least less pressing. Now that the world economy is increasingly dominated by multinational corporations the issue can no longer be ducked.

5.26 Arising from this, corporations are influenced by the sheer strength of public opinion. Members of the public, though they may well hold shares in companies, do not have day-to-day responsibilities for profit-maximising strategies. Free from this constraint, they look with repugnance on activities that seem to violate basic human rights. Responsible organisations have to take account of public opinion, because ultimately it is members of the public who pay for their products.

5.27 **Biodiversity** has been defined as 'the total variety of life on Earth'. In principle, most people support the idea of preserving diversity of habitats, genetic profiles and species. It is a responsibility of organisations to minimise any adverse impact on these areas.

Chapter summary

- An organisation is a social arrangement for the controlled performance of collective goals. Within – or underneath – every formal organisation there is a complex informal organisation.

- A major classification of buying environment distinguishes between organisations in the private sector and those in the public sector.

- There are important differences between the private sector and public sector environments, in terms of: objectives, ownership and control, legal and regulatory control, competition, publicity, budgetary limits, sources of finance, information exchange, and defined procedures.

- Public sector organisations include (amongst others) central government departments, local government authorities, and government agencies.

- Finance for the public sector comes ultimately from the taxpayer.

- Buyers in the public sector are more closely regulated than those in the private sector, eg by EU procurement directives.

- There is a wider range of stakeholders in a public sector organisation than in a private sector organisation.

- Organisations in all sectors are increasingly influenced by the concept of corporate social responsibility. This is an area where CIPS have issued extensive guidance.

Self-test questions

Numbers in brackets refer to the paragraphs where you can check your answers.

1   Define what is meant by an organisation. (1.4)

2   What is meant by a network organisation? (1.15)

3   List areas of difference between buying in the public sector and buying in the private sector. (Table 1.1)

4   What is meant by 'contested goals' in the public sector? (1.45)

5   What is meant by lobbying? (2.6)

6   All finance for public sector activities is collected by central government. True or false? (2.13)

7   Describe the role of a public sector regulator. (3.4–3.7)

8   What are the disadvantages of compulsory open tendering in the public sector? (3.20)

9   Explain the concept of stakeholder theory. (4.5)

10   In relation to what types of issues do firms set objectives reflecting social responsibility? (5.4)

11   What reasons are given by CIPS for the importance of CSR to organisations? (5.11)

12   What key areas of CSR are identified in the CIPS White Paper? (5.15)

CHAPTER 2

Purchasing in the Private Sector

Chapter learning objectives

1.2   Appraise the different types of private sector organisations and the differing demands that they place on those managing the provision of goods and services.

- Different forms, including limited companies, plcs and limited liability partnerships
- Formation and cessation of private sector firms
- Regulation of private sector and impact on purchasing
- Impact of profit motive on purchasing activities
- Transactional activity such as mergers and acquisitions (M&A) together with the role of the Competition Commission

Chapter headings

1   Different forms of private sector organisation

2   Regulation of the private sector

3   Transactional activity

Introduction

In the previous chapter we focused on public sector organisations. We now move on to examine the range of organisations operating in the private and voluntary sectors. Our emphasis is on the differences between the various sectors and the impact that these have on purchasing.

1   Different forms of private sector organisation

The importance of the profit motive

1.1   As we have already seen in the previous chapter, the overriding objective for a private sector organisation is normally to maximise profits. The owners of such an enterprise are normally in business to increase their wealth, and they appoint managers to achieve this for them by making profits.

1.2   It is worth noting that in practice the profit motive is not quite so simple as this analysis makes it appear. In most organisations, owners and managers are different groups. The managers may have their own agenda: for example, they may be concerned with building up their personal power base, or with enjoying benefits such as foreign travel. So not everything they do may be directed single-mindedly towards maximising profits.

1.3   Despite this slight reservation, the pursuit of profits will invariably be an important objective in a private sector firm. Buyers in such a firm may well feel pressure to achieve the lowest possible cost when purchasing supplies. And of course it is true that buyers must always be keenly interested in price as one factor in sourcing supplies.

1.4   This does not mean, however, that buyers will sacrifice all other considerations in order to choose the lowest-cost option. Even in the short term this might not be the best way to achieve profits. For example, a more expensive material of higher quality might lead to lower levels of waste, rework and scrap. This could mean that it works out cheaper than an inferior material.

1.5   More importantly, buyers must look to the long-term benefit of their organisation. This could mean an in-depth assessment of potential suppliers along a number of dimensions, not just price. For example, the long-term profitability of the organisation might be best served by a partnership relationship with a supplier offering technology sharing, just in time delivery, and/or other non-price advantages.

1.6   Individual buyers can contribute measurably to savings on materials, inventory, contract and transaction costs (eg through effective negotiation and contract development, efficient conduct of the purchasing cycle, and effective use of inventory management and e-procurement tools). These savings in turn contribute to bottom line profit.

1.7   If cost reductions are retained within the business, there is an immediate improvement in the bottom line. If the surplus resource is used up by budget holders, there is no direct impact on the bottom line – but there is added benefit.

1.8   Profitability is not solely based on price: the total cost of ownership (or acquisition) of capital items, for example, includes delivery, support, consumables, staff training, inventory/handling costs, inspection, maintenance/repair and so on. Individuals therefore have an impact on profitability through their long-term decisions about quality, supply reliability, supplier selection and so on.

Classifying private sector organisations

1.9   To get a handle on the numerous types of organisation in the private sector, there are various classifications we can use.

- We can distinguish on the basis of size – from very small one-man businesses, through SMEs (small and medium-sized enterprises, perhaps up to 250 employees), to massive organisations such as British Telecom. This is self-explanatory.
- We can distinguish on the basis of business activity – **primary industries** engaged in the extraction of raw materials, **secondary industries** engaged in manufacturing, and **tertiary industries** engaged in services.
- We can distinguish on the basis of ownership and control – for example, partnerships and limited companies. We examine this classification in the paragraphs below.

1.10   In the next chapter we look at the second type of classification, distinguishing between the following types of business activity.

- Manufacturing businesses
- Engineering businesses
- FMCG businesses (fast moving consumer goods)
- Retail businesses
- Technology businesses
- Service businesses

Limited companies

1.11 Private sector organisations may be constituted in various different ways. At the small end, they may comprise just a single individual (a sole trader). All profits earned by the business belong to the single owner. Larger firms may take the form of a partnership, in which the partners share profits in agreed proportions. (We discuss partnerships later.)

1.12 But by far the most common trading vehicle in the private sector is the limited company. And among limited companies, by far the most common type is the private company limited by shares. We begin by describing some of the features of this entity.

1.13 A limited company is a separate legal 'person'. This means that the law recognises a distinction between the company and its owners. The company can own assets and incur liabilities in its own name, and can enter into contracts in its own name. If the company incurs a debt, payment will come from assets owned by the company. The owners of the company cannot be asked to contribute to the payment from their personal funds – they are separate from the company, and the debt is not theirs.

1.14 This is what is meant by the 'limited' in limited company. It means that the liability of the owners is limited to the amount they have invested in the company. The company's own liability for its own debts is unlimited, but the owners cannot be forced to provide new funds if the company runs out of cash.

1.15 This distinction between the company and its owners is sometimes referred to as the 'veil of incorporation'. The idea of this metaphor is that the identity of the owners can be dimly perceived behind the company, but the veil separates them. In certain (exceptional) circumstances the law will 'lift the veil of incorporation', meaning that it will look through the covering provided by the company to find the owners behind it. In such circumstances the law prevents the owners from 'hiding' behind the façade of the company if their aim is to obtain some illicit advantage.

1.16 It is easy to form a limited company. The founder(s) of the company must simply deliver certain documents (along with a small fee) to an official called the Registrar of Companies. Provided he is satisfied with the documents, the Registrar will issue a Certificate of Incorporation. The Registrar will place the documents on file. All files maintained by the Registrar are open to inspection by the public. This simply requires payment of a small fee, and is usually performed nowadays over the internet.

1.17 The initial documents filed with the Registrar (the company's Memorandum of Association and its Articles of Association) form the constitution of the company.

- The Memorandum of Association sets out the name of the company (including 'Ltd' or 'plc'), the location of its registered office and its authorised share capital.

- The Articles of Association set out the appointment and powers of the directors, the rights of shareholders, and the rules in relation to meetings of the shareholders.

1.18 In more detail, the **Memorandum of Association** defines the key components of the structure of the company: its clauses can only be altered according to formal statutory procedures (eg if a company wishes to change from a private company to a public company by re-registration). It includes certain mandatory clauses, to which additional clauses may be added.

- A name clause, stating the company name. A public limited company's name must end with 'public limited company' (plc) and a private limited company's name with 'limited' (Ltd)
- A public clause, stating that the company is a public company (where applicable)
- A registered office clause, identifying the company's registered office (defining legal jurisdiction over the company)
- An objects clause: a short statement of what business the company was formed to undertake. This defines the scope and limits of its power to enter into contracts: anything not authorised by this clause may be invalidated as *ultra vires* – beyond the power of – the company
- A liability clause: statement that the liability of members is limited
- A capital clause: the nominal amount of authorised share capital, as a specified number of shares of a specified value. This sets the value of shares the company is authorised to issue (not necessarily the value of shares actually issued to shareholders nor the amount actually paid to the company for those shares)
- Declaration of association/subscription: agreement by subscribers (a minimum of two, in the case of a plc) to take one or more shares; signed and dated and witnessed by another party

1.19 The **Articles of Association** define the internal administration, rules and procedures applicable to the company and its members: they can, subject to some restrictions, be altered by vote of the members. The company may adopt Table A (model articles laid down in the Companies Act), or devise its own articles. Table A includes more than 100 specific articles, dealing with the internal operations of companies such as:

- The issue and management of shares: calls for monies unpaid on shares, share transfers, alteration of share capital etc
- Requirements for general meetings of shareholders (annual and extraordinary general meetings): notice of meetings, proceedings for conducting meetings (quorum, officers, voting) etc
- Requirements for directors: number of directors; appointment, retirement and removal of directors; powers of directors; directors' remuneration, interests and pensions; regulation of directors' meetings and decision-making processes
- The appointment and duties of a company secretary
- The payment of dividends and capitalisation of profits
- Division of the assets of the company in the event of winding up

1.20 The people who pay for shares are the shareholders, also known as the members of the company. These are the company owners. As time goes by, others may be invited to subscribe for shares in the company. Any money subscribed for shares belongs to the company. The company will not normally return the money to the shareholders, other than in exceptional circumstances (eg when the company ceases to trade and is wound up).

1.21 In the UK, shares always have a 'nominal value'; for example, they may be £1 shares or 10p shares. This is just an accounting convenience, and is not meant to reflect the market value of the shares. The market value depends on the value of the company itself, which will reflect its size, its asset base, its profitability etc. If a small company has issued just 100 shares with a nominal value of 10p each, we say that its total issued capital is £10.

1.22 In a small private company there may be just a very small number of shareholders (possibly just one). For example, many family companies are owned just by a husband and wife. But a private company may be quite substantial and may have a large number of shareholders. Even in this case, however, the shareholders are likely to be connected to each other in some way, because a private company cannot just advertise its shares for sale to the general public.

1.23 The situation is different for a **public limited company**. A public company is a company limited by shares which:

- has a nominal share capital of at least £50,000.
- has at least two members.
- is stated to be a public company in its Memorandum of Association.
- has been duly registered as a public company under the provisions of the Companies Act.

1.24 The name of a public limited company must end with the words 'public limited company', 'PLC' or 'plc'. (The name of a private company ends with 'Limited'.)

1.25 Unlike a private company, a public company is allowed to offer its shares for sale to the general public, which is a means of raising large amounts of finance. To do this, the company must normally publish a prospectus in which detailed financial information is provided as a basis for potential investors to make their decision.

1.26 A private company is any company which is not registered as a public company. It may be limited or unlimited. As we have seen, private companies are often small enterprises in which some (if not all) shareholders are also directors (ie managers). Because owners and managers are the same people, it is unnecessary to impose on the directors the same kind of complex duties and restrictions that are required for public companies, to protect the interests of the owners.

1.27 The main differences between public and private companies (which might be a deciding factor when choosing which is appropriate in a given situation) are listed in Table 2.1.

1.28 Perhaps the most important advantage of the public company is its ability to raise large capital sums from the public; private companies are usually relatively small. On the other hand, if the company wants to be small and to stay within member control, the private company is subject to fewer structural requirements and less red tape.

Table 2.1 *Differences between public and private companies*

Feature	Public company	Private company
Authorised share capital	Minimum authorised capital of £50,000	No minimum requirements
Public subscription	May raise capital by offering its securities to the public, and trade them via the Stock Exchange.	May not raise capital by advertising securities to the public, so securities cannot be traded on the Stock Exchange. Shares are often owned by partners or family members.
Company law	Subject to detailed provisions of the Companies Act in regard to: payment for shares; appointment and duties of directors; requirements for annual general meetings; accounts; and so on.	Some provisions not applicable (eg payment for shares); others partially relaxed (eg in regard to accounting provisions for small and medium-sized companies, loans to directors, AGMs). There is a trend towards deregulation of private companies.
Members and directors	Minimum of two members. Minimum of two directors.	Might have only one member (single-member private limited company). Might have only one director.

Partnerships

1.29 Many sole traders find that a logical way of expanding without taking on the formalities of incorporation is to take on one or more partners, who contribute capital and expertise to the business, and who share the managerial and financial responsibilities. Partnerships often find it easier to raise loans than sole traders, since there are more assets backing the venture than just those of one person.

1.30 A partnership is defined as 'the relation which subsists between persons carrying on a business in common with a view of profit' (Partnership Act 1890).

- There must be at least two partners to constitute a partnership. (One person is a 'sole trader'.)

- The standard maximum number of partners permitted by law is 20 for a commercial partnership, but a professional practice (such as a firm of accountants or solicitors) can have any number of partners.

- The partners must carry on business in common: ie they must be joint proprietors taking a share of the profits.

1.31 Partnership (like sole tradership) is a form of **unincorporated** organisation. The main differences between a partnership and a company are therefore as follows.

- A partnership does not have a separate legal identity from its members; it is merely two or more 'natural persons' in a legal relationship with each other. This means, for example, that partners jointly own the assets of the partnership and are liable for its contracts, and that a change of partners terminates the old firm and begins a new one. Partnership cannot be transferred from one person to another (except by all partners' consent). Interest in a company, in the form of shares, is transferable.

- Partners are usually liable without limit for the partnership's debts. The exception is a registered **limited liability partnership**, in which partners have limited liability. This form of partnership is increasingly being used by firms of professionals, such as accountants, who are prevented by law from operating as limited companies. Liability may extend to retired (and even deceased) partners for outstanding debts incurred during their partnership.

- Partners are entitled to participate in management, and act as agents of the firm (unlike companies, whose owners/shareholders are not necessarily either directors or agents).

1.32 Partnership is a standard form of organisation in the professions (although less common in commerce) because most professions prohibit their members from practising through limited companies. Business people are not so restricted, and generally prefer to trade through a limited company so that, if it becomes insolvent, they are not liable without limit for its debts.

Formation and cessation of private sector organisations

1.33 We have seen above how limited companies are formed. With partnerships there are fewer formalities – two or more individuals may agree to trade in partnership on agreed terms without even drawing up a written document. More usually, though, a written partnership agreement will be produced, setting out such details as how much capital will be invested, how profits will be shared among the partners etc.

1.34 The owners of a business may at any time decide to cease trading. In the case of a partnership, the partners simply split the remaining assets of the business according to any agreed terms (after paying off any liabilities). The situation with a limited company is essentially the same: once liabilities have been settled, any remaining assets are realised in the form of cash and distributed to the shareholders in proportion to their shareholdings.

1.35 In some circumstances a business (partnership or company) may be compelled to cease trading. Usually this will be in cases where the business has been unprofitable and can no longer pay its debts. The usual situation is that any assets remaining in the business are realised in the form of cash and are then distributed to the creditors in proportion to the amounts owing. There will not usually be anything left for the owners of the business – if there was such a surplus, the business would probably not have had to be wound up.

1.36 Insolvency is not the only possible reason why a business might terminate. Another possibility is that the owners take a strategic decision to sell up, perhaps because they no longer want to be involved in that area of activity. In such a case, the normal procedure would be to sell the business as a going concern to someone who sees it as a profitable investment opportunity.

1.37 The acquirer may choose to run the new business as a venture in its own right, or alternatively to close it down. (This could happen, for example, if the acquisition was made by a competitor company wishing to stop the activities of a rival.) In the latter case, there may be many undesirable consequences.

- Loss of employment in the region
- Loss of personal income of the staff

- Loss to the national economy (eg in lost tax revenue, reduced competition, increased burden on the welfare state)
- Loss of business for suppliers, and possibly bad debts if bills are not paid
- Threat to security of supply for former customers
- Loss of investment for shareholders

Summary: classification on the basis of ownership and control

1.38 Table 2.2 summarises some of the key advantages and disadvantages of the different business 'constitutions' we have looked at in this section of the chapter.

Table 2.2 *Classification by ownership and control*

Organisation	Advantages	Disadvantages
Sole trader	Simple to set up and administer Freedom from regulations Owner has complete control All profits belong to owner	Limited in size Owner dependent on own capital and expertise Finance is hard to raise All liabilities belong to owner personally
Partnership	Simple to set up and administer Freedom from regulations Wide range of expertise among partners Easier access to finance than for sole traders	Harder to run, because of need for consultation among partners Profits are shared among partners All liabilities belong to partners personally
Limited company	Limited liability for owners Good access to finance through sale of shares Directors provide expertise without necessarily diluting ownership	Harder to set up Heavily regulated Financial details are public information Share trading can result in unwelcome change of ownership

A note on terminology

1.39 We have several times referred to the share capital of a limited company. It is worth noting some terminology in this area.

- **Authorised share capital** is the amount of share capital the company is authorised (in its Memorandum of Association) to issue. This is sometimes regarded as an impediment to the growth of the company, but this idea is a misconception. If the company wishes to increase its authorised share capital it is a relatively simple matter for the shareholders to do so.
- **Issued share capital** is the amount of share capital actually issued by the company and held by the shareholders. It may be less than the full authorised share capital.
- **Paid up share capital** is the amount that shareholders have paid to the company for the shares issued to them. This may be less than the issued share capital in cases where payments for shares are due by instalments.
- **Unpaid capital** is the amount owing from shareholders in respect of the shares issued to them. Paid up share capital plus unpaid capital adds up in total to the issued share capital.

Sources of finance in the private sector

1.40   There are a number of key sources of finance for private sector organisations.

- Initial capital investment by the owners of the business (eg in the case of a sole trader or partnership) or by venture capitalists

- Share capital: that is, the sale of shares in the company. A public limited company (plc) will, as we have seen, be able to sell shares to the general public on the Stock Exchange. A private limited company (Ltd) can raise finance by selling shares to investment syndicates and associates (eg friends and family members)

- Retained profits resulting from the profit-generating activities of the business, such as sales: that is, profits that are 'ploughed back' into the business (rather than being withdrawn by the owners or paid out to shareholders as dividends)

- Loan finance, such as bank overdraft facilities, or bank loans and debentures (usually secured against the assets of the business)

- The sale of unneeded assets

- Government grants (eg for small business development or other projects and capital purchases).

2   *Regulation of the private sector*

The political scene in the UK

2.1   There are three main political parties in the UK: the Labour Party, the Conservatives and the Liberal Democrats. At the time of writing (May 2010), no party has an absolute majority in parliament, and a coalition government (Conservatives with Liberal Democrats) is in power.   Before that, the Labour party had enjoyed a large majority since 1997; this had followed an 18-year period in which the Conservative Party (most notably under the leadership of Margaret Thatcher) had held the upper hand.

2.2   Traditionally, the Conservative Party has espoused right-wing policies. These have been based on a philosophy of individual self-reliance, free markets, private ownership, and a strong approach to issues such as defence and law and order. The Labour Party, by contrast, has historically been associated with left-wing policies: a strong emphasis on social welfare, intervention in the markets to advance government objectives, and public ownership. In recent years, many critics of the party have objected that it has drifted to the right in its policies, even to the point of becoming indistinguishable from the Conservatives. The Liberal Democrats have traditionally been the party of centrist views (usually slightly left of centre).

2.3   The three main parties (plus a number of more minor parties) pursue their objectives both in central government and in local authorities.

The influence of government on organisations

2.4   There are four main areas in which government influences organisations generally (quite apart from its very direct influence on public sector organisations).

- Governments influence the operation of organisations: what they can and cannot produce, and how they produce it (eg in laying down restrictions on production processes in order to protect the environment).

- Governments influence the costs and revenues incurred by organisations: by the application of taxes and duties on the production and sale of certain goods, and by the effect of taxes on the general level of consumer spending.

- Governments influence organisations by the actions they take in pursuing macroeconomic objectives (eg in establishing exchange rates and interest rates, by the extent to which they stimulate aggregate demand in the economy).

- Governments influence the values and norms that are regarded as acceptable within the national culture, and hence indirectly affect the outputs produced by organisations and the ways in which organisations behave.

Legislation

2.5   An important influence on private sector firms is legislation. There is a wide variety of laws affecting the conduct of business. These derive (in the UK) from three main sources.

- Regulations and directives issued by the European Union
- Acts of Parliament enacted in Westminster
- Case law (ie law deriving from the decisions of judges in interpreting the law of the land)

2.6   The content of such law is wide-ranging.

- Restricting practices that tend to stifle competition
- Protecting employees
- Protecting consumers
- Restricting the types of products that firms can supply (eg forbidding the supply of dangerous goods)
- Restricting the ways in which firms manufacture (eg imposing fines for processes that damage the environment)
- Restricting the uses to which firms can put personal data (eg forbidding firms from passing on customer details without their consent)

Regulation of privatised firms

2.7   Privatised firms are those such as British Telecom that used to be in public ownership but were sold by the government into private hands. In most cases, the firms enjoyed natural monopolies (or near monopolies). This is the case, for example, with both British Telecom and British Gas.

2.8   The existence of a monopoly leaves the public open to abuse, because the privatised firms were mostly free from the restraints imposed by a competitive environment. For example, there was nothing to prevent them from raising their prices to unacceptable levels – consumers had nowhere else to take their custom. Because of this possibility of abuse the government has imposed a regulatory regime on these firms.

2.9   The usual mechanism by which this works is the creation of a regulatory body, such as Ofcom for the telecommunications industry. In principle, this was intended to be a temporary measure, because government policy was to open up these markets to competitor firms who would bring in the disciplines of a more open market place. However, it is likely that true competition in these industries will be a long time coming, if it ever comes, and for the moment the regulatory bodies retain their powers.

2.10 The main power wielded by Ofcom and suchlike bodies is concerned with limiting price rises. The regulator simply instructs the firm concerned that its price rises for a particular period must not exceed a certain percentage, which invariably is less than the general rate of inflation for that period.

2.11 Another important power arises from publicity. Naturally, the activities of an organisation such as British Telecom affect very large numbers of people. There is widespread interest if Ofcom finds fault with any of those activities, which means that the regulator has no difficulty in gaining publicity in the media. This clearly puts pressure on the monopolist firm to fall into line and pursue 'fair' policies.

2.12 Other powers include the following.

- Issuing and renewing licences for firms wishing to operate in the market. In exceptional circumstances the regulator may withdraw a licence to operate, but this would only be in extreme cases involving (for example) a threat to public safety or persistent and large-scale failure to comply with regulatory standards.
- Setting standards of good practice
- Monitoring the activities of firms operating in the market, responding to customer complaints, and seeking to ensure that firms operate to high standards.
- Communication and promotion of market activities to maintain consumer confidence.
- Making periodic reports to the government.

Regulation of other private sector firms

2.13 Governments of all persuasions accept that some regulation of the private sector generally (not just recently privatised firms) is desirable, for the following reasons.

- Governments wish to preserve a balance between consumers and firms. Consumers must be protected in terms of service, quality and price, while firms must be prevented from charging excessive prices for essential services.
- Governments wish to promote competition – see later in this section.
- Governments wish to assist firms to prosper, because their prosperity makes for the prosperity of the nation generally.
- Governments wish to protect national interests, eg by protecting domestic companies from unfair competition from overseas companies.

The impact of regulation on private sector procurement

2.14 Private sector regulators are intended to ensure compliance with defined standards. For example, buyers must ensure that the goods they purchase match up to all public standards and specifications (as well as, obviously, matching up to the specification generated by the buyer himself). This includes compliance with relevant health and safety standards, not just in the products purchased, but in the entire purchase process (eg compliance with manual handling regulations in the delivery and handling of the goods).

2.15 Buyers must also comply with relevant environmental standards.

2.16 Buyers must act with accountability. They must ensure that appropriate processes have been followed to acquire the best possible cost and quality, and must equally ensure that a full 'audit trail' exists so that actions and decisions can be vetted.

2.17 Buyers must ensure that appropriate service levels are achieved in the provision of services, especially when they have delegated the service to an outside provider.

3   *Transactional activity*

Mergers, acquisitions and strategic alliances

3.1 A characteristic of the private sector (and to some extent the public sector) is the frequency of **transactional activity**. This general term covers a variety of situations in which the activities and resources of one firm are combined with those of another. In this section we look at three such situations: mergers, acquisitions and strategic alliances. From the first two of these situations the term **M&A activity** has arisen; this means the same as transactional activity.

3.2 An **acquisition** means that Organisation A develops its resources and competencies by taking over Organisation B. There are various reasons why Organisation A might be motivated to do this.

- It may enable the organisation to enter new product and market areas without the delays normally associated with such processes.
- It may enable the organisation to develop a strategy internally for which it is currently lacking the necessary resources or competencies. For example, Organisation B may have much better developed R&D expertise.
- It may enable the organisation to enter a market of low growth. Entering the market by its own efforts might create capacity in excess of demand, whereas this is not the case if it merely acquires an organisation already present in the market.
- It may enable economies of scale or operating efficiencies.
- It may satisfy shareholder aspirations, eg by delivering rapid growth and improved return on investment.

3.3 However, a strategy of acquisition can lead to problems. In particular, it may be difficult to integrate the new business with the old one, possibly because of a mismatch between the two organisational cultures.

3.4 A **merger** is very similar in outcome to an acquisition. The main difference tends to be in the reasons why the two organisations come together. In an acquisition, Organisation A is actively pursuing Organisation B. There is no certainty that Organisation B welcomes this approach, and in fact it may actively resist. A merger, by contrast, is where both organisations see value in pooling their resources and neither party is dominant over the other.

3.5 The reasons for a merger may be similar to those for an acquisition. Synergistic benefits are more likely in this case to be the main driver for the business combination.

3.6   The reasons given above explain why mergers and acquisitions are so common a part of the business scene in developed economies. However, the same objectives can sometimes be achieved without formally combining the two organisations into a single entity. A variety of **joint venture** and **strategic alliance** relationships is possible.

3.7   Some of the possibilities are illustrated by Johnson and Scholes in their influential text *Exploring Corporate Strategy*: see Figure 2.1.

Figure 2.1 *Types of and motives for strategic alliances*

	Loose (market) relationships	Contractual relationships	Formalised ownership/ relationships	Formal integration
FORMS OF ALLIANCE	Networks Opportunistic alliances	Subcontracting Licences and franchises	Consortia Joint ventures	Acquisition and mergers
INFLUENCES Asset management	Assets do not need joint management	Asset management can be isolated	Assets need to be jointly managed	
Asset separability	Assets cannot be separated	Assets/skills can be separated		Assets cannot be separated
Asset appropriability	High risk of assets being appropriated		Low risk of assets being appropriated	High risk of asset appropriation

3.8   The essence of a strategic alliance or similar relationship is that the two organisations agree to retain their separate identities while collaborating closely over the long term to achieve mutual objectives.

The stages of a business combination

3.9   A merger or acquisition will typically proceed through the stages shown in Figure 2.2.

3.10   The diagram is mainly self explanatory, but the term **due diligence** may be unfamiliar. It refers to the process whereby the potential combination is thoroughly investigated, often employing the services of external specialists such as management consultants and accountants. The aim of the process is to ensure that the combination is likely to achieve the desired objectives and that there are no unexpected surprises awaiting.

3.11   Due diligence will include analysis of accounts, review of past trading activities and future forecasts, investigation of major contracts in existence or in course of negotiation, analysis of customer base, valuation of key assets, analysis and quantification of potential synergies, and preliminary planning of the integration process.

Figure 2.2 *Stages of a business combination*

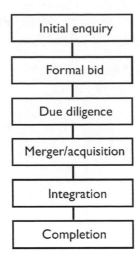

3.12 The role of purchasing in these various activities can be significant. For example, purchasing can help to analyse existing contracts, evaluate potential synergies, and assess risk.

3.13 Purchasing also have an important role during the integration phase.

- One common feature of this phase is a rationalisation of the two supplier bases. Purchasing staff are key to this process.

- Frequently the integration process is managed by external consultancies. Purchasing are best placed to establish the consultancy contract.

- It is essential to keep suppliers informed about changes, and purchasing are best placed to maintain the communication process.

Competition policy

3.14 It is agreed by almost all governments that the public interest is best served by a regime of free competition. It has therefore been a government policy for many years to ensure that monopolies are regulated. Monopolies may arise either from 'natural causes' – eg it was long regarded as natural to have just one body, British Rail, in control of all rail travel in the UK – or from the amalgamation of competing firms through mergers and acquisitions.

3.15 There is a long history of legislation setting up the anti-monopoly machinery. The earliest important Act was the Monopolies and Restrictive Practices Act 1948, which set up the Monopolies and Mergers Commission (now superseded by the Competition Commission).

3.16 This was followed by the Restrictive Trade Practices Act 1956, which was directed at agreements between companies which resulted in monopoly-like behaviour. It required any collective agreements to be registered.

3.17 The Monopolies and Mergers Act 1965 widened the scope of the Monopolies and Mergers Commission to cover mergers; and the Fair Trading Act 1973 replaced earlier legislation, strengthening the role of the Monopolies and Mergers Commission and establishing the Office of Fair Trading (OFT).

3.18 Other Acts in this area include the Resale Prices Act 1976, which consolidated earlier legislation, the Competition Act 1980, the Competition Act 1998 and the Enterprise Act 2002. Much of the legislation is affected by European Union rules.

3.19 The OFT monitors the economy, looking for monopolies and anti-competitive practices. Examples of anti-competitive practices include boycotts of shops stocking rivals' products; and price fixing, where retailers are told what price to charge for the supplier's product. An instance of how the legislation can be manipulated in this area is the fixed price for many items of confectionery; the price is technically **not** a fixed one, as the labels always give the '**recommended** retail price'. In theory, the retailer could charge a lower price.

3.20 If the OFT feels that a firm is abusing a market with its monopoly power, it has the power to refer it to the Competition Commission for investigation. Some monopolies may not be noticed and will therefore continue. The OFT can also go to court to get prison sentences of up to five years for the controllers of the firms involved and can seek to have them disqualified from acting as directors.

3.21 The Competition Commission has the power to investigate both local monopolies, where the market in question is a small, local one, and larger, national monopolies. It is not restricted to the private sector, as it may investigate nationalised industries.

3.22 The powers of both the OFT and the Competition Commission have been increased by the Enterprise Act 2002.

3.23 To prevent abuse of a monopoly position, the government has set up appropriate regulatory bodies for each of the main industries that were previously nationalised but are now in private hands. But this has not prevented public concern about the level of profits earned by such organisations as British Telecom.

3.24 In addition to this concern, the replacement of a public sector ethos by private sector (profit maximising) objectives has led to severe levels of redundancies. Many commentators have also remarked unfavourably on the moves into new markets that privatised firms have embarked upon, mostly without success. In effect, the public has subsidised these efforts without really consenting to do so.

3.25 One significant difficulty experienced by the regulators is that of defining the boundaries of individual firms. This difficulty arises from three causes.

- Increasingly, a single organisation may operate in different markets, making the boundary lines between them unclear.
- Many large organisations are becoming global in scope.
- Many large organisations are pursuing growth and diversification by means of alliances with other organisations.

3.26 From a regulator's point of view, the problem this causes is that it is hard to control the market share of a regulated organisation if it is not clear where the organisation begins and ends.

3.27 The above considerations indicate that the existence of a regulatory body is not necessarily a perfect protection for consumers, or much of an impediment to monopolistic firms. In fact to some extent the existence of regulation strengthens the position of the firms.

- Many of the privatised firms are effectively protected from competition by government rules limiting the extent of rival firms' activities.

- Price caps may prevent excessive increases in price, but do not necessarily drive prices down, as might happen if the firms were subject to full competition.

- In many cases, the firms have proved adept at 'managing' the regulators, either by lobbying politicians or by directly seeking assistance from the government.

Chapter summary

- Private sector organisations are usually profit maximisers. But profit must be considered in the long term.

- The most common type of private sector organisation is the limited company. This is a legal person in its own right, owned by shareholders. A public limited company may raise capital from the general public, whereas a private company is not allowed to do this.

- A partnership is not a separate legal entity. The partners do not enjoy limited liability.

- A private sector firm may terminate because of insolvency, but may also terminate as part of a strategy determined by the owners.

- In the UK, both central government and local government have an influence on organisations.

- Privatised firms are more closely regulated than most private sector organisations. Often the method of control is a dedicated industry regulator such as Ofcom or Ofgem.

- Transactional activity (also referred to as M&A activity) is an important feature of the private sector, and sometimes also of the public sector. Organisations combine their resources and competencies by means of mergers, acquisitions and alliances.

- Most governments believe in the benefits of free competition. For that reason, governments invariably insist on regulation of monopolies and try to stamp out anti-competitive practices.

Self-test questions

Numbers in brackets refer to the paragraphs where you can check your answers.

1   Distinguish between the primary, secondary and tertiary industry sectors. (1.9)

2   What is meant by limited liability? (1.14)

3   What characteristics of a public limited company distinguish it from a private company? (1.23, and Table 2.1)

4   Define 'partnership'. (1.30)

5   What undesirable consequences may occur if a business terminates? (1.37)

6   What are the four main areas in which government influences organisations? (2.4)

7   How do regulators such as Ofcom and Ofgem influence the privatised industries? (2.10, 2.11)

8   Why might one organisation wish to acquire another organisation? (3.2)

9   List the typical stages in a business combination. (Figure 2.2)

10   What is meant by due diligence? (3.10)

11   Summarise the work of the OFT. (3.19)

12   Why has it become difficult to define the boundaries of individual firms? (3.25)

CHAPTER 3

The Impact of Different Business Activities

Chapter learning objectives

1.2   Appraise the different types of private sector organisations and the differing demands that they place on those managing the provision of goods and services.

- Specific types of private sector organisations and influences on purchasing function: manufacturing; engineering; fast moving consumer goods (FMCG); retail; technology; services

1.4   Review the different types of third sector organisations.

- Different types of third sector organisations
- Regulation of voluntary and not-for-profit organisations and impact on purchasing
- Importance of corporate social responsibility (CSR)

Chapter headings

1   The primary, secondary and tertiary sectors

2   The manufacturing sector

3   The engineering sector

4   The FMCG sector

5   The retail sector

6   Technology businesses

7   The services sector

8   The third sector

9   Differences in supply chains

Introduction

In this chapter we continue our discussion of the private sector. In the previous chapter we saw how one possible classification of private sector firms is based on the different business activities in which such firms operate. In this chapter we examine the various activities specified in your exam syllabus and identify the particular features applying in each one.

We also look at the specialised situation of voluntary and not-for-profit organisations.

1   *The primary, secondary and tertiary sectors*

Firms in extractive industries

1.1   It is common to distinguish between three major industry sectors in the UK (and in other developed nations).

- Primary industries are concerned with extracting natural resources from the earth. This sector includes oil extraction, minerals, and perhaps agriculture (though agriculture incorporates some of the features of secondary industry and is often classified as such).

- Secondary industries are those engaged in manufacturing.

- Tertiary industries are those engaged in the development and provision of services (accountants and lawyers, advertising and management consultants, insurance companies and stockbrokers, hairdressers and plumbers etc).

1.2   This classification is not exhaustive; for example, it is not clear that the retail sector or the energy sector fits into any of these categories. Both the retail sector and the energy sector have sometimes been regarded as sectors in their own right.

1.3   It is not surprising to find that purchasing philosophies and operations differ as one moves from one major sector to another. Clearly the organisational characteristics of an oil extraction company are likely to be very different from those of a management consultancy and these differences are likely to be apparent at least to some extent within the purchasing functions.

1.4   In an extractive industry such as mining the following important characteristics may be identified.

- The purchasing spend is very high. This is above all because large, specialised, heavy-duty machinery is often necessary, and because expenditure on spares and tools is a significant element.

- Stock levels are typically high and materials management activities should be planned so as to control the costs of stockholding.

- The specialised nature of most supplies, as well as their high value in many cases, mean that most purchases are routed through a specialist purchasing department, rather than being processed in an *ad hoc* way by operational staff. This enables a good level of control and means that the benefits of professional purchasing expertise are realised.

- Partly as a consequence of the above, it is common to find that purchasing is represented at a senior level in the organisation, possibly on the main board.

- The nature of operations is very different from a continuous manufacturing environment. In particular, the problems of links between one stage and the next in a continuous production line are less urgent, and techniques such as just in time and materials requirements planning are less relevant.

- Another aspect of this theme is the nature of the supplier base. The value of items purchased on a regular basis is proportionately less than in a manufacturing firm, while the value of special purchases is proportionately higher. This can mean that the supplier base changes more often and more rapidly than is common for manufacturing companies.

Supplying remote and difficult locations

1.5 One of the problems peculiar to the primary sector is that managers have no choice in where they locate their operating facilities. No doubt it would be easier to build an oil rig in Lincolnshire than in the middle of the North Sea; but since the oil is in fact situated in the latter location the easy option is not available.

1.6 Similarly, a quarrying company must operate where supplies of, say, slate actually exist in the ground. This may well mean operating half way up a mountain.

1.7 Clearly this makes the provision of the right supplies in the right place at the right time all the more difficult. Purchasing staff must consider:

- how to arrange transport of the materials to the remote location
- how to optimise order quantities bearing in mind the additional logistical problems involved
- how to store materials once they are in place
- the additional costs that all this gives rise to.

Supplier support and service operations

1.8 The same problems impact on suppliers. Suppliers must not only undertake a more difficult task in the actual delivery of materials, but also have less margin for error in both quality and delivery performance. This is because if materials are found to be defective or unsuitable the problem of replacement will be more complex than in the usual case.

1.9 Similarly, a supplier of, say, capital equipment will normally provide support and service operations. In the case of an extractive industry the problems that this leads to are magnified. For one thing, the equipment involved is often of a very large scale, implying that support and service requirements are correspondingly larger. For another, the difficulties of access can pose problems in relation to speed of response and cost.

1.10 The buyer's role in managing these problems is a crucial one. From the beginning, his task is to liaise closely with suppliers in anticipating the difficulties and devising solutions. He needs to ensure that suppliers are fully aware of the particular problems that may apply and of their obligations in overcoming them.

Emergency and standby materials

1.11 One step that will usually be taken to minimise these problems is the provision of emergency and standby materials, invariably in larger quantities than would be necessary for a manufacturing operation of similar size. This of course runs counter to modern ideas on stock minimisation but the particular circumstances of the primary industry sector demand it.

1.12 Once again, the expertise of the purchasing professional is vital. Drawing on experience of historical usage patterns the professional buyer is able to determine a level of emergency and standby materials that balances operational requirements with cost considerations.

2 *The manufacturing sector*

Characteristics of manufacturing companies

2.1 This sector used to be overwhelmingly the largest economic sector in the UK, and remains hugely important to the prosperity of the country, despite the fact that service industries now account for a larger slice of the economic cake. The purchasing literature reflects the fact that very many buyers are employed in manufacturing companies. By implication or explicitly much of the discussion in this text and the standard purchasing literature is based on a manufacturing and engineering background.

2.2 The essence of this sector is that the manufacturer takes a series of inputs from earlier stages in the supply chain and performs operations upon them to create a finished product. The inputs may include raw materials, components, and subassemblies. The manufacturer applies resources (manpower, machinery etc) to convert these into the final output for sale to his customers.

2.3 A few of the distinguishing characteristics of manufacturing companies, as they relate to purchasing, are singled out below, but you should bear in mind that most of what you read in the literature is relevant to this sector.

- Purchasing is a relatively advanced function in many manufacturing companies. Often purchasing staff have strategic responsibilities in addition to their operational duties.

- Partly this has come about through the transformation of manufacturing operations in recent decades. World class techniques such as just in time, total quality management, and materials requirements planning have caused a re-evaluation of the role of supply chain management with a consequent upgrading in the status of purchasing. Representation of the function at main board level is common.

- Purchasing's key internal customer is the production function. The most important task is to ensure that production teams have materials of the right quality available in the right place at the right time in the right quantity, achieving all this at the right price – the traditional 'five rights' of purchasing.

- The value of materials which are bought on a regular basis is a high proportion of total purchasing spend. To achieve the 'five rights' for such materials purchasing strategy has focused on a slim supplier base with close relations between buyer and supplier.

- The role of the purchasing professional typically extends through almost the whole spectrum of organisational activities, beginning with new product development right through to delivery to customers.

The impact of different production methods

2.4 Another impact on purchasing and supply activities is the different ways in which production is organised in the manufacturing firm. It is common to distinguish between project, jobbing, batch, mass and continuous production methods.

2.5   **Project work** is typically carried out in the construction and engineering industries. Each item of production (eg a railway bridge, an office block) is individual and distinct from other projects undertaken by the same firm. The size of such jobs is often very significant, and project management techniques are important. From the purchaser's point of view an implication of this is the need to schedule supplies in a precise order: materials needed for Stage 5 must be available once Stage 4 is complete, but on the other hand are useless if they arrive earlier than that.

2.6   **Jobbing production** is similar to project work in that each customer's order tends to be different. The main difference is in the size of the jobs. Jobbing work might be performed by, say, a furniture manufacturer making items of furniture to specific customer orders. The manufacturer may hold a constant stock of items that are used frequently, but will also need to order materials specially for each separate order.

2.7   **Batch manufacturing**, as the name suggests, refers to identical items produced in small or large batches. For example, this textbook has been printed in a batch of identical copies. Clearly in this kind of environment there is no smooth pattern of demand for materials. On the contrary, there tends to be a large demand for materials when the batch processing begins, and then no demand at all until the next batch is begun. Even so, purchasing staff will often be able to make reliable forecasts of demand provided that the quantities are relatively stable for each batch.

2.8   **Mass production** is typically carried out in the traditional production 'line', where items move steadily from one stage of the process to the next and there is a constant and predictable demand for materials. This makes forecasting relatively easy and encourages use of techniques such as just-in-time purchasing. Mass production is of course very common, and examples are numerous.

2.9   In a **continuous process** it is important to avoid any interruption to the flow, which makes it vital to secure an uninterrupted supply of necessary materials. Examples include oil refining and various pipeline operations (eg supply of gas and electricity). The output of a continuous process is completely standardised, and this is reflected in a similar standardisation of inputs.

2.10   Here are a few areas in which purchasing can contribute to a manufacturing firm's competitive advantage.

- Coordinating the entire supply chain so as to minimise waste and duplication
- Ensuring the quality of bought in materials and parts so as to improve the quality of the firm's output and hence ensure customer satisfaction
- Reducing stock levels at all stages of the production process so as to minimise stockholding costs
- Minimising the firm's cost base by effective negotiation with suppliers on price
- Ensuring full use of information technology to maximise effectiveness of materials usage
- Achievement of efficiency and effectiveness by means of accurate demand forecasting and production planning, combined with efficient control of quality and stock levels.

2.11 In addition to the specific contribution of purchasing, it is possible to identify particular elements that contribute to a successful manufacturing operation.

- The infrastructure assets of such a business (factory premises, machinery, stocks etc) are typically high in value, and the manufacturer must make best use of them by efficiency in operations and by volume processing. This is often enhanced by appropriate use of advanced technology.

- To plan effectively, the manufacturer must have accurate means of demand forecasting. Without this, production runs cannot be predicted with confidence, and either over-production will occur (with possible waste) or under-production (with possible disappointment for customers).

- Effective management of quality issues, ensuring a steady supply of consistently high-quality output. The manufacturer must avoid the costs and disruption caused by waste, scrap and rework.

- Effective management of financial investment. This is essential in view of the very large sums invested in capital assets.

Manufacturing supply chains

2.12 The essence of the manufacturing sector is that the manufacturer takes a series of inputs from earlier stages in the supply chain (including extractors of raw materials, producers of components and subassemblies, and related service providers) and performs operations upon them to create a finished product for sale to customers. Key characteristics of manufacturing which impact on supply chains include the following.

- The introduction of world class techniques such as just in time, total quality management and materials requirements planning has extended the integration of supply networks and the role of supply chain management.

- Operations management is the focal point of the supply chain (and the key internal customer of purchasing): the most important task is to ensure that production processes have materials of the right quality, available in the right place at the right time in the right quantity, at the right price (the five 'rights' of purchasing and supply).

- The value of materials bought on a regular basis is likely to be a high proportion of total purchasing spend. Strategies therefore typically focus on a slim supplier base, with close relations between buyers and suppliers (particularly for strategic items).

- Accurate demand forecasting is vital to avoid over-production (with possible waste) or under-production (with possible customer dissatisfaction): as argued earlier, this requires visibility and integration of demand information through the supply chain.

- The effective management of quality issues throughout the supply chain is essential to ensure a steady flow of consistently high-quality output.

2.13 Several writers have noted that the structure and priorities of the supply chain will depend to a large extent on the complexity of the product manufactured and the level of uncertainty and dynamism in its environment. For complex goods in dynamic environments (eg capital intensive industries such as aerospace, shipbuilding and construction), quality management and supply chain agility are a priority. For complex goods in stable environments (eg consumer durables or automotive), value for money and demand-driven supply may be a priority. For simple goods in dynamic environments (eg fashion, cosmetics, food/drink), short cycle times may be key, in response to short product lifecycles. And for simple goods in stable environments (eg commodities), process efficiency and cost improvement are key, in response to price sensitivity.

3   *The engineering sector*

Types of engineering firm

3.1   There are many different types of engineering firm.

- Civil engineers are engaged in the construction of roads, bridges, railways, buildings etc
- Mechanical engineers are engaged in the design and production of plant and equipment.
- Electrical engineers are engaged in the design and production of electrical and electronic goods.
- Chemical engineers are engaged in the design and production of chemicals and chemical processing plants.
- Software engineers are engaged in the design and development of software systems.

3.2   This list is not meant to be exhaustive, but gives an idea of the scope of engineering activities. All of these different types of engineer are engaged in design activities and will give high priority to protection of their intellectual property.

3.3   There are differences in the kind of work undertaken by engineering firms. Typically these firms will be involved in three main categories of operation.

- New build (eg construction of a road or a bridge, creation of a new software system)
- Renewals (eg major enhancements to an existing construction or project)
- Maintenance (ongoing care and repair of constructions and installations)

4   *The FMCG sector*

Fast moving consumer goods (FMCG)

4.1   FMCG products include confectionery, toiletries, soft drinks, mass fashion items and so on. The FMCG sector is a special example of the manufacturing sector, with focus on production of goods for consumer mass markets. The FMCG manufacturer depends for his success on volume sales.

4.2   Competitive forces in this sector are very strong, with numerous manufacturers attempting to push their products to a position of market leadership. This has led to a vast proliferation of choice for the consumer. Just check out the number of different brands of toothpaste, for example, on display in your local pharmacy.

4.3   One implication of this is the crucial importance of branding. Faced with many competing products, consumers are reassured by recognising familiar brands. Often, brand loyalty is their main reason for selecting one manufacturer's product rather than another's. Purchasers in this industry can expect to be spending large amounts of money on promoting brand awareness, eg by means of media advertising.

4.4   Another feature of this sector is a very short product lifecycle. Although many brands have stood the test of time (albeit with many changes to their basic specifications over the years), there are intense competitive pressures to introduce new products constantly. This is so that manufacturers can respond to every nuance of customers' changing needs and so acquire and defend market share. Purchasers must be constantly alert to the need for different materials, ingredients, packaging etc in order to satisfy this need.

Implications for purchasing

4.5   As we have pointed out, FMCG firms are just one special example of the more general manufacturing sector already discussed. You should refer back to Section 2 of this chapter to remind yourself of the main features of manufacturing companies. Many of these, such as emphasis on production quality and the heavy use of manufacturing plant, are important in the FMCG sector.

4.6   Rapid changes in consumer tastes imply a need for agility in the supply chain. Manufacturers must acquire machines that can swiftly be adapted to production of new or refined products. Purchasers have an important role to play in the sourcing of capital equipment.

5   *The retail sector*

Similarities and differences

5.1   In this section we look at the work of buyers employed by wholesalers and retailers. The task of such buyers is to purchase goods which will then be sold onwards to customers with little or no work having been done to them in the meantime. This contrasts with a manufacturing environment, in which buyers purchase materials that will be converted into finished products.

5.2   It should be obvious that important principles of purchasing are as relevant here as they are in manufacturing environments. For example, modern approaches to quality assurance, stock control and supplier relations remain vital. Even so, the nature of the work is different in important respects, and the objective here is to isolate these differences and discuss their impact for buyers.

5.3   The most crucial difference is that buyers in resale environments are usually much closer to their (external) customers than is common in manufacturing. This is because the decision on what to buy is crucially related to expectations of what will sell. There is pressure on buyers in this sector to find new lines that will entice additional customers and generate additional income. This is very different from the situation in manufacturing and suggests that an important part of the buyer's training should be in marketing and selling. (This is one reason why the CIPS examination syllabus includes an optional paper on marketing.)

5.4   The importance of these distinctions should not be exaggerated. For one thing, the similarities between purchasing activities in different sectors probably always outweigh the specific differences. Some specific differences are being eroded as purchasing disciplines evolve towards a world class standard.

5.5   An example of this is the question of supplier relations. As Van Weele points out, these have typically been less durable in resale than in manufacturing. However, there is a definite trend towards closer and more lasting relationships. One way in which this is evidenced is in the closer involvement of some retailers in the production procedures of manufacturers. This is particularly a feature of the large retail chains such as Tesco and Sainsbury's in the UK.

5.6   Partly this is a matter of quality assurance. A retailer wishes to be able to talk with confidence to his customers about the quality of the goods he offers for sale. This is best achieved by working closely with his suppliers, and this implies long-term relations.

5.7   Partly also it reflects the situation where the distinction between supplier and retailer is vague, as has historically been the case with Marks & Spencer. Marks & Spencer sell their own branded items and their suppliers act, in effect, as the manufacturing arm of the company. For this reason, it is very well known that particularly close relations have existed between M&S and their suppliers. Baily, Farmer, Jessop and Jones (in *Purchasing Principles and Management*) state that M&S have sometimes been called 'a manufacturer without factories'.

5.8   Where an organisation sells 'own-label' products, the role of the retail buyer becomes much more similar to that of the industrial buyer; in each case, purchasing aims to get from the supplier a product which matches the buyer's specification.

5.9   Often a producer will produce both their own branded goods (for sale at a premium price) and equivalent non-branded goods (sometimes referred to as **white label goods**). These latter will be sold to supermarkets who want to apply their own branding. From the producer's point of view, this maximises revenue by satisfying all sectors of the market. The discounted price is affordable to the supplier because the white label version will usually be of lower quality and cheaper to produce.

5.10 A number of issues are increasingly subject to debate among buyers and suppliers.

- Buyers may seek to encourage standardisation and variety reduction among manufacturers.
- Buyers may put pressure on manufacturers to provide training to personnel handling their goods.
- Buyers may look to suppliers for a contribution to advertising costs to the extent that this is likely to benefit the supplier.

The importance of technology

5.11 Technological developments have left few areas of business untouched, but their impact on retailing has been particularly dramatic. Improvements in production technology have led to shorter product lifecycles (ie more rapid introduction of new products) which places increased burdens on the retail buyer to stay abreast of events. One step to this end has been greater involvement of buyers in the product development process.

5.12 Purchase ordering is streamlined to suit the fast turnover that is common in resale organisations. Frequent deliveries are essential, which means that ordering procedures must be simple and rapid. Invariably, advanced information technology is used, including electronic data interchange linking buyers' ordering systems to suppliers' sales systems.

5.13 Once goods are delivered to retail outlets or distribution centres they are recorded in the inventory control system. Many retailers have highly automated systems under which suppliers' performance levels are evaluated at this point in relation to on-time delivery and quality.

5.14 Another important aspect of information technology is the facility it gives to obtain and analyse information about buying patterns among consumers, especially by the use of EPOS systems (electronic point of sale). This is vital for marketing staff in planning prices and promotions and in assessing potential demand for new products. Equally, it gives important clues to buyers as to which products are likely to sell and therefore which products should be bought.

The role of the retail buyer

5.15 The above discussion should have made it clear that buyers in the retail sector may become involved in many different aspects of the business, some of them not conventionally regarded as part of the purchasing function at all.

5.16 For example, buyers may become involved in market research activity, partly to establish what their customers wish to buy but also to monitor the activities of competitors. Statistics provided by suppliers are an important source of this kind of information, but should be treated with caution: suppliers have a vested interest in presenting a picture that will promote sales of their products.

5.17 Buyers should also be involved in the process of setting expenditure budgets. This process involves every layer of an organisation, from the very top down to the lowest levels of managerial control. Within a framework laid down by overall organisational budgets individual buyers must negotiate their own spending limits, and other targets such as sales volume and profit margin to be achieved on particular products for which they are responsible.

5.18 Clearly a major part of the buyer's role is in the selection of products and suppliers. Cooperation with other functional areas such as marketing and merchandising is important in this field. Key decision variables obviously include purchase cost (including discounts and trade credit), but buyers will also be influenced by reliability of supply, the extent to which suppliers invest in new product development, and the level of marketing support given. Marketing support could range from high-profile advertising by the manufacturer to provision of ready-to-sell packaging for point of sale promotional material.

5.19 Buyers are also involved in the management of physical inventory, including storage and distribution. It may or may not be appropriate to use the buying firm's own storage facilities. Often in retail contexts it is **not** appropriate, and a mix of just in time principles and storage at suppliers' premises enables buyers to minimise stock held.

5.20 As already explained, an important part of buying is selling! This is the test of whether the buyer has bought well, and the buyer has an obvious interest in becoming involved in this area.

5.21 A common example is the involvement of buyers in sales promotions; where promotions take place the buyer must be alert to the need for additional ordering to meet the expected increase in demand. For consumers, it is frustrating and a source of ill feeling towards the supplier and stockist if a product advertised and promoted strongly is not available for purchase.

5.22 Buyers are involved in monitoring the sales performance of their products. In many retail organisations the responsibilities of buyers include a certain amount of direct communication with suppliers. In other cases, the centralised nature of the purchasing function makes such communication less feasible. However this may be, it is clearly essential that a buyer monitors sales figures produced by the information system.

5.23 Finally, buyers must be concerned with evaluation of suppliers. Often they will be aided by computer-produced statistics relating to quality and on-time delivery.

Retail supply chains

5.24 The distinctive feature of retail supply chains is the direct relationship between the retailer and the final consumer. Buyers have to identify new lines that will entice additional customers and demand – which requires marketing-oriented competencies in addition to purchasing competencies. Supply chain management will be focused on securing the timely availability or fulfilment of a wide variety of products in response to customer demand.

5.25 Various forms of collaboration have been an increasing feature of retail buyer-supplier relationships, including training of retail sales and service staff by manufacturers, and supplier contribution to retailers' advertising and display costs (where this is of benefit to the supplier). Technological integration has also become widespread, in the form of EDI purchasing, automated inventory control and replenishment, and demand management via electronic point of sale (EPOS) systems.

6 *Technology businesses*

6.1 Important market segments in this area include computer hardware, computer software, telecommunications equipment and systems, and services (systems design, systems maintenance etc).

6.2 The sector is characterised by large-scale research and development, which implies a large capital base for companies wishing to compete effectively. The results of R & D work must be protected by appropriate patents and trade marks, which means that intellectual capital is another important feature of the sector.

6.3 The value of bought out materials, as a proportion of total expenditure, is typically high, which implies a significant role for the purchasing function. Often in this sector it is found that purchasing staff enjoy board level representation.

6.4 The different types of technology businesses have similarities with other businesses discussed earlier. For example, the manufacture of computer hardware is a mainstream activity in the manufacturing sector, sharing many of the characteristics pointed out earlier in Section 2 of this chapter. Similarly, the design of computer software is a type of engineering, which means that the features described in Section 3 of this chapter are applicable (particularly the importance of intellectual property protection).

7   *The services sector*

Characteristics of services

7.1   Services have the following characteristics and features which distinguish them from physical, tangible products.

- **Intangibility**: a service cannot be tasted, touched, seen or smelled before it is purchased. For instance, you will not see the results of going to the dentist before you purchase the service. Because of this a customer will look for other evidence of the service quality, such as the price, the promotional material, the location and the staff who provide the service.

- **Inseparability**: services are produced and consumed at the same time. A service cannot be stored. Using our dentist example again, we can see that both the patient and the dentist have to be present for the service to be provided. Therefore, the influence, personality and performance of the staff providing the service is paramount to success.

- **Heterogeneity**: the quality of a service will be variable. Because of inseparability, the service will be influenced by many factors such as the patient's mood, the dentist's mood, the weather etc. So, it is difficult for a customer to be sure of the outcome of any service he participates in. This is different from buying a tangible product mass-produced on a production line: in this case, it is likely that one unit from the production process is indistinguishable from another.

- **Perishability**: a service cannot be stored so supply of a service is difficult to control. For instance, a dentist cannot store the service of filling a tooth. He may find demand high on some days, while there are no patients on other days. The result of this is that the dentist must always have the capacity to meet high levels of demand, which will be costly during slower periods.

7.2   The result of these distinguishing characteristics is that the marketing and the purchasing of services can be quite complex. Two important features in this context are people and process.

7.3   **People** refers to the actual employees delivering the service. Customer satisfaction can often depend on the person providing the service, because the service is inseparable from the person delivering it. If the employee is inefficient or poorly motivated then interaction with the customer will be affected. It is for this reason that organisations which provide services must be aware of the importance of their 'people'. Attention should be given to recruitment and selection, staff training and motivation in order to minimise heterogeneity of the service.

7.4   **Process** refers to the methods used to provide the service. Procedures for dealing with customers and for supplying the service must be carefully planned and managed to minimise heterogeneity. Many organisations – for example BT and many government agencies such as DVLA – have moved to computerised switchboards to achieve this. Because staff are not involved the customer receives the same standard of service every time he calls the organisation. Additionally, processes must be in place to ensure that the service is provided efficiently during peak hours. For instance, a hairdresser might employ Saturday staff because this is the busiest day of the week. Because a service is perishable the hairdresser will lose custom if he cannot meet demand.

The importance of the services sector

7.5 A major force in increasing the strategic role of purchasing functions has been the development of manufacturing operations. This trend is obviously absent from service companies (though philosophies such as total quality management and continuous improvement are equally relevant to any environment).

7.6 The result is that in many service companies the purchasing function is relatively undeveloped. Indeed, it is sometimes found that many purchasing responsibilities are undertaken by non-purchasing personnel because a centralised purchasing function is either completely absent or ineffective.

7.7 This is an area which is both a concern and an opportunity for the purchasing profession. It is a concern because service companies account for a huge share of gross domestic product in the UK and purchasing disciplines should not be neglected. It is an opportunity because such companies are at present failing to realise benefits which a strong purchasing input could bring.

7.8 Generalisations are always dangerous, but it is probably fair to say that in many service companies purchasing activities are dispersed throughout the organisation, rather than being under centralised control; and to the extent that a centralised function exists at all, its role is mainly clerical and administrative. This situation is changing as increased competition forces service companies to examine value added throughout their supply chains, but the stage of development is less advanced than in manufacturing organisations.

7.9 One characteristic that has retarded the development of purchasing functions in service companies is the absence of a clear link between inputs, processing and outputs. In the case of a manufacturing company this link is very clear: materials are bought in for £X, these are worked on at a cost of £Y and eventually converted into finished products for sale at £Z.

7.10 In a service company this process is much less clear, especially since the value of bought in materials is usually low as a percentage of sales output. For example, whereas a manufacturer might expect, say, 60 per cent of his sales revenue to be absorbed by the cost of bought out materials, for a service company the proportion might be as low as 10 per cent. Most of the inputs of many service companies consist of staff salaries, where purchasing expertise has little to contribute.

7.11 What items are bought out in a typical service organisation? This will obviously depend heavily on the exact nature of the organisation, but the following are likely answers.

- Office equipment and supplies such as stationery
- Computer hardware and software
- Motor vehicles
- Advertising and design services
- Maintenance services (for computers, vehicles and buildings)
- In some cases, capital goods (such as a provider of logistics services who must invest heavily in premises, materials handling equipment, heavy goods vehicles etc)

7.12 Whereas in a manufacturing company a purchasing manager's main 'customer' is the production function, in a service company hardly any of the buyer's effort is directed at 'production'. This is well illustrated by the list above. For this reason among others line managers in such companies have tended to think of purchasing purely as a support function and this has been a factor in the low priority accorded to purchasing expertise.

Modern trends in the services sector

7.13 However, a number of trends are beginning to alter this picture. One is the increased use of **outsourcing**. As service companies focus on core activities they are increasingly likely to outsource such support functions as security, catering, printing, and information technology. The logical conclusion to this development is the use of a facilities management approach under which all such activities are placed under the responsibility of a single facilities manager.

7.14 Another trend with important implications for purchasing is the increased size of service companies and the increased scale of their operations, often resulting from mergers and takeovers which reduce the number of companies operating in any particular sector. Once operations have reached a certain scale the desirability of defined purchasing responsibilities becomes more pressing.

7.15 This is clearer in companies where capital spending is relatively high. Because large sums of money are involved, the impetus to adopt appropriate purchasing techniques may well be present. Without this, the purchase of specialist capital equipment (eg computer hardware and systems) may be left to users whose priorities are not mainly directed to low cost. From their perspective, reliability and quality are vital, value for money less so.

7.16 More generally, it can be said that when responsibility for purchasing decisions is dispersed throughout an organisation, management lose the important 'value for money' perspective. End users of the items purchased are not trained to emphasise this criterion and may instead focus on a solution which has worked reliably in the past, without considering whether better or lower-cost solutions may now be available.

7.17 In all these instances the potential value of a strong purchasing function is clear. If purchasing expertise is directed only at routine low-cost items the scope for cost efficiencies is much reduced. By extending the scope of purchasing involvement senior managers can obtain cost benefits that may be vital in securing competitive advantage.

7.18 This sounds easy enough, but in practice difficulties are encountered. The first hurdle to overcome is at the level of senior managers. Unless they can be persuaded of the strategic importance of the issue any initiative from the purchasing department is likely to be stillborn.

7.19 Even with the support of senior management, there are obstacles that must be removed. Chief among these is the probable reluctance of operational managers to hand over purchasing responsibility. They may perceive purchasing staff as having different priorities from themselves, and may resist what they see as merely a cost cutting exercise. Purchasing must be able to convince them that, while cost is important, operational priorities (such as reliability and delivery lead time) will also be addressed with no less enthusiasm than in the past.

Service supply chains

7.20 In service organisations, the value of bought-in materials is generally a low proportion of sales output and total input: such organisations are highly labour-intensive. However, physical supply may be important if services are based on the use of physical or 'hard' assets: property (as in a hotel or bank branch), vehicles (as in a logistics company or airline) or machinery (as in a computer bureau or printing service). In addition, service organisations commonly buy in goods and services for their own use: office equipment and supplies, computer systems, vehicles, advertising/design services, maintenance services and so on.

7.21 Various trends can be observed in service supply chains.

- Services are increasingly about the management and supply of information: financial services, information and research, entertainment and transport bookings, consultancy, advertising and design and so on. Many information storage, query and processing functions have been automated – and can now be offered direct to the consumer through the internet, interactive kiosks, ATM machines and so on. Supply chains are thus shortening to direct interaction between the service provider and consumer, increasingly on a self-service basis.
- Information can replace inventory (eg in the case of Dell's assembled-to-order computers).
- Services are increasingly outsourced, as organisations focus on core activities and subcontract support functions such as security, catering, printing, IT, sales and customer service, fleet management, HR selection and training, logistics and facilities management.
- The combination of automation and outsourcing has enabled the development of virtual service organisations and networks. Financial services are a good example: mortgages, insurance and investment products are often supplied by a network of providers, drawn on by brokers who interface with consumers.

7.22 Perhaps the key point about service supply chains is the importance of people in delivering service and differentiating one service provider from another. Training, motivation, empowerment and cultural values are important factors in service supply. Supply chain management will also contribute to competitive advantage through cost efficiency and the integrated management of information.

8 The third sector

Different types of organisation

8.1 In addition to the commercial firms that we have considered so far there are many organisations that do not exist primarily to make a profit. These include, for example, charities, educational institutions (in both the private and public sectors), museums, hospitals, prisons etc. (Local and central government departments are also included in this sector, but were discussed in the previous chapter.) Your syllabus refers to these organisations as the third sector: presumably private and public are the first two sectors.

8.2 Organisations in this sector have typically been set up to achieve a defined objective (eg a charitable purpose) rather than to maximise profit. They usually derive their income from donations, legacies and grants, but may also have a trading arm (eg the high street Oxfam shops). They are often owned by their members (or by a charitable trust) and are managed by trustees, or by a board of directors.

8.3 The term 'non-profit' or 'not-for-profit' should not be interpreted as implying a disregard for commercial disciplines. On the contrary, in some respects such disciplines are more important than in the private commercial sector. And it is worth noting that some such organisations certainly enjoy a surplus of income over expenditure, even if it is not described in their accounts as a profit.

- Charities are anxious to devote as much as possible of their income to the charitable work for which they are instituted. A healthy regard for cost control contributes towards this aim.

- Public sector educational institutions, hospitals etc are typically constrained by cash limits placed on them by funding authorities. They are obliged to keep expenditure within these limits, and consequently their financial objective is to get the greatest benefit possible from each pound spent.

8.4 These considerations should indicate that purchasing professionals have as important a role to play in non-profit organisations as in commercial enterprises. Some of the organisations discussed here are vast in scope and make many millions of pounds worth of purchases in a year. Moreover the regulatory framework under which they operate often calls for particularly specialised purchasing skills.

The regulatory environment

8.5 A significant factor affecting buyers in the not-for-profit sector is that they are performing a stewardship function. That is to say, they are spending money that has been derived not from the organisation's own trading efforts, but from someone else's donations or taxes. For this reason, purchasers in this arena are more closely regulated than buyers in the private commercial sector. There is a strong emphasis on accountability and stewardship.

8.6 As an example of this, consider the work of the Charities Commission, the regulatory body for UK charities.

8.7 The purposes of the Commission's regulatory activities are as follows.

- To ensure that charities meet the legal requirements for being a charity, and are equipped to operate properly and within the law
- To check that charities are run for public benefit, and not for private advantage
- To ensure that charities are independent and that their trustees take their decisions free of control or undue influence from outside
- To detect and remedy serious mismanagement or deliberate abuse by or within charities

8.8 The steps the Commission takes to ensure compliance by charities include the following.

- To operate as a charity, the organisation must first register with the Commission. The Commission will scrutinise their application to ensure it is appropriate.

- The Commission organises visits to hundreds of charities each year to review their activities, constitution and administration, identifying good and bad practice

- The Commission evaluates complaints or other evidence of possible causes for concern. Where this indicates that something may have gone seriously wrong, the Commission opens a formal investigation.

- In the case of mismanagement or abuse, the Commission has powers to intervene in charities to protect charity assets.

Corporate social responsibility (CSR)

8.9 This is an area that we have discussed at length in an earlier chapter. For our purposes here it is sufficient to note that the organisations we are currently discussing tend to have a particular concern for CSR. This is because they are public bodies, and therefore come under public scrutiny which stimulates them to observe modern principles of CSR. They also lack a profit motive, which means they have less incentive to skimp on their obligations in this area.

9 Differences in supply chains

Differences in supply chains

9.1 Having examined a large number of different industry sectors, it is useful to consider the differences that may arise in the supply chain of an organisation. This is particularly of interest in connection with the means by which organisations sell their products. A useful distinction is between organisations that supply consumer products and those that sell industrial products.

9.2 The differences in the supply chains of such organisations are illustrated in Figure 3.1. (We return in Chapter 6 to the distinction between consumer products and industrial products.)

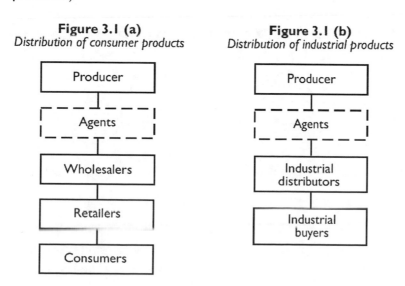

Figure 3.1 (a)
Distribution of consumer products

Figure 3.1 (b)
Distribution of industrial products

9.3   The use of agents depends very much on normal practice within the industry sector, as indicated by the dotted lines in Figure 3.1.

9.4   Figure 3.1 illustrated the downstream distribution of a producer's goods to the eventual customers. We might equally illustrate the upstream supply chain: see Figure 3.2.

Figure 3.2 *Example of an upstream supply chain*

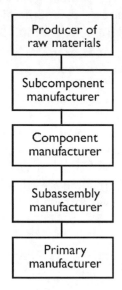

9.5   In a retail environment, the supply chain looks very different. See Figure 3.3, which is due to Baily *et al* in *Purchasing Principles and Management*.

Figure 3.3 *Supply chains in retailing*

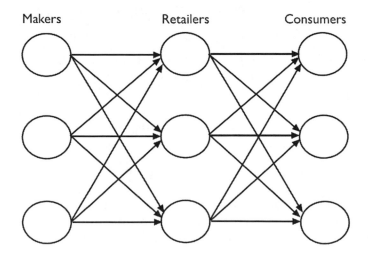

Chapter summary

- Primary industries are concerned with extracting natural resources from the earth. Particular problems for buyers in this sector include supplying remote and difficult locations and the provision of emergency and standby materials.

- In the manufacturing sector, purchasing is a relatively advanced function, often represented at board level.

- The nature of the production process in manufacturing firms will affect the work of buyers. It is usual to distinguish between project work, jobbing production, batch manufacturing, mass production and continuous processes.

- The engineering sector comprises civil engineers, mechanical engineers, electrical engineers, chemical engineers and software engineers, among others.

- In the FMCG sector, competitive forces are strong, and there is an emphasis on branding. Short product lifecycles are also an influence on the work of buyers.

- In the retail sector buyers must have a close interest in sales and marketing activities, because their job is to buy what will sell. Technological developments are vitally important in this sector (eg EPOS).

- In the technology sector the value of bought out materials is a high proportion of total spending, which means that buyers have an important role to play.

- In the services sector the purchasing function is sometimes relatively undeveloped. Many purchases are initiated by users rather than going through a specialist buyer.

- The term 'not-for-profit sector' does not imply a disregard for commercial disciplines. Charities and similar organisations must avoid waste in order to spend as much of their income as possible on their objectives.

Self-test questions

Numbers in brackets refer to the paragraphs where you can check your answers.

1   List key characteristics of extractive industries from the perspective of buyers. (1.4)

2   List key characteristics of manufacturing industries from the perspective of buyers. (2.3)

3   List ways in which purchasing can contribute to a manufacturing firm's competitive advantage. (2.10)

4   What three main categories of operation are undertaken by engineering firms? (3.3)

5   Explain how buyers in the FMCG sector are influenced by short product lifecycles and branding. (4.3, 4.4)

6   What is meant by white label goods? (5.9)

7   What specialised areas may buyers become involved in when working in the retail sector? (5.16–5.23)

8   What are the main market segments in the technology sector? (6.1)

9   List four distinguishing characteristics of services. (7.1)

10   What kinds of items are purchased by a firm in the services sector? (7.11)

11   What are the purposes of the Charities Commission's regulatory activities? (8.7)

12   Illustrate the different supply chains that may apply to consumer products and industrial products. (Figure 3.1)

CHAPTER 4

Organising the Purchasing Function

Chapter learning objectives

1.5   Evaluate the context of the purchasing function and different purchasing situations.

- Purchasing as a discrete organisational function within the supply chain
- The various functional models for purchasing: centralised, decentralised, centre-led action network (CLAN), lead buyer/business partnering and matrix structure
- Typical division of roles and responsibilities within purchasing
- The part-time purchaser

Chapter headings

1   Purchasing as an organisational function

2   Functional models for purchasing

3   Purchasing roles and responsibilities

4   The part-time purchaser

1   Purchasing as an organisational function

The level at which purchasing operates

1.1   Recent years have witnessed a change in perspective in relation to the role of purchasing. In broad terms, the older perspective of purchasing as a clerical and administrative support function is giving way to a perspective in which the strategic contribution of supply chain management is recognised.

1.2   This change is in some cases a sudden one. For example, a new chief executive may be appointed with different views from his predecessor and a determination to re-shape the role of the purchasing function. Or the purchasing function may itself be headed by a new manager sufficiently dynamic to change the perceptions of senior management.

1.3   Often, though, the change comes about gradually as modern techniques, policies and procedures slowly win acceptance. While this process is taking place the position of purchasing in the organisation may gradually change. In general, the level at which purchasing operates in the organisation will increase as its strategic importance is more widely recognised.

1.4   Lysons identifies three hierarchical levels at which purchasing may operate.

- At the lowest level, purchasing is a routine clerical function. As Lysons states, this may well be the case in a small business, or perhaps in a group situation where centralised policies and procedures leave little scope for initiative at local level.

- As purchasing advances, it may become a middle management function. The head of purchasing, whatever his title, reports to a level well below that of the main board, perhaps to a production director if purchasing is seen as a support service for production. This situation may also apply if purchasing is seen as one element in a materials or logistics management structure.

- At the highest level, the head of purchasing may be a member of senior management, perhaps on the main board of the company or group.

1.5   The progression through these stages may well be driven by growing consciousness of purchasing's effect on profitability. As the proportion of external spending rises relative to internal spending the scope for purchasing to improve bottom line profits increases. Another stimulus is given by the rise in automation, leading to very high levels of investment in capital assets; in this area, the need to 'get it right' dictates that specialist purchasing skills are used.

The structure of the purchasing function

1.6   The way in which purchasing tasks are divided among members of staff obviously depends mainly on the size of the department. In a very small purchasing department there may be just a single buyer with perhaps an assistant and a small number of support staff. The organisation structure for the department might be something like Figure 4.1.

Figure 4.1 *Organisation of a small purchasing department*

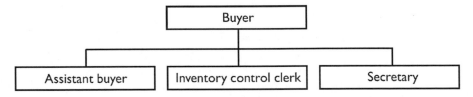

1.7   Clearly this structure leaves little scope for specialisation. Most buying policies and decisions will be initiated by the buyer, with routine matters delegated as far as possible to the assistant buyer.

1.8   In larger organisations the purchasing department is likely to be more developed, with more staff and greater specialisation. A structure such as that in Figure 4.2 may exist.

Figure 4.2 *Organisation of a medium-sized purchasing department*

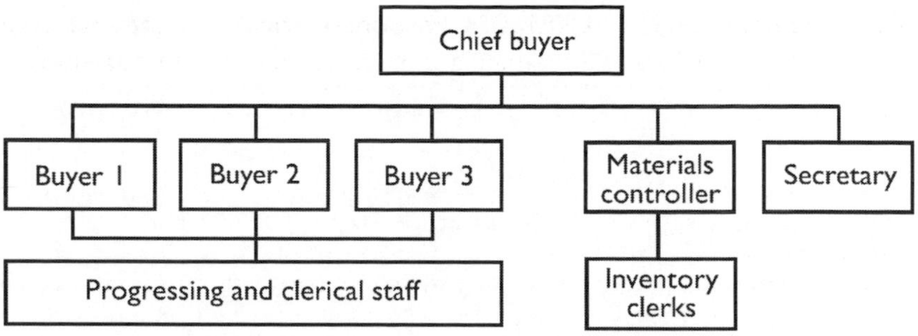

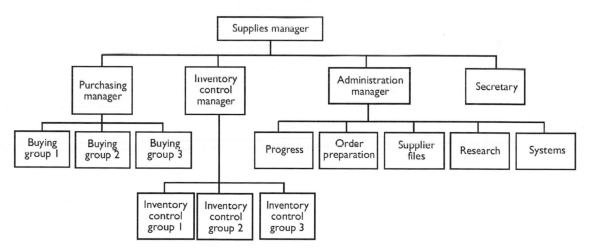

1.9   In this kind of organisation, the chief buyer will be responsible for purchasing policy, as well as for managing the smooth running of the department, but many (perhaps most) of the day-to-day purchasing decisions will be taken by the buyers who report to him. These have the opportunity to specialise.

1.10   One possibility is that each buyer deals with a particular range of items. Another possibility relevant to project-based organisations (eg construction companies) is to allocate responsibility for each project to a particular buyer. At any given moment a buyer may be purchasing all the materials required for a number of particular projects, while his colleagues are doing the same for other projects.

1.11   Specialisation of course increases as the size of the department grows. In a large department a structure such as that in Figure 4.3 may be apparent. The problems of communication and control are evidently much greater in such a large department and must be addressed carefully if optimum performance is to be obtained.

Figure 4.3 *Organisation of a large purchasing department*

1.12   The responsibilities of the purchasing function can be analysed according to the familiar division into strategic, tactical and operational responsibilities. These are set out in Table 4.1.

Table 4.1 *The responsibilities of a purchasing function*

Strategic responsibilities	Tactical responsibilities	Operational responsibilities
Developing guidelines and procedures	Preparing specifications	Preparing orders
Developing performance monitoring systems	Preparing value analysis programmes	Expediting
Major sourcing decisions, such as single vs multiple sourcing, reciprocal trading	Selecting and contracting with suppliers	Monitoring and evaluating supplier performance
Major decisions relating to capital investment or make-or-buy	Preparing certification programmes for suppliers	
Establishing long-term partnership and co-makership relations	Agreement on corporate and/or annual supplier agreements	

Purchasing as a subsidiary function

1.13 So far we have assumed that there is a dedicated purchasing function in the organisation. But what if there is not?

1.14 In such cases, purchasing usually reports through another functional head, and there are generally three possibilities.

- **Production/operations**. The focus of attention for any purchasing activity will be on production-related logistical difficulties. Purchasing will be unlikely to make a valuable contribution to design, marketing and competitiveness, given that it will not secure the involvement of suppliers in value engineering, value analysis or bidders' conferences.

- **Finance**. Reporting through the finance department can suppress the purchasing professional's creativity. Responsibility for purchasing expenditure and the management of supplier credit can be used as crude short-term braking mechanisms, which in turn stifle partnership arrangements and can jeopardise long-term goals and aspirations for strategic purchasing activities.

- **Commercial**. This probably represents the best choice from a bad lot. A commercial director who also acts as purchasing manager should have individual responsibility for the final decision on proposals and quotations. There should be a formal set of procedures to examine the appropriateness of any bid to overall corporate strategy.

Departmentation

1.15 The paragraphs above discuss the structure of the purchasing function as an entity in itself. However, the purchasing function is of course just one part of the overall organisation. There has been much study of how organisations are structured, and although this topic does not appear to be specified in your syllabus, we discuss it here because it may possibly be examined (and in fact it was touched on in the May 2007 exam).

1.16 A key issue in organisational structure is the division of labour between different departments (departmentation). In a very small company, people can simply share the tasks between them according to their skills. Once an organisation grows beyond a certain size, however, systematic specialisation is required. This typically involves the grouping together and allocation of specific aspects of the work to different departments. This can be done on the basis of criteria such as:

- Functional specialisation
- Geographical area or territory
- Product, brand or customer.

We will look at each of these in turn.

Functional organisation

1.17 In a functional structure, tasks are grouped together according to the common nature or focus of the task: production, sales and marketing, accounting and finance, purchasing and so on. An example of a functionally structured organisation is shown in Figure 4.4.

Figure 4.4 *Functional organisation*

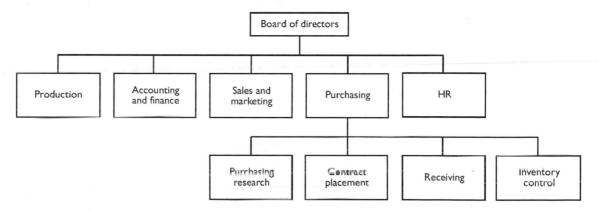

Geographical organisation

1.18 In a geographical structure, tasks are grouped together according to the region in which the activity takes place, or within which target markets or market segments are located. Multi-site organisations (eg a purchasing function organised by plant) and sales departments (with allocated 'territories') are often organised this way. An example of a geographically-structured organisation is shown in Figure 4.5.

Figure 4.5 *Geographical organisation*

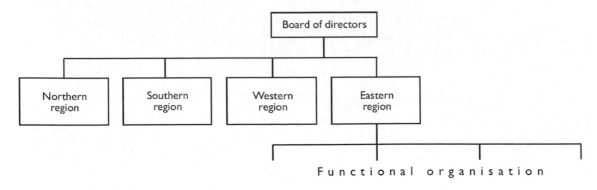

Product/brand/customer organisation
Product/brand/customer organisation

1.19 In a product structure, tasks are grouped together according to the product, product line, customer or brand they relate to. Companies with distinct brands (such as Coca Cola or Persil) often organise in this way, so that there is specialisation of brand marketing and identity – and separate brand accountabilities. Similarly, companies with key customer types, such as publishers (for example trade (bookshops), educational institutions, libraries) may group together tasks in this way. In purchasing, the equivalent may be organisation by items purchased: Figure 4.6.

Figure 4.6 *Product/brand/customer organisation*

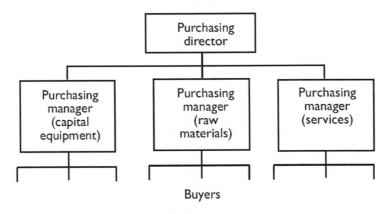

Advantages and disadvantages of different structural forms

1.20 The advantages and disadvantages of the various forms of organisation are summarised in Table 4.2.

Divisionalisation

1.21 Divisionalisation is the division of the organisation into more or less autonomous strategic business units, as the business diversifies into new areas. Divisions may be:

- **Profit or investment centres within a company**. Strategic planning and other technostructure and support activities (such as finance, HR, research and development and perhaps purchasing) are undertaken at a central board or 'head office' level. Divisions may be based on function (retail division, manufacturing division), product (hardware division, software division) or region (Asian-Pacific division, European division). Each division may then be organised in an appropriate way: see Figure 4.7.

- **Subsidiary companies grouped under a holding company**. When businesses grow through acquisition, or require a high degree of differentiation in product or regional divisions, they may form a group of independent public or private companies, owned or controlled by a holding company.

Table 4.2 *Different structural forms*

Organisation	Advantages	Disadvantages
Functional	• Pools and focuses specialised skills and knowledge • Share specialised technology and equipment for efficiency • Facilitates the recruitment, training and management of specialist staff • Avoids duplicating functions within area/product departments: enables economies of scale	• Focuses on inputs/processes rather than outputs/customers (necessary for customer satisfaction) • Creates vertical barriers to cross-disciplinary communication (necessary to flexibility and coordination)
Geographical	• Decision-making at the interface between organisation and local stakeholders (with distinctive needs) • Cost-effective (because shorter) lines of supply and communication to local markets or plants	• Duplication of functional activities • Loss of standardisation, due to local differences
Product/brand/customer	• Clearer accountability for the profitability of different products/brands/customer groups • Specialisation of production and marketing expertise • Coordination of different functions by product managers	• Increased managerial complexity and overhead costs • Possible fragmentation of objectives and markets

Figure 4.7 *Divisional structure*

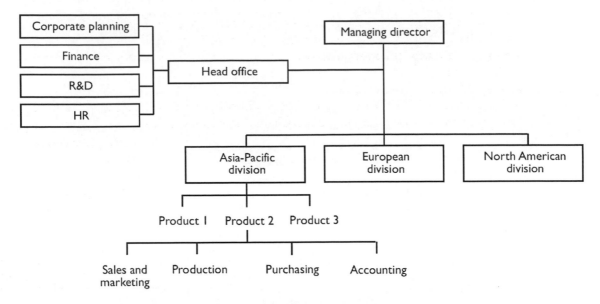

1.22 The advantages and disadvantages of divisionalisation can be summarised as follows.

- **Advantages**

  – Clear accountability for each division as a profit/investment unit
  – Sensitivity to region/product-specific demands and opportunities
  – Efficiencies and economies of scale available from centralised functions
  – Co-ordination available from centralised strategic planning and control.

- **Disadvantages**

  – Potential fragmentation of overall objectives and markets
  – Potential conflict between central management and divisional specialists
  – Potential competition between divisions for centrally-allocated resources
  – Units may not be large enough to support managerial overheads.

Hybrid structures

1.23 'Hybrid' simply means 'crossed' or 'mixed'. As you may have noticed from the various organisation charts shown above, businesses generally combine a variety of organisational forms. For example, they may be organised by region or product at divisional level, with functional departments within each division. Hybrid structures allow the advantages of each form of organisation to be leveraged in appropriate ways: brand identity to be reinforced by a product division, for example, with regional knowledge to be capitalised on by its sales departments and economies of scale to be gained by a specialised purchasing department.

Matrix structures

1.24 The 'matrix' structure emerged at American aerospace company Lockheed in the 1950s, when its customer (the US government) became frustrated at dealing separately with a number of functional specialists when negotiating defence contracts. The concept of the 'project co-ordinator' or 'customer account manager' was born.

1.25 The essence of matrix structure is dual authority: staff in different functions or regions are responsible both to their departmental managers, in regard to the activities of the department, and to a product, project or account manager, in regard to the activities of the department related to the given product, project or account.

1.26 The matrix can be illustrated as follows, in the case of an advertising agency: Figure 4.8.

Figure 4.8 *Matrix organisation*

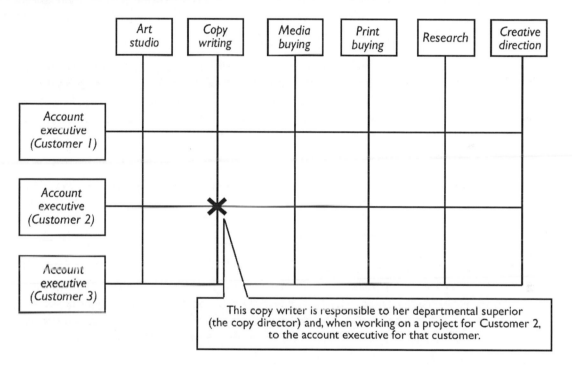

This copy writer is responsible to her departmental superior (the copy director) and, when working on a project for Customer 2, to the account executive for that customer.

1.27 The advantages and disadvantages of matrix structure can be summarised as follows.

- **Advantages**
    - Combines functional efficiency with product/project accountability
    - Fosters interdisciplinary cooperation in pursuit of project goals
    - Develops tolerance of flexibility and ambiguity: improved change, learning
    - Focuses all functions on customer satisfaction and results: more satisfying
    - Brings conflicts of authority into the open.

- **Disadvantages**
    - Potential competition/conflict between dual managers
    - Potential stress on staff 'caught' between competing or conflicting demands
    - Potential inefficiency of ambiguous priorities and switching between tasks
    - More complex (potentially slower) decision-making processes
    - Costs of added management layer, meetings and so on.

2   *Functional models for purchasing*

Centralisation and decentralisation

2.1   An important organisational issue is the extent to which purchasing responsibilities should be centralised, ie placed in the hands of a single department reporting to a single executive.

2.2   One particular context in which this arises concerns service firms. In such firms it is common to find that purchasing is carried out by users rather than by purchasing specialists. (And this practice is by no means confined to service firms.)

2.3   This situation gives rise to no real differences of opinion in the purchasing literature: almost without exception, commentators suggest that responsibilities for purchasing should lie as far as possible with purchasing specialists. Although user departments have an important role in decision making, actual selection of suppliers and processing of orders falls to the purchasing function.

2.4   The position is far more complex when multi-site operations are in question. Clearly, an organisation that operates through a number of branches or divisions, perhaps separated by considerable distances, may consider a single purchasing function at head office (centralisation) or separate functions at each division (decentralisation). The choice is rarely clear cut, and an aim of this section of the text is to review the advantages and disadvantages of each option.

2.5   Before doing so, however, it is worthwhile to consider whether it is always feasible to centralise purchasing operations. In cases where it is not feasible, clearly a decentralised structure is the only option.

2.6   The main reason why centralisation is sometimes not feasible is that the various divisions in the group use and purchase entirely different materials. Strictly speaking, it is still feasible to adopt centralised purchasing even in this case, but more realistically it would not make sense to do so. The main advantages of centralisation, as we will see below, are to do with consolidating the requirements of several divisions, and this aim is undermined if there is no similarity between the requirements.

2.7   However, firms are sometimes too quick to reach this conclusion without proper examination of the nature of their requirements. In practice, it will rarely happen that divisions of a single firm use **completely** different materials. More probably, they use materials which differ in detail but belong to the same major categories, and hence can be sourced from the same suppliers. This situation reinstates the advantages of centralisation and the topic is once again open to discussion.

2.8   Another reason why centralisation may not be feasible is concerned with geographical dispersion. Modern transport and communications have reduced the importance of this factor, but where divisions are very widely dispersed the practicality of a fully centralised purchasing function must be questionable.

Advantages of centralisation

2.9   In most cases, both centralisation and decentralisation are realistic options. The problem then is to decide which policy offers the greater advantages. In this section we look at the advantages of centralising the purchasing function. In the next section we will consider the advantages of decentralisation.

2.10 To begin with it is worth pointing out that the choice is not necessarily between two extreme possibilities. There is a spectrum of organisational arrangements bounded at one end by full centralisation and at the other by full decentralisation. In between, there are arrangements in which some activities are centralised while other matters are decided at local level. Most organisations operate somewhere in the middle of the spectrum rather than at its extremes.

2.11 A major advantage claimed for centralisation of purchasing is the greater specialisation that is possible among purchasing staff. If 100 purchasing staff are scattered around 10 divisions each of them must have general responsibility for a wide range of his division's requirements. General responsibilities lead to general knowledge, and highly specialised knowledge may be absent.

2.12 By contrast if 100 purchasing staff are based at a single centralised location, there is opportunity to divide tasks among them on the basis of specialised skills. Each buyer can focus on a particular area and develop his knowledge to greater depth. This has great benefits when a wide range of complex materials are required by the organisation.

2.13 A further advantage is that the requirements of different divisions can be consolidated. This reduces the frequency of very small orders for a particular material and enables buyers to obtain better prices and service. The number of suppliers is likely to be smaller, and order administration and processing is more streamlined. This advantage is particularly evident if the divisions are relatively small, because in such a case there is a high likelihood that their individual requirements might be for uneconomic amounts.

2.14 Greater coordination of purchasing activities may result from a centralised structure. For example, uniform purchasing policies and procedures can be introduced and standardisation is facilitated. Staff training and development can be undertaken systematically.

2.15 Centralisation generally enables greater **standardisation** of procedures and specifications, avoiding 'maverick' buying and requirements.

- Standardisation of procedures should enable greater consistency of action, better performance monitoring and management (against consistent measures), better control and improved compliance.

- Standardisation of specifications should enhance quality and efficiency in a number of ways: facilitating the consolidation of orders; larger (but fewer) orders, for economies of scale and reduced transaction costs; a reduced supplier base (with fewer 'specialist' requirements); reduced inventory and handling costs (less variety and greater utilisation); improved quality management (ease of inspection etc); simpler and more accurate ordering; and simpler internal and supply chain communication.

2.16   Centralisation of purchasing can also avoid price anomalies between group companies or divisions. Even more importantly, it can avoid actual conflict between them in times when supplies of a particular material are scarce.

2.17   Finally, the vital area of purchasing research is often neglected if individual divisions are expected to carry it out. This is partly because it is a specialised area, and specialised skills may not be available at divisional level. Partly also it is because the need for divisional purchasing staff to conduct a wide range of activities may mean that some areas receive too little attention; purchasing research is often the Cinderella in this scenario.

2.18   If purchasing is centralised, it is usual to establish the function at head office and to appoint an overall manager or director reporting at board level. Apart from operational buying, the function will handle planning, purchasing research, specialised buying, and negotiation of long-term contracts.

2.19   The benefits of centralisation are often held to be compelling and adoption of centralised structures in some cases has spread even beyond organisational boundaries. This is the case for example in **buying consortia**, which has been a notable trend in UK local government authorities. For example, Baily, Farmer, Jessop and Jones in *Purchasing Principles and Management* cite the example of the Yorkshire Purchasing Organisation that buys on behalf of several local authorities. We discuss buying consortia in the next chapter.

2.20   Centralised purchasing suffers from the disadvantage that communication is difficult. However, this can to some extent be countered by developing detailed purchasing manuals, arranging regular visits to divisions by central purchasing personnel, and by training courses emphasising group policies. Electronic links are also extremely important in overcoming this difficulty.

Advantages of decentralisation

2.21   Although the above considerations are powerful arguments for centralisation, things are rarely so clear cut as they might suggest. There are also significant advantages in devolving purchasing responsibilities to local level.

2.22   One reason for doing so is to maximise coordination between purchasing and operating departments. Buyers are close to users and develop a close understanding of their needs and problems. Face-to-face discussions are easy to organise and can help to crystallise problems and stimulate solutions.

2.23   Another benefit of decentralisation is that local buyers can respond more quickly to user needs. Centralised purchasing can run into difficulties if things do not go exactly according to plan. Reacting quickly to changes in schedules or unforeseen problems is easier if buyers are close to the scene of operations. Relying on long-distance communication inevitably means that response times are longer.

2.24   Locally based buyers also have the advantage of knowing locally based suppliers. There are great advantages – of cost, delivery time etc – in sourcing from short distances, and a centralised purchasing function will have difficulty in identifying good local suppliers.

2.25 Finally, there is an important management principle that supports a policy of decentralisation. This is the principle that a divisional manager can only be held accountable for the performance of his division if he has genuine control over its operations. This is not the case if the vitally important area of procurement is taken out of his hands and given instead to a centralised purchasing function.

2.26 If purchasing is carried out at local level, it is likely that there will still be a need for a centralised purchasing function to carry out specialised activities, such as purchasing research or buying of specialised materials. Often long-term contracts may be negotiated by the central purchasing office with divisional buyers calling off requirements against the contracts.

2.27 Lysons suggests that a mix of centralised and decentralised purchasing is common in practice. Both local and central purchasing functions exist, with a division of duties somewhat as indicated by Table 4.3.

Table 4.3 *Duties of local and central purchasing functions*

Local purchasing function	Centralised purchasing function
Small order items	Determination of major purchasing policies
Items used only by the local division	Preparation of standard specifications
Emergency purchases (to avoid disruption to production)	Negotiation of bulk contracts for a number of divisions
Items sourced from local suppliers	Stationery and office equipment
Local purchasing undertaken for social 'community' reasons	Purchasing research Staff training and development Purchase of capital assets

Centre-led action network (CLAN)

2.28 A modern trend in the organisation of a purchasing function is the centre-led action network (CLAN). This is a relatively decentralised model that has become popular in many large organisations. Its basic principles are well explained in an article by Peter Smith in *Supply Management* (April 2003 issue). The notes below are based on Smith's article and the replies to it which appeared in subsequent issues of *Supply Management*.

2.29 According to Smith, the CLAN model is based on procurement staff located in many different business units (as opposed to a centralised model, where all or most procurement staff are located in a single unit). These staff report primarily to the local management of their business unit, though they also have a responsibility to a small procurement centre usually located at corporate HQ. This is an example of a **matrix management structure**, where some staff report to more than one boss.

2.30 The procurement centre leads the network, sets standards, encourages the spread of best practice and persuades the different elements of the network to cooperate. Often this is achieved by the concept of a **lead buyer**.

2.31　The lead buyer approach involves delegating defined purchasing responsibilities onto a designated individual within a user department. For example, a member of the manufacturing department is given responsibility for certain purchasing activities. This has the advantage that the user department is closely involved in purchasing decisions. The disadvantage is that the lead buyer is not a professional buyer.

2.32　To make this concept work, it is essential that the purchasing function give appropriate support to the lead buyer. If this is successful, the benefit is better communication and improved relations between purchasing and user departments.

2.33　A similar benefit is claimed for the concept of **business partnering**. This is where a member of the purchasing team works within a different functional area, typically one in which there is a very large external spend. The business partner – ie the purchasing specialist – liaises closely with members of the other function, acting in effect as a representative of the purchasing department. It is his task to identify situations where the involvement of the purchasing function can add value.

2.34　Peter Smith argued that despite its advantages, CLAN was losing favour with many large organisations. In some cases its replacement is a model that Smith refers to as SCAN – strategically controlled action network. This too is based on a matrix structure, but the difference is that the primary reporting responsibility of local procurement staff is to the central procurement unit. Their responsibility to local management of their own business unit becomes secondary.

2.35　In a SCAN structure there is a central core of procurement staff with a small team looking at strategy, policy, training, competence, exchange of good practice and performance management. There is a team of category managers responsible for those goods and services that have a high degree of commonality across the organisation. And there are business purchasing teams that work closely with the individual business unit.

2.36　Smith argued that CLAN offers advantages: procurement is identified closely with local needs and can react quickly to business needs. But there is a potential loss of leverage (as in all decentralised models), and it needs constant energy from the centre to drive cooperative activity. On the other hand, the SCAN model suffers from the disadvantages of centralised operations generally; these have already been discussed above.

3　*Purchasing roles and responsibilities*

Introduction

3.1　It used to be a relatively simple matter to define the work performed by purchasing staff. This was because the purchasing function used to be regarded as a reactive support service, responding to the needs of other functions as they arose by performing routine clerical and administrative tasks.

3.2　This outlook has changed radically over the years. The view of the purchasing function is now typically more strategic in nature: the range of tasks to be completed is broader and the complexity of the purchasing operations is greater. However, it is still possible to distinguish a number of broad areas of responsibility.

3.3 Clerical and administrative tasks remain vital even in a more strategic environment. Record keeping, origination and processing of purchase orders and other documentation, and storage and retrieval of data are essential to the smooth running of the department. These tasks are usually to a greater or lesser degree automated and the amount of man hours expended on such activities is a declining proportion of overall purchasing effort.

3.4 Negotiating and buying are perhaps the core activities of a purchasing function. This category of work includes locating, assessing and selecting potential suppliers, as well as settling terms and conditions between buyer and seller.

3.5 Expediting, like other non-value adding activities, is increasingly tackled by automation and by approaches that seek to eliminate the need for follow-up. In an ideal world suppliers would perform exactly as required by the time required and no follow-up would be necessary. Until that happy day dawns, though, we must recognise that expediting is an essential part of purchasing work.

3.6 The importance of purchasing research has never been greater. The pace of change in the environment generally, and in supply markets in particular, make it essential to dedicate staff to monitoring activities. The objective is to improve the quality of buying by collecting, classifying and analysing relevant data to help in decision making. This area embraces economic forecasting, demand projections, analysis of prices and availability of materials, and analysis of potential suppliers.

3.7 Management of the purchasing function includes development of policies, procedures and controls; management of resources; the building of relationships within the purchasing and supply chain; and dealing with specific problems in supplier and commodity management.

Typical roles and responsibilities

3.8 Your syllabus refers to 'typical division of roles and responsibilities within purchasing'. The word 'typical' is important: naturally, there will be much variation in the way that roles and responsibilities are divided among staff members. In particular, such division will be much more a feature of large purchasing departments than small ones.

3.9 Guidance issued by CIPS indicates that the following roles are considered 'typical'. We will look at each of them in turn.

- Head of Purchasing
- Senior Purchasing Manager
- Purchasing Manager
- Contracts Manager
- Supplier Manager
- Expediter
- Purchasing Analyst
- Purchasing Leadership Team

The Head of Purchasing

3.10   The Head of Purchasing may have a title such as Procurement Director. In many organisations, this will be a position on the main board.

3.11   As the job title suggests, the Head of Purchasing takes overall responsibility for all the work of the purchasing function. In particular, he provides strategic leadership in areas such as policy formulation. The strategic aspect of this role is vital, particularly in a large organisation. The Head of Purchasing should be able to rise above the day-to-day operational pressures in order to give overall direction to the work of the purchasing function.

3.12   In practice, it is unlikely that the Head of Purchasing will be able to exercise control over every aspect of purchasing. This is because it would be impractical in most organisations to centralise purchasing to such an extent. Even in a strongly centralised environment, there is always likely to be a role for user departments in purchasing routine, low-value items.

3.13   As head of the entire function, the Head of Purchasing is also responsible for representing the function in its dealings with other departments. This calls for strong leadership and communication skills, especially in the need to convey to other departmental heads the benefits offered by the purchasing function.

Senior Purchasing Manager

3.14   The Senior Purchasing Manager (SPM) will be next in seniority to the Head of Purchasing. Typically, he will be leader of a team of Purchasing Managers. His team leadership role will involve coordination of all activities undertaken by his subordinates.

3.15   The SPM will work within the strategic framework laid down by the Head of Purchasing. Following this guidance, he will be responsible for broad decisions on market evaluation, sourcing, appraisal and selection of suppliers, negotiations with suppliers, and award of contracts.

3.16   Depending on the organisational structure, the SPM may be responsible for just a single category of purchase (eg IT expenditure, or expenditure on raw materials or commodities), or alternatively his brief may extend across all categories of external spend. A relatively common structure in large organisations would involve an SPM in charge of one large category of expenditure, with a number of Purchasing Managers reporting to him, each of whom takes responsibility for a subdivision of the SPM's spending.

Purchasing Manager

3.17   The Purchasing Manager has responsibilities similar in scope to those of the SPM, though of course at a lower level. He may be a single individual, or one of several reporting to the SPM. Like the SPM, his role may be confined to a single category of spend, or it may be more wide-ranging. This largely depends on the size of the purchasing function as a whole.

3.18   The Purchasing Manager will not generally become involved in the day-to-day running of established contracts. His role typically ends with the award of a contract, leaving others to deal with subsequent contract management.

Contracts Manager

3.19   A Contracts Manager will be needed in cases where a large and complex contract has been awarded. In such a case it becomes important to manage all the issues specified in the contract: monitoring that supplier performance is up to standard, ensuring that payments to suppliers are made in line with the agreement, checking and approving changes to the contract if any are necessary.

3.20   This is a closely defined role, and the Contracts Manager will not become involved in wider issues. For example, general relations with the supplier are the province of the Supplier Manager; the Contracts Manager is concerned solely with ensuring that both parties fulfil their contractual obligations.

Supplier Manager

3.21   Once a contract has been awarded (typically by the Purchasing Manager) it becomes important to manage relations with the successful supplier. The Supplier Manager will be concerned to evaluate the supplier along a number of different dimensions (the term 'balanced scorecard' is sometimes used to describe this approach). For example, the supplier will be interested in quality management systems, supplier involvement in new product development, supplier development, information sharing etc.

3.22   To distinguish the roles of Contract Manager and Supplier Manager it is important to realise that there may well be more than one contract with any particular supplier. The Contract Manager will be concerned with strict compliance to the terms of a particular contract; the Supplier Manager will be concerned with broader aspects of the relationship with the supplier.

Expediter

3.23   As the name suggests, the role of the expediter begins once an order has been placed. At that point, it is rarely sufficient to sit back and trust that the supplier will deliver on time. More realistically, it will be necessary to expedite: ie to chase the supplier so as to ensure timely delivery of the correct items ordered. Without this, we risk late or inaccurate delivery, with damaging knock-on effects on production.

Purchasing Analyst

3.24   Purchasing analysis (or purchasing research) is a vital role in a large purchasing function. The role of the Analyst is to investigate the supply market, to gather data, and to organise it into information that can be used by other members of the purchasing team. This is essentially a support role for the purchasing function as a whole, and as such is sometimes neglected in all but the largest purchasing departments. The focus of the Analyst's attention may be on suppliers or on the items and materials purchased by the organisation.

Purchasing Leadership Team

3.25 As the name suggests, this is a team comprising senior members of the purchasing function, particularly in large organisations. The team is naturally led by the Head of Purchasing and provides a means by which he can communicate with the senior members of staff reporting to him. The focus of meetings will be on the strategic direction envisioned by the Head of Purchasing.

4 *The part-time purchaser*

What is meant by part-time purchasing?

4.1 Earlier in this chapter we looked at the advantages and disadvantages of centralising the purchasing function. We commented that in practice there is a spectrum of possibilities between full centralisation and full decentralisation. Unless an organisation is at the extreme 'centralisation' end of the spectrum, part-time purchasing will be present. The term refers to purchasing activities undertaken by people who are not members of the purchasing function, and whose main activities are nothing to do with purchasing.

4.2 Why does part-time purchasing take place? There are three main reasons.

- In some organisations, part-time purchasing was a regular occurrence at a time before the introduction of a dedicated purchasing function. (Remember that the development of the purchasing profession is a relatively recent trend.) In such organisations, a legacy of part-time purchasing remains for historical reasons.

- Sometimes it is found that user departments believe themselves best qualified to make purchasing decisions. This is particularly the case where the items to be purchased are very technical in nature: users may not trust the purchasing function to have sufficient technical understanding.

- Finally, there is the phenomenon of 'maverick spending': users sometimes deliberately keep spending decisions away from the purchasing department. This may be because they simply wish to keep power in their own hands, or may reflect distrust of purchasing's objectives, which are sometimes perceived to be solely concerned with cost reduction.

Advantages and disadvantages of part-time purchasing

4.3 There are obvious disadvantages associated with part-time purchasing.

- There is a high risk of committing company funds unwisely if the people responsible for spending have no professional expertise.

- There is a risk that a part-time purchaser is too preoccupied with his main role to give sufficient attention to his purchasing activities.

- There are serious difficulties in budgeting and controlling spend if responsibilities for purchasing are dispersed throughout the organisation.

4.4   However, it would be foolish to disregard the existence of part-time purchasing, and given that it exists, it makes sense to identify any advantages that it may bring.

- In the case of routine, low-value purchases it may be sensible to devolve responsibility to user departments. This frees up time for professional purchasers to devote to more difficult tasks.

- It is no bad thing to take advantage of the technical skills and knowledge that may be spread throughout the organisation. Part-time purchasing, if properly controlled, is a way of achieving this.

- The purchasing function should be concerned to communicate purchasing disciplines as far as possible throughout the organisation. Once again, a properly controlled part-time purchasing operation may be a means to this end.

Chapter summary

- Lysons identifies three levels at which purchasing may operate: a routine clerical function, a middle management function, and a senior management function with strategic responsibilities.

- The structure of the purchasing function will depend on (among other things) the size of the organisation. In larger organisations, greater specialisation will be possible.

- In some cases, centralisation of the purchasing function is not feasible. But when it is feasible, there are many advantages to such an arrangement (eg greater specialisation, consolidation of requirements to achieve economies of scale etc).

- Despite this, there are some advantages of decentralisation (eg coordination between buyers and end users, more rapid response to local needs etc).

- A CLAN organisation is an example of a matrix structure, often achieved by the concept of a lead buyer. A modification of this is a SCAN structure.

- A typical division of roles in a purchasing function will include places for a Head of Purchasing, a Senior Purchasing Manager, a Purchasing Manager, a Contracts Manager, a Supplier Manager, an Expediter, a Purchasing Analyst, and a Purchasing Leadership Team.

- Part-time purchasing takes place for a variety of reasons: historical reasons, particular qualifications of end users, maverick spending.

Self-test questions

Numbers in brackets refer to the paragraphs where you can check your answers.

1 Describe the three levels at which (according to Lysons) purchasing may operate. (1.4)

2 Use a diagram to illustrate the typical organisation of a purchasing function in a large organisation. (Figure 4.3)

3 Where there is no dedicated purchasing function, what three main possibilities are there for the reporting lines through which purchasing activities are conducted? (1.14)

4 Why may it not be feasible to centralise purchasing operations? (2.6, 2.8)

5 List advantages of centralising the purchasing function. (2.9ff)

6 List advantages of decentralised purchasing operations. (2.21ff)

7 What is meant by a CLAN structure? (2.29)

8 What is the concept of business partnering? (2.33)

9 What typical roles may be found in a large purchasing department? (3.9)

10 Describe the role of a contracts manager. (3.19, 3.20)

11 Give three reasons why part-time purchasing may take place in an organisation. (4.2)

12 What advantages may part-time purchasing bring? (4.4)

CHAPTER 5

Purchasing as Part of the Supply Chain

Chapter learning objectives

1.5   Evaluate the context of the purchasing function and different purchasing situations.

- Relationship between the purchaser and a supply market
- Customers of the purchasing function
- Merits of internal versus external outsourcing of supply
- Role of a shared services unit (SSU) and how it can be measured for effectiveness
- Merits of consortium buying with other independent organisations

Chapter headings

1   Relationships within the supply market

2   Supply chains and networks

3   Customers of the purchasing function

4   Outsourcing the purchasing function

5   Consortium buying

1   Relationships within the supply market

Competitive advantage and the supply chain

1.1   An organisation operates somewhere in a supply chain, between the suppliers of original raw materials or services and an end consumer. Suppliers to a company will have suppliers of their own, and the customers of a company might not be the end consumer, but will have customers of their own. The position of an organisation in the supply chain can be described in terms of the number of 'tiers' of suppliers and customers it has: see Figure 5.1.

1.2   The significance to an organisation of suppliers and customers at each tier of the supply chain will vary according to their potential influence over its competitive position. Michael Porter (*Competitive Strategy*) identified four external influences on the competitive position of an organisation. These were:

- the threat from potential new entrants to the market.
- the threat from substitute products, which customers might switch to buying.
- the strength of the bargaining power of any of the organisation's suppliers.
- the strength of the bargaining power of any of the organisation's customers.

Figure 5.1 *The organisation in its supply chain*

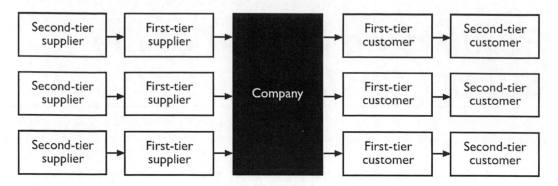

1.3   The threat to an organisation's competitive position from 'supplier power' is likely to be high when:

- there is a small concentration of supply of a key item from just a small number of suppliers, so that the organisation is restricted in its choice of suppliers.

- the cost (and risk) of switching to a new supplier would be high. This could be due to the fact that there is special equipment or facilities used to obtain supplies (eg a dedicated pipeline or cable) and similar equipment or facilities would have to be put in place if a new supplier were selected.

- a supplier might make a strategic move down the supply chain, and become a competitor to the organisation.

- the organisation is not a major customer of the supplier; therefore the supplier is not greatly concerned about developing a long-term relationship.

1.4   The threat of 'buyer power' to the competitive position of an organisation will be high in any of the following circumstances.

- There is only a small concentration of customers in the market, so that the organisation relies heavily for its business on a small number, perhaps just one, customer.

- There are so many suppliers to the market that a customer can switch easily to an alternative supplier.

- The supplier's product or service makes up a very large percentage of the customer's total costs. The customer will therefore want to source its purchases competitively, and this will result in squeezed profit margins for the supplier.

- A customer might make a strategic move up the supply chain, and become its own supplier for the product or service supplied by the organisation.

1.5   An organisation faces competition from rival firms, but the external influences listed above affect its ability to compete successfully. Purchasing is just one aspect of business operations, but effective purchasing can contribute significantly to competitive advantage.

1.6   Competitive advantage is gained by:

- providing competitively-priced goods or services. (In Porter's terminology, 'cost leadership' in a market is won when a firm can dictate prices to the market, by being the lowest-cost supplier.)

- providing differentiated products or services.

'Competitive advantage results from a firm's ability to perform the required activities at a collectively lower cost than rivals, or perform some activities in unique ways that create buyer value and hence allow the firm to command a premium price.' (Porter, *Competitive Advantage: Creating and Sustaining Superior Performance*).

Buyer power and supplier power

1.7   We have mentioned the importance of buyer power and supplier power above. Cox and others (in *Supply Chains, Markets and Power: Managing Buyer and Supplier Power Regimes*) have taken the analysis further and use the following diagram to illustrate the possible relationships between buyer and supplier.

Figure 5.2 *Relationships between buyer and supplier*

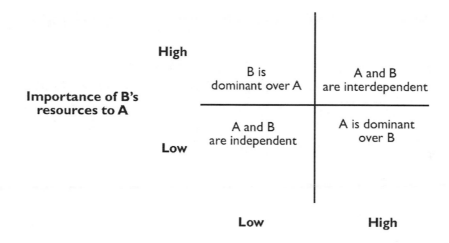

1.8   What the diagram indicates is that where B is important to A, but A is not important to B (top left sector), then B is the dominant partner in the relationship. The bottom right sector indicates the opposite situation: A is important to B, but B is not important to A, so A is dominant. In the top right sector, each partner is important to the other and their relationship is one of interdependence. In the bottom left sector, neither partner is important to the other: they are independent of each other.

1.9   In certain special cases, this kind of market situation is sufficiently important to have earned a name. We look below at the four special cases of monopoly, oligopoly, monopsony and cartel.

1.10   A **monopoly** is a market in which just one supplier exists. It is doubtful whether any pure monopoly exists, because almost always there are alternative possible suppliers. However, there are markets in real life which approximate closely to monopolies in that it would hardly be realistic to contemplate any supplier but one. For example, in the UK, most households will have their water supplied by the local water company, and it is not feasible to look beyond this.

1.11 In a monopoly situation the single supplier clearly has great power over buyers. This opens up the possibility of abuse, but governments are alert to the danger and in most cases markets that are monopolies or near monopolies are closely regulated.

1.12 An **oligopoly** is a market dominated by just a few large suppliers. For example, in the UK the telecommunications industry is dominated by just a handful of very large companies such as British Telecom. Once again, this places suppliers in a very strong position relative to buyers.

1.13 A **monopsony** is a market in which just one buyer exists. As with monopolies, it is hard to think of a pure monopsony. However, a close approximation in the UK was the market for rolling stock in the days before British Rail was split up into fragments. In a mirror image of the monopoly situation, monopsony confers great power on the single buyer.

1.14 A **cartel** is a market in which the suppliers (usually few in number) agree to collude and fix prices among themselves. This enables them to maintain a higher price for their products than would be possible if they were competing with each other. The most familiar example of a producer cartel is OPEC (the Organisation of Petroleum Exporting Countries). By restricting the supply of oil, OPEC members can force the price up to unnaturally high levels.

2 *Supply chains and networks*

Supply chain management

2.1 What exactly is meant by supply chain management (SCM) or supply chain networks management (SCNM), and how does it differ from simple 'purchasing' or 'procurement'? The essence of the distinction is that an SCM philosophy is based on the idea that an organisation is just one link in a chain of suppliers and customers. Along the whole chain the objective is to increase value and reduce waste, but this will not be done most effectively if buyers concentrate only on the organisation they happen to work for. They need to adopt a wider perspective.

2.2 This does not imply any sacrifice of the buyer's own organisational objectives. Rather, buyers learn to think that the best way of achieving such objectives is to cooperate strategically with other organisations upstream and downstream. This way of thinking has led some commentators to coin the phrase 'extended enterprise', meaning that buyers look beyond the boundaries of their own organisation to focus on the needs of a lengthy chain of suppliers and customers.

2.3 Although this mode of thought first surfaced in connection with manufacturing companies, it has also been applied to service organisations. Organisations in all sectors have been driven to adopt the more strategic perspective by factors such as the following.

  • Cost pressures – traditional purchasing disciplines have not been sufficient to eliminate waste (eg the costs incurred in holding stocks). To achieve this objective, buyers must study potential waste throughout the supply chain.

- Reduced lead times – customers have been educated to expect faster delivery of existing products, and reduced time to market for new products. Again, it is difficult (or impossible) for an organisation to deliver this in isolation, because each organisation is reliant on a number of others.

- Increased demand for quality – organisations have come to realise that quality issues can surface upstream. It is not enough to ensure quality procedures within the organisation itself – the problem must be tackled throughout the supply chain.

2.4 Supply chain thinking has an important effect on commercial relationships. Buyers are keen to optimise their relationships with suppliers in order to achieve competitive advantage. This may involve departures from the traditional adversarial relationships that have prevailed between buyers and suppliers in the past. Ideas such as partnership relations, transparency, and strategic alliances have become prominent as a result of this.

2.5 The overall effect is a tightening of the links in the chain. Buyers and suppliers attempt to integrate their activities more closely. Often this leads to greater sharing of information along the supply chain.

2.6 The benefits claimed for an SCM approach may be summarised as follows.

- Reducing non-value-adding (waste) activities throughout the supply chain. ('Often there are many activities that do not create value involved in trade between two companies. Jointly locating and eliminating these activities, as well as developing co-operative goals and guidelines for the future, can focus resources on real improvements and development possibilities.' *Jespersen and Skjøtt-Larsen*)

- Reducing cycle times: supporting innovation (through faster new product development), faster and more precise delivery times (through shorter order cycles), lower inventory (eg just in time) and supply chain agility

- Improving responsiveness to customer requirements (by emphasising the continuous flow of value towards the customer) – with a knock-on effect on customer loyalty and sales revenue

- Giving access to complementary resources and capabilities: joint investment in research and development; technology and innovation sharing; and so on.

- Enhancing quality and service (through collaborative quality management, continuous improvement and enhanced supplier motivation and commitment)

- Improving supply chain communication (through increased information sharing and integration of systems for faster and more accurate information flows). This in turn offers planning and co-ordination benefits such as reduced stockouts, potential for just-in-time supply and so on.

- Reducing total costs (through better co-ordination and planning, reduction of inventory and better capacity utilisation, elimination of wastes, fewer inspections and defects, systems integration reducing transaction costs and so on).

- Optimising the balance of service levels and costs by measuring them across the supply chain, avoiding sub-optimal conflicts and trade-offs.

External relationships

2.7 Purchasing must establish effective relationships with suppliers. This is the process **of supplier relationship management** (SRM). The nature of an effective supplier relationship will vary with circumstances, and on the relative importance to the buying organisation of the supplier's product or service. However, it is interesting to look at five stages of development in the selection of a supply base, identified in an exercise by the Treasury's Central Unit on Procurement in 1986 (*Procurement Practice and Development*). These are as follows.

Table 5.1 *Selection of a supply base*

Stage	Supply base
Innocence	The organisation uses a large number of suppliers and selects them in a random fashion. There is clear scope for improvement.
Awareness	The organisation still uses a large number of suppliers, but most spending is on just a few of them.
Understanding	The organisation has reduced the number of its suppliers still further, and appreciates the benefits of a good working relationship with suppliers.
Competence	There is a partnership with suppliers for key procurement items. There is multi-sourcing of other (non-key) items.
Excellence	There is a continually-reviewed programme to optimise the supply base so as to achieve strategic objectives.

2.8 Until comparatively recently, little attention was paid to the idea of buyers and suppliers working together in long-term relationships. The received model of business relations was based on the idea that buyers and suppliers were on opposite sides in a competitive struggle. Tactics were developed with a view to one side or the other gaining the upper hand.

2.9 Often, such tactics depended on an implicit assumption of short-term links: if a buyer could not get the price or quality he wanted from Supplier X he would have no hesitation in moving to Supplier Y instead.

2.10 More recently, these ideas have given way to strategic and long-term approaches which emphasise the essential partnership between buyers and suppliers. This is not to say that the old model has suddenly disappeared. On the contrary, many firms have hesitated to adopt the newer philosophy and pursue the same practices as have benefited them over decades. Even where new ideas have been welcomed, they may not be considered relevant to **every** aspect of purchasing.

2.11 A key feature of the new ideas is the attempt to avoid the **zero-sum game** that was inherent in previous approaches. (A zero-sum game is one in which any gain for one contestant represents an equal loss for another contestant. In purchasing terms, a buyer would compete by trying to secure concessions from a supplier, each such concession being a gain for the buyer and an equal loss for the supplier.)

2.12 Nowadays, the task is to increase the total value of activities so that by mutual cooperation both buyers and suppliers can increase their profitability. This recognises that the entire process of obtaining raw materials and transferring them to end users, after perhaps many stages of conversion, is a single activity. All businesses involved in the process are working to the same end and can benefit by cooperation.

2.13   The concept underlying this is that of an integrated 'supply chain' in which each supplier is linked to a buyer, who in turn acts as supplier to a later link in the chain. The final link is the ultimate consumer. The idea of a chain neatly captures the way in which each member is dependent on all the other members: if one link snaps, the chain is broken.

2.14   In a series of research papers, D R Towill has analysed further how supply chains should work together seamlessly. He has emphasised in particular the concept of 'flow' in the supply chain. There are several items that 'flow' through the supply chain; to demonstrate what this can mean we shall use the example of a supply chain that links the miner of gold (A) to the purchaser of a necklace (Z).

- Order – each party in the supply chain except A and Z will place orders with a supplier and fulfil orders from a customer. It follows that there is a flow of orders, which may become very complex, and if there is a hold-up at one point in the chain it can have a great effect further up the line.

- Money – each party in the supply chain, except (arguably) A, pays money to its supplier; each party (except Z) receives money from its customer. Therefore there is a flow of money; if there is a hold-up here, say because one party has cashflow problems, again delays can occur.

- Goods/services – each party in the supply chain (except A) receives goods or services from its supplier and (except Z) passes them on, after some kind of further processing, to its customer. There is a flow of goods and services, which again may be very complex, and problems with which could conceivably cause the chain to snap.

- Information – in order to facilitate the flow of the other components the parties in the supply chain (except Z) must have information about what their customers want and (except A) about what their suppliers can provide. Information may be delayed and distorted as it flows through the supply chain if it becomes out of date, which may cause inefficiencies, delay and extra costs.

2.15   The analogy of the chain should not be pressed too far – of course buyers do not confine themselves to just one supplier for all their needs – but it does capture an important feature of the partnership model. This is that buyers work to reduce the supply base.

2.16   Partly this is a necessity for the buyer: the kind of relationship envisaged here requires very detailed assessment of and cooperation with the suppliers concerned. It would not be possible to do this if suppliers were too numerous, or if relationships were entered into and broken off very rapidly. Equally, though, it is a necessity for the supplier: to meet the very stringent requirements that will be laid down by a buyer-partner the supplier needs to feel security in the relationship.

2.17   Table 5.2 summarises some of the benefits which are perceived as arising from this kind of thinking.

Table 5.2 *Benefits of the supply chain concept*

Managerial benefits	Fewer suppliers – easier to manage Increased stability because of supplier loyalty Less time spent on competitive bidding procedures Joint planning increases chances of satisfying customers Improved service from suppliers (reduced lead times, higher quality)
Technological benefits	Supply partners may share technology and innovation Partners may contribute to product development Supplier expertise may improve quality and reduce time to market
Financial benefits	Joint investment in research and development Just in time supply leads to reductions in stock holding costs Long-term commitment leads to more stable prices

Network sourcing

2.18 The term 'network sourcing' refers to a pattern of buyer-supplier interaction that has grown up through development of certain elements in the Japanese-style subcontracting system. The term is explained, and the pattern elucidated, by Peter Hines. Hines gives credit to the Japanese authority Professor Itsutomo Mitsui for first expounding the network viewpoint.

2.19 According to the analysis of Hines, the network sourcing model embodies ten characteristics which are summarised in Table 5.3 below.

Table 5.3 *Characteristics of network sourcing*

•	A tiered supply structure, with heavy reliance on small firms
•	A small number of direct suppliers with individual parts sourced from one supplier but within a competitive dual sourcing environment
•	High degrees of asset specificity among suppliers and risk sharing between customer and supplier alike
•	A maximum buy strategy by each company within the semi-permanent supplier network, but a maximum make strategy within these trusted networks
•	A high degree of bilateral design employing the skills and knowledge of both customer and supplier alike
•	A high degree of supplier innovation in both new products and processes
•	Close, long-term relations between network members involving a high level of trust, openness and profit sharing
•	The use of rigorous supplier grading systems increasingly giving way to supplier self-certification
•	A high level of supplier coordination by the customer company at each level of the tiered supply structure
•	A significant effort made by customers at each of these levels to develop their suppliers

2.20 Each of these ten characteristics requires some explanation.

2.21 **A tiered supply structure, with heavy reliance on small firms**. This refers to a 'pyramid' arrangement in which the final assembler sits at the peak and is served by a small number of first-tier firms, who themselves are supplied by a larger number of second-tier firms and so on down the pyramid. At each level, the customer tier organises and supports the tier below.

2.22 **A small number of direct suppliers with individual parts sourced from one supplier but within a competitive dual sourcing environment**. Customers typically have few suppliers, and suppliers typically have few customers. Linkages between companies in the network are minimised, meaning that there is time to give detailed attention to each link.

2.23 **High degrees of asset specificity among suppliers and risk sharing between customer and supplier alike**. 'Asset specificity' refers to readiness on the part of suppliers to make investments that are aimed at satisfying one particular customer only. This of course exposes the supplier to risk, but the general framework of network sourcing gives him the encouragement he needs.

2.24 **A maximum buy strategy by each company within the semi-permanent supplier network, but a maximum make strategy within these trusted networks**. In other words, each participant in the network seeks to buy out as much as possible of his needs, sourcing of course from network partners; meanwhile, the network as a whole seeks to make as much as possible, minimising recourse to outsiders. The result is that value added ratios are low by Western standards: for any individual manufacturer most parts are bought out and a minimum of value is added internally.

2.25 **A high degree of bilateral design employing the skills and knowledge of both customer and supplier alike**. Network partners place emphasis on cooperative value engineering in which suppliers and customers work together to develop products of high quality and low cost. This is quite different from the familiar focus in Western companies on securing low cost by hard negotiation with suppliers.

2.26 **A high degree of supplier innovation in both new products and processes**. In a network system, suppliers are increasingly willing to come up with technically innovative improvements that benefit the customer.

2.27 **Close, long-term relations between network members involving a high level of trust, openness and profit sharing**. This point may already have become apparent from some of the comments made above.

2.28 **The use of rigorous supplier grading systems increasingly giving way to supplier self-certification**. This has resulted from a general raising of standards among suppliers, itself due in part to the kind of relationship that we are describing. With 100 per cent performance becoming the norm, the need for grading suppliers is disappearing.

2.29 **A high level of supplier coordination by the customer company at each level of the tiered supply structure**. The success of the network concept has been due not to chance, but to the great effort invested by Japanese firms in **kyoryoku kai** (literally 'cooperative circles', though Hines suggests the term 'supplier associations' as a good English equivalent). These are somewhat similar to the familiar concept of quality circles, but operate between different firms rather than internally within a single firm. A key feature is a constant two-way flow of strategic information between customers and suppliers.

2.30 **A significant effort made by customers at each of these levels to develop their suppliers.** This too has been greatly promoted by the efforts of **kyoryoku kai**.

2.31 Hines concludes his analysis by pointing to the dangers of Western firms emulating the characteristics of network sourcing in a half-hearted 'cherry-picking' manner. The success of the scheme in Japan has come about through recognition of the effort required and a full commitment to achieving results in the long term.

3 *Customers of the purchasing function*

Internal relationships

3.1 The supply chain can be seen as a long sequence of operations and activities, some of them carried out by the organisation itself, and some by suppliers or customers. Within an organisation, operations can be seen from an overall 'macro' perspective, as a single whole operation. It can also be seen as a number of separate operations that have to be carried out to transform the original inputs into the final finished output or service.

3.2 For example, an operation in an advertising agency to prepare a campaign for a client can be seen as a single overall operation, but it can also be seen as a number of 'micro operations', such as TV advertisement production, copy writing and copy editing for magazine advertisements, artwork design and production, media selection, media buying, and so on. Within each of these micro operations, there are other operations. Producing a TV advertisement, for example, involves micro operations such as story boarding and script writing, film production, the shooting of the film, film editing, and so on.

3.3 Each micro operation needs its input of resources, which might include both externally-purchased materials and services and input from another department or work group in the organisation. Each micro operation is supplied, both internally and externally.

3.4 The concept of internal supply leads on to the idea that within any organisation there are **internal suppliers** and **internal customers**.

3.5 For example, a road haulage company might have operational units for maintenance and servicing of vehicles, loading and driving. One micro process within the overall operation is the repair and servicing of vehicles. The mechanics servicing the vehicles are the internal supplier in the process, and the drivers of the vehicles are the internal customers. Similarly, the team that loads the vehicles is an internal supplier in the loading operation, and the drivers are the internal customers.

3.6 In most respects, an internal customer should be treated as any external customer should be treated. The aim of the organisation should be to deliver a product or service that meets the customer's needs.

3.7 The main difference between an internal and an external customer is that in many cases, the internal customer has no freedom of choice of suppliers, and must use the internal supplier.

3.8 The concept of the internal customer is that within an organisation, internally-delivered goods and services, as well as externally-obtained goods and services, should meet the requirements and expectations of the internal customer. To do this, the needs of the internal customer have to be identified. The needs of the internal customer can only be properly established by having a dialogue with the customer.

3.9 Effective purchasing will therefore make use of cross-functional teams (CFTs), with representatives of the internal customers included within the team.

Internal customers of purchasing

3.10 Like all functions in an organisation, purchasing must be sensitive to the needs of customers. Purchasing staff must understand customer requirements because of their increasing strategic role in all aspects of organisational activities from product design onwards.

3.11 An extension of this basic idea is to regard each function in the organisation as having its own 'customers', who may be customers internal to the organisation, or who may be external to it. For example, purchasing staff may regard the production function as a 'customer', because the needs of production – for the right materials in the right place at the right time – must be met at least in part by efficient purchasing.

3.12 This attitude of treating other departments as customers encourages an effective, market-led approach to organising purchasing activities.

3.13 Too often in practice, the benefits of purchasing's involvement are resisted by internal users who are antagonised and alienated by their misconception of purchasing's role. In particular, they often believe that purchasing is solely concerned with the objective of low price, while ignoring other objectives legitimately pursued by user departments. This misconception must be overcome by a genuine philosophy of 'customer-friendliness' among purchasing staff.

3.14 The value of this perspective on internal customers is that it encourages purchasing staff to plan proactively. Merely responding to requests from production (or other customer functions) as they arise is insufficient to ensure that internal customers are getting the service they require.

3.15 The primary roles of purchasing are as follows.

- To provide service to internal customers, such as production departments
- To reduce the costs incurred by the organisation
- To reduce the risks faced by the organisation
- To assist in quality issues, particularly in the early stages of product development
- To provide a satisfactory interface with other functions and with external customers

Setting internal objectives

3.16 To ensure that all of these roles are carried out satisfactorily (particularly the first and last ones), a logical approach is required to the organisation of the purchasing function.

In particular, purchasing should not be a reactive function: work should be undertaken in line with agreed objectives and a predetermined strategy.

3.17 The objectives that may be identified for a purchasing function are very varied. They may include any or all of the following.

- To identify and select effective suppliers, and to manage relations with them in a constructive and profitable manner
- To protect the organisation's cost structure
- To ensure availability of required materials without undue stockholding costs
- To maintain constructive relationships with other organisational functions
- To ensure that value for money is obtained in managing the purchasing function

3.18 To attain these objectives, detailed plans capable of guiding day-to-day operational decisions must be made. These plans should cover such issues as:

- sourcing policy – single or multiple sourcing, or a combination depending on the materials concerned?
- make internally or source from outside?
- capture and analysis of purchasing-related information
- standardisation of products or emphasis on differentiation?
- links with other functional areas.

3.19 Once the plans are in place it is important to monitor their workings in practice. To what extent are they contributing to the objectives of purchasing and of the organisation as a whole? What changes might be made to improve the system?

3.20 Formalising the process of setting objectives and defining plans has great advantages. Above all, it imposes a discipline on purchasing functions which ensures that staff do not simply drift from one task to another without a clear sense of direction.

The status of purchasing in the organisation

3.21 Purchasing will achieve its maximum contribution to organisational goals only if its status in the organisation is sufficiently recognised. If the function is still seen primarily as providing administrative and clerical services, the opportunity to influence organisational achievement and delight internal customers will be severely limited.

3.22 Historically, the purchasing department has often been regarded as a support function, subordinated to production. This perception has gradually changed. Nowadays it is common in large organisations to find that the head of purchasing either reports directly to a main board director or is himself a director on the main board.

Who are the internal customers?

3.23 One of the prime purposes of a defined organisational structure is to ensure smooth liaison between different functions in order to achieve organisational objectives. Purchasing is just one example of this: links between purchasing and other functions are vital if purchasing itself is to perform to its optimum.

3.24 Purchasing's main internal customers, with whom it must establish and maintain links, include design and engineering, production, accounting and finance, and marketing. Some of the main areas of interaction are summarised in Table 5.4.

Table 5.4 *Purchasing's links with internal customers*

Internal customer	Links with purchasing
Design and engineering	Value engineering and value analysis Quality assurance Evaluation of availability and price of materials Preparation of specifications
Production	Preparation of delivery schedules Control of inventory and scrap Make or buy decisions Cooperation in implementing world class manufacturing techniques Planning to avoid costly special production runs
Accounting and finance	Budget preparation, and monitoring of actual input costs against budget Administration of buying, eg in processing of invoices and progress payments Stock valuation, stocktaking and insurance of stock
Marketing	Purchasing's role in enhancing product features, particularly price Ensuring prompt deliveries in to meet promised deadlines for delivery out Cooperation on reciprocal trading

3.25 Poor relationships between purchasing and other departments will lead to inadequate understanding by purchasing of requirements elsewhere in the organisation and inefficiency in translating these requirements into the necessary materials support actions.

3.26 The other side of the coin is that purchasing's own activities will be hampered through inadequate information, and in extreme cases by actual obstruction caused by inter-departmental frictions.

3.27 A traditional example is the conflict that sometimes arises between production and sales departments. To secure a particular sale, it may be necessary to institute a special production run. This may be resisted by production staff wishing to optimise the efficient running of their own department, with insufficient regard to overall corporate profitability.

Information networks

3.28 A great aid to reducing conflict and increasing communication and cooperation with internal customers is provided by information networks – in which different managers and different departments can all hook on to the same central information source. A network is merely a means of connecting together two or more computers.

3.29 In detail, the following operational benefits may be expected from such systems when dealing with internal customers.

- Reduction in the time spent by purchasing staff on clerical tasks such as order processing and expediting
- Increased time available to purchasing staff for value added activities where their professional expertise can enhance organisational performance
- Dramatic reduction in delivery times to, say, production departments by increased speed of processing orders
- Dramatic reduction in costs and other problems associated with high volumes of paperwork.

Managing the service provided by purchasing

3.30 If purchasing is regarded as providing a service to internal customers, then it is appropriate to manage the service, just as if we were servicing an external client. One important step to this end would be a system of measurement and control.

3.31 There are various measures that could be used to evaluate the effectiveness of purchasing's service to its internal customers. Here are some possibilities.

- Average lapse of time between requisition and delivery
- Average cost of processing a requisition through to delivery
- Number of complaints from user departments
- Cost savings achieved for user departments

3.32 The task of managing the purchasing function naturally falls to the Head of Purchasing, whose task includes ensuring a quality service for internal users of the purchasing service. As part of this process, Head of Purchasing has a duty to communicate effectively with users of the purchasing service.

Shared service units

3.33 Shared services are those support functions that are used by many different departments within a large organisation (finance, IT, human resources etc). A shared service unit (SSU) is a dedicated provider of such services to internal users. Individual business units, eg regional divisions, retain their autonomy but in effect 'outsource' their need for specialist services. The difference compared with conventional outsourcing is that the outsource provider is not an external company, but an internal function.

3.34 The SSU is responsible for managing the costs, quality and timeliness of its services. They employ their own dedicated resources, and usually have contractual agreements with internal customers based on service level agreements.

3.35 Advantages claimed for this approach include cost savings (cost of back-office processes is usually reduced when they are taken out of individual business units), common standards across the organisation, and a strengthening of corporate value. The approach works best when there is a good measure of uniformity among the business units within the organisation; it is less effective if business units are very diverse in their nature and activities.

3.36 In an article in *Supply Management* (issue of 7 June 2007) the head of shared services at Surrey County Council identified the following benefits as having arisen from the introduction of a shared services centre in the Council.

- It is easier for external customers to do business with the Council.

- Faster, simpler and more accurate handling of routine administrative or support work that otherwise takes up a lot of customers' time and can be a source of frustration.

- Answers to queries and access to expertise through a single point of contact.

- Ability to use information on a 'self-service' basis that previously was likely to have been done elsewhere or by somebody else. This includes, for example, managers using financial information and staff selecting training and updating their own personal records.

- Consolidation of end-to-end purchasing processes.

- Opportunities to identify and obtain economies of scale.

3.37 However, there are also criticisms of the SSU approach.

- They may encourage a centralised approach that stifles innovation and initiative.

- Their value and performance levels are not easily measured.

- They may sacrifice effectiveness in favour of efficiency in order to achieve predetermined service levels.

- Workers in SSUs may be remote from end users.

3.38 Managers of SSUs should possess a number of important qualities.

- Good understanding of functional issues

- Empathy with 'customers'

- Good communication and motivational skills

- Strong organisational abilities

4 Outsourcing the purchasing function

When to outsource

4.1 Like any other activity, purchasing can be considered as a candidate for outsourcing. More and more firms are following a strategy of focusing on their core competencies, while outsourcing more peripheral functions, and purchasing is not exempt from this trend.

4.2 Lysons and Farrington identify a number of situations in which outsourcing of the purchasing function should be considered: see Table 5.5.

Table 5.5 *When purchasing should be outsourced*

Circumstances	What activities to outsource
Purchasing is a peripheral rather than a core activity (ie low or generalised skill requirements, internally focused responsibilities, well-defined or limited tasks, jobs that are easily separated from other tasks)	Purchase orders Locally and nationally procured needs Low-value acquisitions Brand name requirements Call-offs against framework agreements Administration and paperwork associated with purchasing needs
Supply base is small and based on proven cooperation and there are no supply restrictions	Well-defined or limited tasks Jobs that are easily separated from other tasks Jobs that have no supply restrictions
Supplier base is small, providing non-strategic, non-critical, low-risk items	Outsource purchasing to specialist purchasing and supplier organisations, or to buying consortia

4.3   Of course, there are risks associated with outsourcing the purchasing function.

- The organisation loses a critical commercial skill.
- The organisation may lose control over vital intellectual property.
- An additional management layer is needed to manage the outsource provider.

4.4   However, these must be balanced against the possible advantages.

- Managers free up time to focus on core activities.
- The organisation gains administrative efficiencies.
- The organisation gains the benefit of specialist expertise provided by the outsource provider.
- Problems of seasonal or uneven demand for purchasing staff become a worry for the outsource provider rather than for us.
- Particularly for small organisations, there may be economies of scale if purchasing is outsourced to a specialist provider purchasing on behalf of many different organisations.

5   *Consortium buying*

Introduction

5.1   A buying consortium is a group of separate organisations that combine together for the purpose of purchasing goods or services. The idea is that by combining together, the buying organisations can use their combined 'muscle' to negotiate with suppliers, in order to obtain better terms.

5.2   A buying consortium might be created when a group of organisations see mutual benefit in combining their 'bargaining power'. This could happen when one organisation on its own is not sufficiently important to attract special attention from suppliers. Together, however, the total value of their purchases gives them greater value as a customer.

5.3   The consortium is represented in discussions with suppliers by a centralised buying unit, which will be the purchasing section of one of the buying organisations. The other organisations in the consortium will share the costs of the purchasing operations and administration.

5.4   With a buying consortium, the relationship with the supplier is likely to be transactional, because it could be difficult for a supplier to develop long-term supply partnership relationships with a collective group of different organisations. This is particularly the case when the members of the consortium change over time, with some new members joining and existing members leaving the group.

5.5   Buying consortia can be found in both the public and the private sectors. In the UK, several local government authorities might form a consortium with a centralised buying unit. Similarly, there are buying consortia in parts of the automotive industry. There are also buying consortia in the training market: a group of several small accountancy firms might form a consortium to negotiate the provision of training from a training provider for their employees taking their professional examinations.

Costs and benefits of consortia

5.6   The benefits of consortia purchasing may be summarised as follows.

- By means of enhanced bargaining power, the consortium can obtain discounts that would not be available to individual consortium members. (There may be difficulties in allocating such discounts fairly among the members, but at least it must be beneficial that the discounts can be obtained.)

- A consortium can establish framework agreements with suppliers which simplifies purchase administration for consortium members. This can lead to significant reductions in admin costs, especially in the case of low-value items where the admin cost is disproportionate in relation to the purchase price of the item.

- Where a high level of technical expertise is needed for particular purchases, consortium members can pool their individual expertise.

5.7   However, it is not all good news. There are some costs and disadvantages associated with consortium purchasing.

- There are costs and effort associated with communication and coordination, staff development and policy development.

- There is an issue of transparency between consortium members. A buyer working for a single organisation needs full information about the activities of the organisation in order to make informed purchasing decisions. In the context of a consortium, this implies that the buyer should know all about the activities of each consortium member. Some members may balk at sharing such information.

- Consortia may suffer from long-winded decision processes, which are bad for efficiency and may also deter some suppliers from dealing.

- Members are not obliged to purchase to the agreed specification.

- Some consortia may fall foul of EC competition rules.

Chapter summary

- An organisation operates within a supply of chain extending from distant suppliers to ultimate consumers.

- Professor Michael Porter identifies situations where an organisation's competitive position may be threatened by supplier power and buyer power.

- Different market structures include monopoly, oligopoly, monopsony and cartels (among others).

- The supply chain management philosophy is based on the idea that an organisation is just one link in a chain leading from suppliers to customers. Some commentators have used the phrase 'extended enterprise' to describe this notion.

- Concepts of supplier relationship management have undergone changes over the years. Nowadays there is increasing emphasis on long-term partnership relations.

- Network sourcing is one model of supplier relations, based on a tiered supply structure.

- Purchasing staff must give the best possible service to their internal customers. Effective purchasing will make use of cross-functional teams.

- It is important to manage the service provided by purchasing. To do this, organisations may establish measures of purchasing's effectiveness.

- Shared services are those support functions that are used by many different departments within a large organisation. A shared service unit (SSU) is a dedicated provider of such services to internal users.

- Increasingly, organisations are looking to outsource non-core activities. In some organisations, purchasing is a candidate for such treatment.

- A buying consortium is a group of separate organisations that combine together for the purpose of purchasing goods or services. By doing so, they aim to obtain bulk discounts and other improvements in economy and efficiency.

Self-test questions

Numbers in brackets refer to the paragraphs where you can check your answers.

1 In what circumstances is the threat to an organisation's competitive position from supplier power likely to be high? (1.3)

2 Draw Cox's diagram illustrating the possible relationships between buyer and supplier. (Figure 5.2)

3 What is meant by a monopsony? (1.13)

4 Describe the concept of supply chain management. (2.1)

5 What is meant by a zero-sum game in the context of purchasing? (2.11)

6 What are the benefits of the supply chain concept? (2.17)

7 List characteristics of the network sourcing model. (2.19)

8 What is the main difference between an internal customer and an external customer? (3.7)

9 What are the primary roles of the purchasing function? (3.15)

10 What objectives may be identified for a purchasing function? (3.17)

11 Who are the main internal customers of purchasing? (3.24)

12 What is meant by a shared service unit? (3.33)

13 What are the risks associated with outsourcing the purchasing function? (4.3)

14 What are the main benefits of consortium buying? (5.6)

CHAPTER 6

Classifying Products and Customers

Chapter learning objectives

2.1   Analyse and explain different types of product and customer requirements.

- The difference between customers and consumers
- Contribution of purchasing to customer satisfaction
- How customer feedback is collated and used
- The contrast/difference between consumer products and industrial products
- Key requirements in goods for resale
- Regulatory framework for protection of consumers
- Impact of corporate social responsibility (CSR) on consumer confidence

Chapter headings

1   Customer groups and their different needs

2   Customer feedback

3   Purchasing and customer satisfaction

4   Consumer protection

5   Corporate social responsibility

6   Goods for resale

1   Customer groups and their different needs

Customers and consumers

1.1   Why does an external customer purchase an organisation's goods or services? If the organisation does not understand the process, it will not be able to respond to the external customer's needs and wishes.

1.2   Traditional views of marketing tend to assume that people purchase according to the value-for-money that they obtain. The customer considers the functional efficiency of the alternative products, and arrives at a decision by comparing this with the price. While this set of beliefs is demonstrably inadequate in explaining **consumer** behaviour, in **industrial** purchasing it is somewhat closer to the truth.

1.3 Owing to the differences that often exist between 'consumer buyers' (those who purchase items for personal consumption), and 'industrial buyers' (those who purchase items on behalf of their organisation), it is traditional to split buyers into these two broad groups for the purpose of analysis. While a company may sell to other businesses (its **customers**) buyers must also have an eye to the eventual **consumers** of their products, who may be further along the supply chain than the immediate customers.

1.4 In industrial marketing, the buyer is frequently not the customer or the user. For example, a seller of grinding wheels may have a company as a customer. The buyer is a member of the purchasing department and the user is a grinding machine operator. As a result there are major differences between consumer and industrial selling.

1.5 An industrial buyer is motivated to satisfy the needs of the organisation rather than his individual needs. Often, purchases are repeat orders when stocks have fallen below a certain level and thus the buying motive is clear (avoiding stockouts). With significant one-off purchases, the motivation will be the achievement of the organisation's goals or targets. Thus a profit target may mean the buyer placing an emphasis on cost minimisation. A growth target expressed in terms of sales motivates a purchase that will promote that goal.

1.6 An industrial purchase may be made by an individual or group. The individual or group is buying on behalf of the organisation but the buying decision may be influenced by the behavioural complexion of the individual or group responsible.

1.7 Each organisation will have its own procedures and decision-making processes when purchases are made. Large centrally controlled organisations will often have centralised purchasing through a purchasing department. The purchase decisions will tend to be formal with established purchasing procedures. In small organisations there will not be a purchasing department. Purchasing decisions will tend to be made on a personal basis by persons who have other functions as well in the organisation. Personal relationships between the supplier and the buyer will often be very important.

1.8 The seller must therefore identify and understand the buyer in the organisation. As the buyer may be a department, the term decision-making unit (DMU) is sometimes used. The DMU is the group of people (there may only be one in the group in some instances) who has some influence on the purchasing process.

1.9 An industrial buyer appraises a potential purchase in a more formal way than a consumer buyer. Written quotations, written tenders and legal contracts with performance specifications may be involved. The form of payment may be more involved and may include negotiations on credit terms, leasing or barter arrangements.

1.10 Finally, purchases by an industrial buyer will tend to be on a much larger scale than those made by consumers.

Consumer products and industrial products

1.11 A product is anything that satisfies a customer need or want. We often consider products as tangible objects that a customer buys, but we need to remember that the customer is buying something to satisfy a need or want. This satisfaction might be achieved through the purchase of a service. The term product is used very generally to describe whatever is produced by an organisation, whether in the form of tangible products or in the form of services.

1.12 It is useful to make a distinction between consumer products and industrial products.

- A consumer product is one that is designed to appeal to, and be purchased by, a consumer, ie the person who will actually 'consume' the product.

- An industrial product is one that will be purchased by an organisation rather than an individual. The organisation may need the product as raw material for the manufacture of its own products, or for use in the running of its business, or for a variety of reasons.

1.13 Some authorities subdivide each of these two categories of product into further classifications. One possible categorisation is shown in Table 6.1.

Table 6.1 *Classifying consumer and industrial goods*

Consumer goods	Industrial goods
Convenience goods: those that a consumer purchases without much thought, including fast-moving consumer goods (FMCG)	Capital goods: large-scale purchases for the purpose of increasing an organisation's productiveness, often 'one-off' in nature, with a lengthy decision-making process
Speciality goods: these have distinctive features which often encourage brand loyalty (eg cars, designer clothes)	Materials and components: raw materials, parts, components, subassemblies etc for use in manufacturing
Shopping goods: these are usually quite substantial in terms of bulk, price etc (eg furniture, electronic equipment, white goods). The consumer will usually think long and hard before selecting among competing brands	Supplies: other items, not for incorporation into finished output, but enabling the organisation to function (eg indirect production materials, administrative supplies etc)
Services: the special features of services are discussed in Chapter 10	Accessories: capital items which do not in themselves generate revenue but which are nevertheless necessary (eg computer systems)

Customer groups

1.14 In some contexts it is important to identify the different groups of customers that may be served by an organisation. For example, a timber yard may sell to consumers intending to do a carpentry job in their own homes, but may equally sell to a major building company intending to build an estate of houses.

1.15 To satisfy different groups of customers the organisation may need to consider different marketing routes, different production processes, different payment methods etc. This can clearly create additional work for the organisation, but is compensated by the additional business that becomes possible.

1.16 There is also the issue of internal customers. We saw in an earlier chapter that a purchasing department, for example, has various internal customers whose needs must be considered alongside those of external customers. Apart from purchasing, departments such as finance, human resources, and IT all provide services to internal customers.

1.17   The examiner for this unit points to an interesting difference in perspective between supplier and customer. Whereas the supplier is focused on effectiveness and efficiency in operations, the customer is concerned with effectiveness and quality of the product he buys. It is easy to see that there may be a conflict of interest here. For example, the supplier can improve efficiency by eliminating an inspection process which might detect flaws in the finished product. But this would not be good news for the customer.

2   *Customer feedback*

Introduction

2.1   Organisations naturally wish to obtain feedback from their customers so that they can identify problems early and plan for improvements. Some feedback will come naturally to the organisation without any special effort – sometimes a customer just wants to complain about a product he has purchased, or to praise an instance of outstanding service. Such feedback should be recorded and acted upon. However, this is not sufficient for the organisation's needs.

2.2   To get a more thorough picture of what is going right or going wrong, an organisation will need to be systematic in collecting and collating feedback from its customers. There are many techniques for doing this. In the paragraphs that follow we discuss a few of them: observation, experimentation, depth interviews, focus groups, market research surveys, test marketing, and online research techniques

2.3   **Observation** is a data collection technique that can be used without actually speaking to any participants. It means watching and observing people and the way they behave in different situations.

2.4   There are many uses of observation in marketing research. In most of the larger retail outlets it is now usual that our actions are recorded. The retailer will observe the way we walk around the store, the things we select from shelves, whether we read labels, and the length of time we queue to pay for our purchases. In fact, many stores are designed based on information gathered from observational studies.

2.5   One of the main advantages of this type of approach is that often we are being observed without our knowledge. This means that the researcher is gaining information from natural, unaffected behaviour.

2.6   The major disadvantage of observation is the lack of depth to any information that is gained. The researcher cannot observe opinions and attitudes or indeed identify what people are thinking. Therefore, it is a quantitative tool rather than a qualitative one.

2.7   **Experimentation** is 'a data collection method in which the market researcher tries out some marketing action on a small scale, carefully observing and measuring the results'.

2.8 An example of experimental research is the **hall test**. People are recruited off the street and taken to a hall (hence the name) where they are shown products or advertisements. The researcher can test preference and attitude for the product or advertisement. The purpose of experimentation is to test each variable in isolation without the impact of competitors' activities, economic conditions, the weather or any other environmental influence.

2.9 **Depth interviews** normally involve either individual depth interviews or a **focus group**.

2.10 The individual depth interviews are usually quite unstructured and the interviewer will have a list of subjects that require discussion rather than formal questions which should be asked. The interviewer will be trained to create questions and probe for in-depth responses.

2.11 Depth interviews are very useful if the subject is confidential or potentially embarrassing (for example on how much alcohol a person consumes) or where a detailed understanding of complicated behaviour is required. Depth interviews might be used for industrial research where executives will be interviewed on a one-to-one basis.

2.12 A depth interview can provide valuable qualitative information but it is an expensive data collection technique. Bear in mind that each interview might last from one to three hours.

2.13 **Focus groups** consist of a group of 5 to 25 respondents. According to Peter Chisnall, '... group depth interviewing studies the interaction of group membership on individual behaviour. It is this interaction – this free exchange of ideas, beliefs, and emotions – which helps to form the general opinion of people sharing common interests and responsibilities'.

2.14 Focus groups are often used for the following purposes.

- Generating ideas for new product concepts and new products
- Exploring consumer response to promotional and packaging ideas
- Conducting preliminary research before carrying out further research, for example to establish customer knowledge and vocabulary before designing a questionnaire

2.15 Again, the focus group is an expensive technique. The researcher will have to organise suitable accommodation for the discussion to take place and should pay respondents' expenses. The success of this technique will also depend largely on the skill of the interviewer to generate the right mood and atmosphere. Often, focus groups will be recorded so that full analysis can take place later. Analysis is difficult as, again, the research is dealing with qualitative information.

2.16 **Survey research** is based on collecting data originating from answers to questionnaires. Questionnaires can be issued in four ways.

- By post where the respondent receives a questionnaire at home or work and is expected to complete the questionnaire and return it.
- By telephone either at home or at work. The respondent simply answers questions asked.
- Face-to-face or personal interviewing involves dealing with respondents individually and asking questions from the questionnaire.
- On the internet (effectively the same as a postal survey).

2.17 **Test marketing** means that the entire marketing programme for a newly developed product can be tested, in miniature, in a limited geographic area. This means that the full marketing mix can be tested in a selected geographical area which is representative of the whole market.

2.18 Because the smaller test market will emulate what will happen when the product is launched nationwide, the marketer hopes to be able to forecast with some accuracy the profit potential of the product.

2.19 The marketer can test a range of marketing decisions, such as changes in the marketing mix elements, so that he can launch the optimum mix on a national basis. He will attempt to eliminate any weaknesses in the product and the marketing mix at this stage.

2.20 Increasingly, organisations attempt to investigate their markets by means of **online techniques**. Often this involves the use of surveys conducted via the internet. Although the practice is still in its infancy, the increasing impact of information technology on marketing activities is likely to lead to rapid growth.

2.21 What are the benefits of conducting research online?

- Large numbers of respondents can be reached in a single hit.
- The geographical range of the survey can be worldwide.
- Costs are low. Many thousands of individuals can be reached without undue expense.
- Rapid results are possible – it takes very little time to collect and analyse responses.

2.22 The significant benefits of online marketing research should not blind marketers to some disadvantages. Nobody is arguing that online methods have completely superseded more traditional methods.

- It is difficult to draw a truly representative sample. By definition, all respondents will be internet users, and will be drawn from that small subset of the population who are prepared to answer online questionnaires.
- There is only limited guidance governing the ethical and methodological aspects of conducting internet surveys.

Internal customers

2.23 As always, internal functions must remember that they have internal customers too. We have already seen in a previous chapter that it is important for purchasing (and other internal functions) to obtain feedback from other departments on the effectiveness of the service provided.

Database management and customer satisfaction

2.24 To ensure customer satisfaction, organisations wish to know as much as possible about the individual tastes and preferences of the people who buy from them. Increasingly, this is achieved by the development of a customer database.

2.25 This is defined by Kotler as 'an organised collection of comprehensive data about individual customers or prospects, including geographic, demographic, psychographic and buying behaviour data'. Kotler states that the database can be used to locate good potential customers, tailor products and services to the special needs of targeted consumers, and maintain long-term customer relationships.

2.26 A customer database contains much more than the customers' names and addresses. Kotler suggests that the details required will depend on whether the business is dealing primarily with other businesses (B2B trading) or primarily with consumers (B2C trading): see Table 6.2.

Table 6.2 *Details included in a customer database*

For a B2B business	For a B2C business
• Products and services that the customer has bought	• Products and services that the customer has bought
• Past volumes and prices	• Customer demographics (age, income, family members, birthdays)
• Key contacts (and personal details about them, such as their birthdays, their families)	• Psychographics (activities, interests, opinions)
• Competitive suppliers	• Buying behaviour (buying preferences)
• Status of current contracts	
• Estimated customer expenditures in the next few years	
• Assessment of competitive strengths and weaknesses in servicing the account	

2.27 Clearly, the use of information technology is crucial in this entire process.

3 Purchasing and customer satisfaction

Direct impact of purchasing on customer satisfaction

3.1 It may appear that purchasing can have little impact on external customers because the focus of the purchasing function is primarily towards suppliers. However, this is a simplistic assumption. In fact, purchasing has both a direct and an indirect impact on customer satisfaction.

3.2 An obvious example of purchasing's direct impact on customers is the case of retail buyers. Their job is to buy goods that customers will want to buy in turn. Purchasers must therefore have a good insight into what the eventual customer will like.

3.3 Purchasers also source services that are directly passed on to customers. This can include such items as product warranties.

Indirect impact of purchasing on customer satisfaction

3.4 More usually, the impact of purchasing will be an indirect one. Purchasing is part of the overall organisational system. Unless all the organisational subsystems, including purchasing, are functioning well, the likely consequence is faulty or defective output, which will lead to customer dissatisfaction.

3.5 Purchasing staff are heavily involved in the acquisition of inputs to the organisation. They need to ensure the timely purchase of high-quality inputs. If they succeed, there is a good chance of satisfying the customer by the timely delivery of a high-quality output. If they fail, customer dissatisfaction is again the likely result.

3.6 Good buyers will reduce the overall costs suffered by their organisations. In turn, this will enable the organisation to offer their products at competitive prices, which is an important benefit to customers.

3.7 Purchasing has an important role to play in the development of new products. This too has a benefit for customers, because it means that their changing needs and requirements can be catered for.

3.8 Purchasing also source peripheral goods and services that add to the customer's experience of the organisation's products. For example, purchasing are involved in buying packaging, in sourcing transport to retail outlets or direct to customers etc.

4 *Consumer protection*

The legal framework

4.1 In the UK, as in most developed economies, there is a framework of legal regulations designed to protect the rights of consumers. The assumption is that an individual consumer is less powerful than a commercial organisation. The commercial organisation might take advantage of the consumer's weakness by selling products of poor quality, or on unfavourable trading terms. Consumer protection legislation is designed to prevent this.

4.2 The Sale of Goods Act 1979 gives a consumer automatic statutory rights when purchasing **goods** from a commercial business. For example, the goods must be of satisfactory quality, must be fit for their purpose, and must correspond to any description applied to them.

4.3 If a consumer finds that the goods are not up to scratch, he can seek various remedies. Depending on the circumstances, he may be able to get a refund of his money, or compensation in the form of a payment for damages, or a repair or replacement.

4.4 The Supply of Goods and Services Act 1982 provides similar protection to consumers purchasing **services**. When work is carried out by a trader, the consumer is entitled to expect that it will be performed with reasonable care and skill, in a reasonable time and for a reasonable charge. If any goods are supplied along with the service they must meet the same standards as specified by the Sale of Goods Act.

4.5   The Trade Descriptions Act 1968 forbids firms from making misleading descriptions of their products and services.

4.6   The Consumer Protection Act 1987 imposes a liability on producers and suppliers for damage caused by defective products. The Act also requires firms to ensure that goods comply with general safety requirements.

4.7   The Unfair Contract Terms Act 1977 allows a consumer to challenge contractual terms that may be unfair to him. The producer or supplier will not be able to rely on such terms. In particular, it is not permissible for a firm to include terms limiting the consumer's statutory rights, as laid down by the legislation already discussed.

5   Corporate social responsibility

The impact of CSR on consumer confidence

5.1   We discussed the importance of CSR in an earlier chapter and you should refer back to refresh your memory of this important topic. In the present context, the relevance of CSR is concerned with maintaining consumer confidence.

5.2   An important trend in recent years has been the increasing weight accorded by consumers to principles of ethical business practices. This is seen in many different sectors. A frequently quoted example is the Body Shop, an organisation which has made ethical trading a key feature of its marketing message. Another example is the growth in ethical investment funds: increasing numbers of investors are choosing to put their money into funds supporting companies whose trading policies are ethically acceptable.

5.3   In this climate it is natural that consumers are paying more attention to the CSR policies adopted by companies. Media reports suggesting that particular companies are not up to scratch in this area can have a very damaging effect on the organisations concerned. This appears to be the case particularly where the perceived abuses are damaging to third world countries. Consumers in developed Western economies do not want the organisations they buy from to engage in exploitation of cheap labour in less developed countries, and are prepared to 'vote with their feet' if they are not satisfied on this issue.

5.4   Where organisations are slow to upgrade their CSR policies they risk attracting unwelcome media attention. Often this originates with the various consumer watchdogs who increasingly see CSR issues as part of their brief. Organisations such as the Consumers' Association are formed to protect the interests of consumers, and increasingly see this as including the need for organisations to act ethically.

5.5   The other side of this coin is that companies who do adopt robust CSR policies can expect to benefit from increased consumer confidence. Their reputation will be enhanced compared to competitors with less developed CSR. The loyalty of their customers will be strengthened. They will avoid damaging media criticism. Their CSR principles will extend along the supply chain, so that their suppliers too benefit. They will be increasingly able to attract the best staff because they are seen as good organisations to belong to.

6 Goods for resale

6.1   The work of buyers in the resale sector, and the characteristics of goods for resale, were discussed at length in Chapter 2. The reference to this topic in this area of the syllabus duplicates what we have already covered, and you should simply refer back to Chapter 2 to refresh your memory on this area.

Chapter summary

*   There are important behavioural differences between consumer buyers and industrial buyers. In particular, the industrial buyer is frequently not the customer or the user.

*   In an industrial context, the buyer may be a department; the term decision making unit or DMU is often used.

*   Consumer products are designed to appeal to end users; industrial products will be purchased by an organisation rather than an individual.

*   Feedback from customers may be obtained by a number of techniques: observation, experimentation, depth interviews, focus groups, survey research, test marketing, and online research techniques.

*   To ensure customer satisfaction, organisations increasingly rely on the information in customer databases.

*   Purchasing staff can have both a direct and an indirect impact on customer satisfaction.

*   There is a framework of consumer protection legislation in the UK, including the Sale of Goods Act, the Supply of Goods and Services Act, the Trade Descriptions Act, the Consumer Protection Act and the Unfair Contract Terms Act.

*   Consumer confidence is heightened when organisations display a commitment to corporate social responsibility.

Self-test questions

Numbers in brackets refer to the paragraphs where you can check your answers.

1   Distinguish between customers and consumers. (1.3)

2   What is meant by a DMU? (1.8)

3   Distinguish between consumer products and industrial products. (1.12)

4   What is the major disadvantage of observation as a technique for obtaining customer feedback? (2.6)

5   What is meant by a hall test? (2.8)

6   For what purposes are focus groups used? (2.14)

7   What are the benefits of conducting customer research online? (2.21)

8   What details might be included in a customer database for a B2B business? (Table 6.2)

9   In what ways may purchasing have an indirect effect on customer satisfaction? (3.4ff)

10   What rights are given to consumers by the Sale of Goods Act 1979? (4.2, 4.3)

11   What adverse consequences may occur if an organisation fails to adopt robust CSR policies? (5.4)

CHAPTER 7

Different Methods of Purchasing (I)

Chapter learning objectives

2.2   Identify and explain different methods of purchasing.

- Classification of supply chains, tiered supply, managed services and the role of an agent
- The purchasing cycle, its key stages and its relative transferability
- Importance of cross-functional teams, varying cross-functional requirements and the impact of this on purchases
- Methods of purchase: spot-buying and one-off purchases; low-value orders including use of purchasing cards; typical purchase-to-pay (P2P) methods
- Long-term supply relationships
- Framework agreements and call-off arrangements
- Consumables
- Call-off orders

Chapter headings

1   Classification of supply chains

2   Managed services and the role of an agent

3   The purchasing cycle

4   Cross-functional teams

5   Methods of purchase

6   Low-value orders

1   Classification of supply chains

Defining the supply chain

1.1   A supply chain is a term covering all activities associated with the flow of goods from the raw materials stage through to the end user. Supply chain management is the art of integrating these activities through improved supply chain relationships in order to obtain sustainable competitive advantage.

1.2   A supply chain may be very short. As an example, you may have driven past a farm and noticed a sign advertising fresh eggs for sale. The farmer is producing the goods and selling direct to his customers with no intermediaries.

1.3   In other cases the supply chain may be very long. For example, if you purchase a washing machine from a department store there will clearly have been many organisations involved in the stages leading up to your purchase. To analyse the supply chain you would have to go right back to the extraction of a metallic ore forming the main material of the washing machine.

1.4   Some supply chains are controlled through ownership. This is the case, for example, with the large oil companies. Typically, these companies have control over all the main stages of exploration, production, refining and retailing. These activities are carried out by organisations within the overall ownership of the oil company.

1.5   In most cases, though, supply chains are controlled through contracts between unrelated parties. A supplier contracts to provide his customer with required goods or services. The customer may process these supplies before selling them onwards to his own customer, or he may simply on-sell them (in the case of a retailer or wholesaler). These transactions are subject to the contractual terms that prevail between the parties concerned.

Tiering of suppliers

1.6   An important strategic issue facing supply organisations is the structure of their supply chains. One such issue is easily illustrated. Suppose that a manufacturer wishes to maximise his own part in the value adding process by taking in only a minimum contribution from outside suppliers. For example, the manufacturer buys in parts from a number of suppliers, and assembles them through a number of stages before the finished product is complete. The structure of the supply chain in such a case is as illustrated in Figure 7.1.

Figure 7.1 *All manufacturing performed by top-level purchaser*

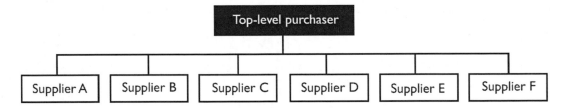

1.7   By contrast, suppose that the manufacturer sees strategic advantage in outsourcing all activities other than the final stages of production. In that case his direct relationship may be (in simplified terms) with a single supplier or (more realistically) with a single tier of suppliers.

1.8   Each supplier in this first tier would have an extensive role to fulfil in the manufacture of the final product. He would discharge this responsibility by making use of 'second tier' suppliers. The structure of the supply chain now looks like Figure 7.2.

Figure 7.2 *Top-level purchaser outsources most manufacturing*

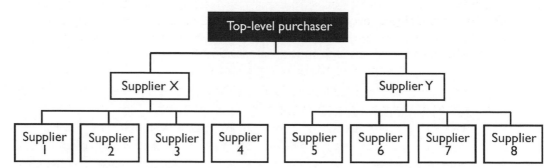

1.9 An organisation might adopt a deliberate policy of tiering its suppliers, so as to reduce the number of first-tier suppliers (suppliers with which it deals directly), and so 'reduce its vendor base'.

1.10 An organisation deals directly only with first-tier suppliers. Second-tier suppliers are suppliers to first-tier suppliers, and deal with the first-tier supplier, not the 'original equipment manufacturer' (OEM).

1.11 For example, an original equipment manufacturer might have 180 different suppliers with which it deals directly. In order to rationalise its commercial relationships, the OEM might pursue a policy of reducing the number of its first-tier suppliers to, say, 20 within a given time frame. To the extent that the OEM still needs products or services from some of the 180 suppliers who are no longer in the first tier, it will be the task of one of the first-tier suppliers to organise the other suppliers, who will become second-tier suppliers.

1.12 In a manufacturing operation, such as automobile manufacture, the OEM is the producer of the end product. First-tier suppliers would tend to be specialist assemblers, each making a particular subassembly. Second-tier suppliers would be component manufacturers, who would supply their products to a first-tier supplier.

1.13 The relationship between an OEM and its first-tier suppliers will be critically important, because each first-tier supplier will be organising the second-tier suppliers for the benefit of the OEM. The OEM will have a limited number of first-tier supplier relationships, and can focus on developing these as a long-term partnership. The first-tier suppliers will be expected to work with the OEM in making improvements and adding value throughout the supply chain, and in developing innovations in products and practices. Improvements in the supply chain will depend heavily on the contributions of the first-tier suppliers.

1.14 The reasons for tiering of suppliers might include any of the following.

- The OEM wants to develop long-term relationships with key suppliers, but only has the time and resources to develop a limited number of such relationships.
- Standardisation of parts and variety reduction has reduced the number of parts required, so that the OEM needs fewer suppliers than in the past.
- There has been consolidation of suppliers within the supply market.

Benefits of tiering

1.15   The benefits of tiering may be any or all of the following.

- The OEM has fewer commercial relationships to manage, and can direct its attention to improving these key relationships.

- The OEM can have strategic focus, without having to worry so much about the transactional and operational details of procurement.

- The OEM can share an objective to improve the supply chain with its first-tier suppliers: a shared effort is likely to bring more and better improvements.

- When responsibility is devolved to first-tier suppliers, operational decisions might be taken with a greater understanding of the operational detail, combined with a knowledge of the objectives and requirements of the OEM.

- First-tier suppliers might be able to co-ordinate supply activities more efficiently.

Characteristics of a first-tier supplier

1.16   The characteristics of a typical first-tier supplier are as follows.

- It is a direct supplier to the OEM.

- It is usually a supplier of a high-cost or complex subassembly.

- It is heavily dependent on the OEM, which in turn is heavily dependent on the first-tier supplier. It might even purchase assets dedicated to use on jobs for the OEM.

- There is a close and long-term buyer-supplier relationship with the OEM, and the partnership should ideally operate as a partnership of equals. The OEM should not be a dominant partner.

- It will often be involved in discussing new product ideas with the OEM.

- It is responsible for dealing with a number of second-tier suppliers. This number could be quite large. In effect, the first-tier supplier is put in charge of a section of the OEM's vendor base.

- It understands and shares the 'mission' of the OEM.

- It disseminates the standards and working practices of the OEM to the second-tier suppliers with which it deals.

- It must be a competitive producer to justify selection by the OEM.

- The supplier must also have the management capabilities to manage the second-tier suppliers efficiently.

- The relationship with the OEM is a long-term partnership. For example, the supplier will negotiate ways of removing costs from the supply chain (partnership relationship) rather than negotiate the allocation of costs between the buyer and the supplier.

The effects of tiering: upstream management

1.17   What are the effects of these different structures on management of the supply chain, from the perspective of buyers in the purchasing company at the top of the chain?

1.18   An immediate effect is that such buyers find themselves with far fewer transactions to handle and far fewer suppliers to manage. This greatly simplifies many operational tasks of purchasing.

1.19   At the same time, the purchaser must recognise the extent to which responsibility for his firm's product has been handed over to outsiders. This makes it necessary to ensure that the outsiders are thoroughly up to scratch in all relevant areas. In other words, it suggests that the relationships with suppliers, though fewer in number, will be closer and deeper than under the alternative model.

1.20   In particular, it is likely that the final purchaser will want to drill down through tiers in the supply chain to ensure that appropriate quality is present all the way down. This means that influences on lower-tier suppliers will come not only from the firms immediately above them in the chain, but potentially also from the very top of the chain.

1.21   For first-tier suppliers the implications are also significant. In effect, these suppliers have to take on the main responsibility for investment in product and process development. This implies a need for such suppliers to feel secure of continuing business from the top-level purchaser. Once again, this points to a partnership model of buyer/supplier relationships.

1.22   The competitive environment raises additional issues, particularly in relation to this last point about investment by first-tier suppliers. The top-level purchaser must consider carefully his attitude to these suppliers servicing his competitors as well as his own operations. In some cases, he may feel that this is unacceptable and will make it a condition of awarding the business that first-tier suppliers do not deal with competitors.

1.23   However, this will not always be an option. An important consideration is the level of investment required of the first-tier supplier. If this is very large, the supplier will have to cast his net widely to find other customers and so recoup his outlay. Inevitably, this will mean dealing with firms in the same or similar industries, and this is bound to mean that some customers are competitors of each other.

2   Managed services and the role of an agent

Managed services

2.1   In this section we look at two factors that impact on the design of an organisation's supply chain. This follows on from the discussion in the previous section relating to structural issues in supply chains. The two factors we examine are managed services and the role of an agent.

2.2   Managed services is a term that has recently come into common use, but it describes a situation that has prevailed for many years. In the construction industry it is common for a single main contractor to be appointed, whose task is to identify, commission and manage appropriate subcontractors. This is the concept of managed services in action: the main contractor is the provider of managed services.

2.3   In this situation the supply chain can look very simple indeed from the ultimate client's perspective: see Figure 7.3. The client deals with just one organisation, the main contractor. It is the main contractor's function to deal with all the subcontractors. Notice the similarity of this situation to the tiered supply chain discussed earlier in the chapter.

Figure 7.3 *Managed services in the construction industry*

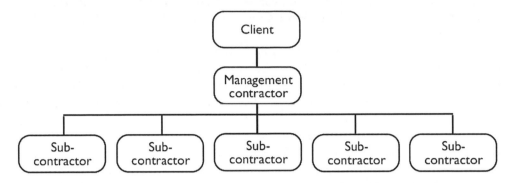

2.4   This familiar situation in the construction industry has plenty of parallels in other sectors. For example, an organisation may hire an agency to look after all of its advertising or wider marketing activities. The main agent will need to deal with numerous suppliers: designers, media, printers etc. But from the client's perspective there is only one supplier to deal with, namely the main agent.

2.5   Other applications include outsourcing of IT activities, telecoms, or entire facilities management contracts. In this latter case, the facilities management provider will have to deal with a host of suppliers, while the client is free to concentrate on core competencies.

2.6   There are obvious advantages in adopting a managed services approach.

•   Administrative simplicity: instead of dealing with numerous suppliers, the client deals with just one

•   Access to specialist expertise: the client naturally chooses a main contractor with relevant experience, and will benefit from this accordingly

•   Potential cost reductions: if the main contractor is well chosen, the client will save administrative and management costs

2.7   However, these must be weighed against certain disadvantages.

•   Risk: if the wrong choice of main contractor is made, the consequences may be disruption and unnecessary expense

•   Cost: there will be a fee to pay, and this may not be recouped in efficiency savings

•   Loss of control: the client hands over control to the service provider

•   Loss of market knowledge: the client distances himself from the market

The role of an agent

2.8 An agent is a person who acts on behalf of someone else. A purchasing agent is not himself a party to the transactions he undertakes on behalf of his principal; instead, he is an intermediary. He acts on the instructions of his 'employer' and enters into contracts that bind that employer to third parties.

2.9 From the employer's point of view, dealing with an agent means that he does not need to deal with the numerous third parties that the agent deals with. This has the effect of streamlining his supply chain.

2.10 Historically, agents acting on behalf of buyers or sellers have been an important part of the supply chain. This is still the case in some industries. For example, in the sale of domestic and industrial property it is common for the seller to appoint an agent to act on his behalf. The role of an agent in situations includes a variety of tasks: bringing together a buyer and seller, assisting in the process of selling, representing his principal in negotiations, obtaining and providing market information etc.

2.11 However, in many markets the role of agents in the supply chain is decreasing. Many sellers who previously dealt routinely through agents are now finding it more effective to deal directly with their end customers. A good example of this is in the insurance industry. In bygone years, it was commonplace for insurance companies to deal only with brokers, who in turn would deal with customers. Nowadays, companies such as Direct Line have 'disintermediated', ie they have eliminated the intermediary and now deal direct with customers.

3 *The purchasing cycle*

Introduction

3.1 Purchasing procedures of course vary widely from one organisation to another. However, there are certain stages which almost any purchasing transaction will have to progress through. In the language of your syllabus, this means that the purchasing cycle is **transferable**: no matter what sector you work in, or what you are trying to buy, you will typically follow the stages in this cycle, or something very similar.

3.2 The main stages are shown below in Figure 7.4. In this section of the chapter we look briefly at what happens during each stage. The descriptions we give accord with best practice but of course cannot incorporate all of the variation that will be experienced in the course of your professional work in different organisations. Each organisation will lay down policies (outlining the broad objectives to be achieved) and procedures (detailed guidelines for each stage of the process). You will follow the policies and procedures of your own organisation in your day-to-day work, but you should find that they accord closely with the descriptions that follow.

Figure 7.4 *The basic purchasing cycle*

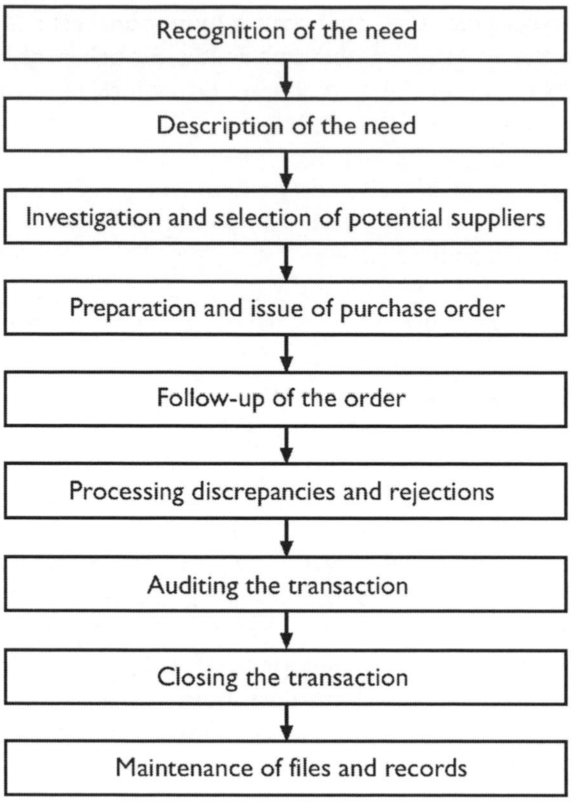

```
┌─────────────────────────────────────────────────┐
│           Recognition of the need                │
└─────────────────────────────────────────────────┘
                       │
                       ▼
┌─────────────────────────────────────────────────┐
│           Description of the need                │
└─────────────────────────────────────────────────┘
                       │
                       ▼
┌─────────────────────────────────────────────────┐
│  Investigation and selection of potential suppliers │
└─────────────────────────────────────────────────┘
                       │
                       ▼
┌─────────────────────────────────────────────────┐
│      Preparation and issue of purchase order     │
└─────────────────────────────────────────────────┘
                       │
                       ▼
┌─────────────────────────────────────────────────┐
│             Follow-up of the order               │
└─────────────────────────────────────────────────┘
                       │
                       ▼
┌─────────────────────────────────────────────────┐
│     Processing discrepancies and rejections      │
└─────────────────────────────────────────────────┘
                       │
                       ▼
┌─────────────────────────────────────────────────┐
│            Auditing the transaction              │
└─────────────────────────────────────────────────┘
                       │
                       ▼
┌─────────────────────────────────────────────────┐
│            Closing the transaction               │
└─────────────────────────────────────────────────┘
                       │
                       ▼
┌─────────────────────────────────────────────────┐
│         Maintenance of files and records         │
└─────────────────────────────────────────────────┘
```

Recognition of the need

3.3 Before any purchasing transaction can even begin, someone must notice that something is needed which is not currently available. This need must be notified to the purchasing department.

3.4 The need may be identified by a user department; for example, a designer may recognise a need for enhanced computer equipment or software for use in his work. Or the impetus may come from a stores department; perhaps the storekeeper's check on stock levels reveals a shortage of a component used in production.

3.5 In either of these cases the normal procedure would be for the department concerned to issue a purchase requisition. This form describes the item needed and instigates action by the purchasing department. Typically, the originator of the requisition would keep a copy of the form while the other copy is forwarded as appropriate.

   • If the originator is the stores department, the copy is forwarded to purchasing for action.

   • If the originator is a user department, the copy is forwarded to stores. Stores will meet the need if the item is in stock, and if not will pass the copy on to purchasing.

3.6   In some cases the identification of need is signalled not on a purchase requisition, but on a **bill of materials**. The approach is to forecast the manufacturing schedule for finished products, and then to calculate the requirement for parts needed in those products. Purchasing then have the task of ensuring that sufficient parts are in stock to meet the production schedule.

Description of the need

3.7   Whether a requisition or a bill of materials is used, the form will contain details of the required item(s) in a standardised form. It would be wrong to assume that purchasing simply act on this description without enquiry. On the contrary, purchasing must check the requirement carefully, drawing on their past experience of the item and on records of past purchases.

3.8   In many cases it will be appropriate to refer the requisition back to the originator. This may simply be for clarification if the requisition is unclear, but may also be to suggest alternatives that offer better quality or lower price than the item specified. Purchasing should not make such changes without consultation because they cannot know all the factors that the originator may have had in mind when drawing up the requisition. But neither should they accept requisitions without question.

3.9   The discussion so far relates to description of the need **within** the organisation. Of course, the eventual supplier also needs a detailed description of the buyer's requirement – ie a specification. However, it is worth mentioning at this point that this is not solely the responsibility of the buyer. The user of the item must also play a part in ensuring that the supplier is providing what is needed to satisfy the requirement.

Investigation and selection of potential suppliers

3.10   There may well be a large list of potential suppliers. Buyers will be aware of them partly from past experience and partly from the department's records. The task at this stage is to narrow down the possibilities.

3.11   Where the item required is a standard or routine one the task is usually simple. Preferred suppliers will already be known. However, if a non-standard item is needed it is important to investigate the possible suppliers. The extent of this investigation must be in proportion to the value of the item.

3.12   In the case of major purchases buyers will need to conduct extensive investigations, perhaps involving discussions with salesmen and visits to suppliers' premises. Eventually the list will be narrowed down to a small number of suppliers who, in the buyer's opinion, are well qualified to supply the item(s) required.

3.13   At this point it will be necessary to establish price and availability of the required item(s). The easiest situation is where a low-volume standard item is in question. It is usually possible in such cases to simply refer to suppliers' catalogues and price lists.

3.14   In more complicated cases – for example where large sums of money are at stake, or the item is a non-standard one to be manufactured specially – this approach is insufficient. The buyer must then choose either to negotiate with a small number of suppliers over price and availability, or to solicit quotations.

Preparation and issue of purchase order

3.15 When all this is complete, the buyer makes out a formal purchase order. In most cases this will be a standard form produced within the organisation. The effect of the form will be to create legal obligations, and for this reason firms are careful to design their purchase orders very carefully, usually including the legal terms on which they propose to do business.

3.16 In some cases an order may be placed by telephone. This may be because some kind of blanket order system is in place (see later in this chapter). If this is not the case, then any telephone order should be confirmed later in writing.

3.17 A number of copies of the purchase order are prepared so that appropriate departments can be informed. Obviously the top copy goes to the supplier. Often the supplier receives a second copy too, so that he can sign and return it as evidence that he accepts the order and the legal terms contained on it. One copy will be retained by the purchasing department. Other copies may be sent to the stores department, finance department, and user department, depending on the system within each organisation.

Follow-up of the order

3.18 It is not safe to assume that the transaction is now complete. Often there will be a need to follow up the order. For example, a buyer may chase the supplier to return the acknowledgement copy of the purchase order. Or it may be necessary to check with the supplier that the delivery will be on schedule.

3.19 Usually, these routines are triggered by review of outstanding orders. In some organisations this may mean reference to a manual file or folder of such orders. More often nowadays, purchase orders are logged on a computer system which will automatically flag when follow-up routines are needed.

Processing discrepancies and rejections

3.20 There are many cases where the transaction does not flow through exactly as anticipated. For example, the supplier may deliver the wrong goods, or the wrong quantity. Alternatively, there may be a problem with the quality of the goods delivered; this might be detected by the inspection department.

3.21 In all such cases the buyer will need to liaise with the supplier to ensure that the matter is resolved. If this leads to disruption to schedules, or to increased costs of inspection, the buyer will seek financial compensation from the supplier.

Auditing the transaction

3.22 The buyer must ensure that the transaction is completed in a way that gives the organisation value for money. There are several aspects to this.

- The goods delivered by the supplier must correspond to what was ordered. This involves agreeing goods received documentation to the purchase order.

- The goods must be of satisfactory quality. This will often be the responsibility of an inspection department.

- The amount charged by the supplier must correspond to the price agreed. This involves checking the supplier's invoice. If the details on the invoice match the goods that were ordered and the goods that were actually delivered, and if the prices on the invoice are those that were agreed before the order was placed, the buyer can approve the invoice and pass it to accounts for payment.

Closing the transaction

3.23 We have already mentioned that outstanding orders must be reviewed periodically with a view to taking follow-up action. This may be particularly tricky if part deliveries are made; for example, for an order of 6,000 components a supplier may make three separate deliveries of 2,000 each. Until the final delivery is made the order remains incomplete.

3.24 Once all goods have been received, and the supplier's invoice has been received and checked as described above, it is time to close the transaction. It is usual to do this by noting on the purchase order the details of goods received documentation showing that the goods ordered have actually been received. Similarly, the order may be annotated to reflect the receipt and vouching of the supplier's invoice.

3.25 Once all this has been done, the order may be filed along with other completed orders.

Maintenance of files and records

3.26 Finally, it is important to ensure that all files and records relating to purchase orders are maintained in good order. This makes it easier to investigate any queries that arise later. It also gives buyers a permanent record of how a particular order was satisfied. This can be a vital aid in future purchasing decisions. For example, if the records show that Supplier X performed badly in supplying Component Z then buyers will not make the mistake of using that supplier again.

3.27 The use of computers has greatly simplified this process of record keeping. In addition, once data has been entered onto a computerised system it is easy to generate reports. For example, it would be a simple matter for a computer to summarise all transactions with a particular supplier, or all transactions relating to a particular part or material. This is a great help to buyers in planning future purchases.

Authorisation of the need

3.28 The above completes our outline description of the 'typical' purchasing transaction. However, one further aspect should be mentioned: the question of control over the process.

3.29 Buyers spend huge sums of money, often a very large proportion of the total earned by the organisations that employ them. It is vital to ensure that the organisation receives full value for the sums spent. To a large extent this is achieved by reliance on the professional expertise of buyers, but that might be insufficient without a defined system of controls.

3.30 In particular, purchasing staff depend on user departments to identify needs. While buyers can use their experience to question requisitions, in the last resort the user department has the most detailed knowledge of their own requirements. This means that care must be taken to avoid inappropriate or irresponsible requisitions.

3.31 This is achieved by authorisation procedures, which take effect at three main points in the purchasing cycle.

- When a requisition is originated it must be signed by an authorised individual before being passed to purchasing. This gives purchasing the assurance they need that the requisition is for an item that is genuinely needed.

- When the purchase order is completed, it must be signed by an authorised person within the purchasing department. The person signing it will usually do so with sight of the requisition and any other relevant documentation.

- When the supplier's invoice is received it is not passed for payment to the accounts department until purchasing staff have carried out the checks already described.

Limitations of traditional ordering procedures

3.32 There are many situations where the traditional ordering procedure is insufficient. For example, the requirement may be for a large number of the same item, but with the exact quantity unknown. This is often the case with MRO supplies. Alternatively, the quantity may be known but the exact timing is difficult to predict because it depends on how production schedules work out.

3.33 Another possibility is that the price is uncertain. This might happen if delivery is to take place over an extended period during which underlying costs may fluctuate. Or it might happen because in a large contract it is difficult for either buyer or supplier to estimate underlying costs in advance, and a fixed price would place all the burden of uncertainty on the supplier.

3.34 These possibilities are not mutually exclusive. There may, for example, be situations where both quantity and timing are uncertain. To cope with this, purchasing professionals have evolved a large number of variations on the basic theme described above, some of which we describe in the remaining sections of this chapter.

4   Cross-functional teams

Why are cross-functional teams necessary?

4.1 A cross-functional team, as the term suggests, is a group of individuals taken from different organisational functions so as to work together. The purpose of doing this is to ensure that the correct range of skills and expertise is available to achieve the intended task. Members of the purchasing function might form part of such a team for dealing with, for example, new product development. Other members of the same team might come from finance, marketing, production etc.

4.2   Lysons and Farrington identify a number of reasons why this kind of teamwork has become more common in recent years.

- Purchasing staff have increasingly become engaged in strategic procurement decisions.

- Increasing adoption of a supply chain philosophy has meant that organisations see a need to deal with work flow in an integrated way.

- It needs teamwork to make best use of increased availability of information and communications technology.

- Advanced world class systems such as materials requirements planning require teamwork for their effective implementation.

- Purchasing staff increasingly need expert support to deal with new complications in global sourcing and other modern developments.

- Organisations realise that teams out-perform individuals.

4.3   Teams may be formed either for short-term project work, or for longer-term purposes. Their functions may be to deal with such issues as global sourcing, outsourcing, new product development, quality management or the purchase of capital equipment.

4.4   Lysons and Farrington, citing the work of G M Parker, list the competitive advantages that may arise from successful implementation of cross-functional teams.

- Reduction in the time it takes to get things done

- Improvement in the organisation's ability to solve complicated problems

- Improvement in the organisation's customer focus

- Improved creativity brought about by the interaction of individuals from different backgrounds

- Improved organisational learning

4.5   *Burt et al* identify four key roles for a supply management professional on a cross-functional team: providing process knowledge/expertise (eg in supply base research or negotiation); providing content knowledge (eg of a specific market or commodity area); liaising with supply staff to ensure project needs get attention and priority; and putting forward the supply management point of view (eg re trade-offs, priority-setting and policy decisions).

4.6   Cross-functional teams are particularly valuable in increasing team members' awareness of the big picture of their tasks and decisions – and therefore dovetailing functional objectives with overall strategy.

4.7   They enable a wider pooling of viewpoints, expertise and resources, and represent a wider range of stakeholder interests. This can help to generate innovative and integrative solutions to problems, suggestions for performance or process improvements and organisational learning.

4.8   Cross-functional teams are a key tool for co-ordinating work flow and communication across vertical organisational boundaries. This is an important element in aligning business processes, so that the flow of added value towards customers is not impeded by vertical barriers. It can also reduce the time it takes to get things done!

4.9 Product development and innovation, partnering, networking and learning are all horizontal activities, requiring the free exchange of information across functional boundaries. Cross-functional teams contribute significantly to the flexibility and responsiveness of organisations in competitive and fast-changing environments. They support innovation through the pooling of different expertise and knowledge, and they enable swift decision-making by avoiding lengthy vertical channels of communication and authorisation.

4.10 However, there are difficulties to cross-functional teamworking.

- While representing different viewpoints and interests can enhance decisions (and their acceptability), it also adds potential for time-consuming complexity, conflict and consensus-seeking.

- Horizontal structures may lack clear authority structures: members may need to exert informal influence through persuasion, politics, negotiation or personal leadership in order to have their functional perspective heard.

- All teams take time to develop before they perform effectively: to overcome conflict, build trust, allocate roles and determine a shared working style.

- There may be difficulties of dual authority structures and conflicting demands, if cross-functional team members also report to their individual departments.

- There may be practical difficulties of organising meetings and information flows, given different functional work patterns, locations and so on. (ICT links may be used to support 'virtual' teamworking, meetings, data-sharing and so on.)

Managing the cross-functional team

4.11 The examiner for this subject has suggested a three-tier structure for the management of a cross-functional team.

- The programme owner (or sponsor) is the person who takes overall responsibility for achievement of the team objectives. This will be a senior individual, most likely the Head of Purchasing, who will lead the project, setting objectives and delegating authority to team members.

- A steering committee will be composed of senior managers from relevant functions within the organisation. It will be chaired by the Head of Purchasing and will provide advice and support in running the project.

- A programme manager is responsible for operational matters day to day, with the task of ensuring that deadlines are met and standards of work upheld.

5   *Methods of purchase*

Relations with suppliers

5.1 There is a continuum of relationships that a buyer may have with a supplier, ranging from an arm's length 'transactional' relationship, to a closer 'partnership' relationship at the other extreme. In practice, it is rare to achieve full partnership relations and usually there will be much less commitment on both sides.

5.2 In ascending order of commitment we might identify the following possible relationships.

- Spot buying. This means that a buyer contacts a supplier as a one-off transaction as and when required. See below for more detail on spot buying.

- Regular trading. Very common in practice, this describes the situation where a buyer looking for a particular item on a regular basis usually chooses a particular supplier to satisfy the need.

- Blanket ordering (sometimes called a call-off contract). The buyer sets up an agreement on terms and conditions (a **framework agreement**) in relation to a particular item or items. As and when necessary, the buyer 'calls off' his requirements and asks the supplier to deliver in accordance with the framework agreement. A variation on this is known as **system contracting**. Again, see below for further detail.

- Fixed contract. This is one step on from blanket ordering. The additional element is that the fixed contract specifies the total quantities that will eventually be called off.

- Partnership sourcing. Buyer and supplier work together to achieve mutual benefits. For example, the supplier may be involved in early design stages of a new product.

5.3 What factors might influence the choice of relationship in particular cases? Here are a few of the possibilities.

- Importance of the item being purchased. If the buyer is dealing with a critical item he is more inclined to favour a close relationship with the supplier.

- Capabilities of suppliers. Close relationships usually involve shared approaches to total quality management and other 'world class' techniques. Some suppliers will simply not be able to cope with this.

- General conditions in the supply market. If there are many competing suppliers, all involved in markets requiring constant innovation, a buyer may be reluctant to commit to a long-term deal with any one of them, because he may be 'backing the wrong horse'.

- Geographical location. It is more difficult to maintain close relationships with a supplier who is geographically distant, though of course modern communications technology is gradually changing this.

Spot buying

5.4 Spot buying is a natural and simple method of purchasing. The buyer sees a need, and simply contacts a supplier to fulfil the need – end of story. There is little administrative effort needed and transaction costs are low. Buyer and supplier simply need to agree on price.

5.5 The examiner for this subject suggests that spot buying should be used for purchases fulfilling the following criteria.

- The goods are easily specified.
- The goods are needed immediately.
- The order can be fulfilled at once, and payment can be made at once.
- Agreed terms of trade exist.

5.6   Of course, there are dangers. Where prices fluctuate over time, there is a risk of buying at an unfavourable moment. This is particularly the case with volatile commodities such as agricultural crops.

Blanket ordering

5.7   One of the simplest and most common of the variations is **blanket ordering**. This is an agreement under which a supplier undertakes to provide an estimated quantity of items over an agreed period of time at an agreed price. Sometimes the price is not specified in monetary amount, and instead the agreement contains a formula for determining it. For example, the agreement may specify 'market price' and include a method of defining the market price at any time.

5.8   When the buyer needs a delivery of the items he initiates a simplified 'release' procedure which avoids the need to go through all the stages of the traditional purchasing cycle. In simple cases, the buyer simply telephones the supplier and calls for a particular quantity, specifying the blanket order under which the supply has been agreed. Indeed, once the basic agreement has been established it may not be necessary for purchasing staff to become involved in calling for releases. This can be left to user departments instead, though they would be acting under authority delegated by purchasing.

5.9   The quantity of items to be supplied is not usually agreed in advance. Instead, the agreement specifies that the purchaser is to supply all the buyer's requirements for that particular item over an agreed period. In this case, the buyer will provide the supplier with an estimate of requirements in advance, but actual quantities will not be finally known until the end of the agreement.

5.10   The great advantage of this type of agreement arises in the case of items with low unit value, but for which there is a large requirement. The exact number required may be difficult to calculate, and the exact timing of requirements may be even trickier, but the approximate pattern over a period of, say, one year is well enough known for the supplier to be able to plan production and respond when required.

5.11   A typical application for this technique is in the ordering of **consumable office supplies** such as computer stationery. The advantages are that it cuts out the staff time and paperwork that would be involved in numerous small orders, and assures regular supply.

5.12   Buyers must work hard to ensure that blanket orders are handled in a way that makes them satisfactory to suppliers. Otherwise, it will be difficult to obtain agreement. A common problem in this context is unrealistic (inflated) estimates of annual requirements. However, if handled properly blanket orders carry benefits to suppliers as well, particularly in the elimination of selling costs once the order is in effect and in the assurance of a good sales volume for a defined period ahead.

Systems contracts

5.13   A systems contract is a closer form of cooperation between buyer and supplier than a blanket order. Like a blanket order, a systems contract is designed to minimise administrative time and cost in dealing with materials that are subject to constant and repetitive demand. Unlike blanket orders, a **systems contract** (as the term is usually understood) does not relate to a single item or small group of items, but instead covers a large group of materials or supplies. Typically, it is for a long (even indefinite) period.

5.14 The procedure involves negotiation of a master contract specifying the items included in the agreement, the price of each and the terms of delivery. Quantities are not usually specified. When demand arises, appropriate staff (normally from user departments rather than purchasing) call for releases against the contract. Requisitions and purchase orders are not used, so cutting down administration.

5.15 The use of systems contracting implies a high degree of trust on the part of both buyer and supplier. Invariably, the buyer is placing the contract on an exclusive basis (ie no other supplier is to be used when demand arises for one of the specified products). The supplier is faced with uncertain demand and a high requirement for service performance. It is usual to treat the supplier in effect as an extension of the buyer's stores function, and expected delivery times are similar to what would be expected if that were indeed the case. Both buyer and supplier must be prepared for a level of interdependence.

5.16 To make the concept work, there must be a catalogue of the products covered by the agreement. This will contain price details, which is one reason why paperwork is minimised: accounts staff do not need copies of purchase orders in order to check prices, and indeed there is usually no need for a purchase order at all. The supplier receives payment on a periodic basis, say monthly, for all requisitions supplied during the period.

5.17 If the agreement works well, there are significant benefits to the purchaser.

- Administration is reduced.
- Delivery times are rapid.
- Stocks are reduced. This is the effect of having the supplier act like an extension of the stores function, and for this reason systems contracting is sometimes referred to as stockless purchasing. It is usually a condition of the contract that the supplier holds a certain level of stock to meet urgent orders from the buyer.
- Purchasing staff are freed up to perform more useful work on high-value items and to play a more strategic role in the organisation.

5.18 The supplier benefits too from the reduction in paperwork and administrative effort. As with blanket ordering, there is also a saving in sales effort for the supplier.

Partnership relationships

5.19 Blanket ordering and systems contracts are examples of **long-term supply relationships**. An extreme development of such ideas is the concept of partnership relationship.

5.20 The idea here is that buyer and supplier are not adversaries, but partners working together to maximise efficiency along a supply chain. In other words, there is an attempt to break down barriers between the buying organisation and the supplier, and to regard the supply chain as a single entity.

5.21 There are potentially large advantages of this approach.

- Each party can benefit from the other's expertise.
- Each party has a thorough knowledge of how the other operates, which can lead to identification and removal of inefficiencies.
- World class techniques, such as just in time production and purchasing, become feasible because of close collaboration between buyer and supplier.
- Costs of re-tendering and of switching suppliers are avoided.
- Suppliers may offer preferential terms in return for a long-term agreement.
- There is greater focus on quality rather than on winning the next order.

Criticisms of partnering

5.22 Partnering has become a fashionable topic in recent years, but its importance should not be exaggerated. In most organisations, it is still the exception rather than the rule.

5.23 This is because the favourable view of partnership relations is far from universal. Indeed, some substantial criticisms of this approach have been made.

- Without the need for continual re-tendering there is a danger of relations becoming too close, possibly leading to complacency on the part of the supplier and lack of innovation.
- The administrative and management time involved in establishing this kind of relationship are prohibitive for many companies. Even for those who favour the idea, the approach may be restricted to a small number of key supplies.
- The buyer can become overly dependent on the supplier, which restricts options.
- A long-term relationship may not be able to cater for changing requirements over time.

Why long-term supply relationships sometimes fail

5.24 It is commonly assumed that all relationships have a beginning, grow to mutually satisfying maturity, decline and finally end. Long-term supplier relationships are likely to decline (grow stagnant or less successful) and eventually be terminated. The reasons for failure could be any of the following.

- The buyer has changed the type of products it makes or the markets it sells to, and no longer needs the products or services provided by the supplier.
- The buyer makes a strategic shift in its sourcing strategy (eg using low-cost country suppliers), so that the supplier is no longer relevant or competitive.
- The supplier makes a strategic shift into other supply markets, and no longer makes the products the buyer wants.
- New suppliers enter the market offering a product, service or terms that the existing supplier cannot match (eg as a result of lower labour costs or technological innovation).
- Problems arise within the relationship because it has become too 'cosy' and complacent: it no longer achieves the continuous improvements and added value that were stimulated by supplier competition.

- Either or both parties change personnel, culture or systems – creating fresh incompatibilities which the other party may not be able to resolve.

- Performance problems, shortfalls or disputes arise, leading to a rift between customer and supplier. This may be made worse by complacency about contract management. It may become 'terminal' if improvement commitments are not agreed and met over time.

Managing relationship decline

5.25 In 'downgrading' a relationship from partnership to transactional, the organisation may need to take any or all of the following steps.

- Set and reinforce pragmatic and objective criteria for purchasing decisions, with well-defined price data and so on – to re-establish competition-based decision-making and supplier selection.

- Redefine the roles of people assigned to administer supplier relationships.

- Increase resources assigned to indirect purchasing.

- Establish precise price bases and quality requirements for indirect purchases, in order to 'de-mystify' the process and give clear guidelines for comparison and supplier selection.

- Re-emphasise to all stakeholders the benefits of using free-market competition to reduce costs and improve service quality.

- Be prepared to switch suppliers if necessary – effectively terminating or suspending the relationship.

Suspending or terminating relationships

5.26 As indicated above, a commercial relationship may have to be suspended in a range of circumstances, and these will dictate how the process should be handled. In some cases, the relationship may be mutually terminated or suspended by notice or agreement (eg at the end of a contract period), while other cases may be adversarial or disciplinary in nature (eg breach of contract or unsatisfactory performance by a supplier). Even in the former cases, it is useful to manage the termination constructively, so as to:

- maintain the possibility of future relationship

- learn from the past relationship, in order to improve relationship management in future.

5.27 In cases of dispute, however, the need for careful management is even greater, because of the potential negative consequences for both parties: loss of co-operation, escalating disputes, legal actions and so on. A comprehensive approach to managing termination would include steps such as the following.

- Clearly defining and communicating what will be construed as a breach of contract or shortfall in performance

- Setting and agreeing remedies or penalties which will be sought

- Defining formal procedures for pursuing a dispute

- Paying attention to relational and ethical aspects: giving balanced, constructive feedback; acknowledging the value of work done; attacking the problem (not the people) and setting improvement targets for contract renewal or replacement (so that the door is left open).

Managing relationship growth

5.28 Just as a relationship may shift from partnership to transactional, due to a number of internal and external changes, so in the 'growth' phase of the relationship there may be a shift from transactional to longer-term partnership relationships.

5.29 Managing the shift towards intentional longer-term relationships may require consideration of factors such as the following.

- Monitoring and managing the risks of longer-term ties, given environmental changes and potential areas of incompatibility
- Improving communication at all levels and points of contact between the organisations
- Implementing or improving performance monitoring and measurement
- Ensuring strategic and operational 'fit' between the organisations (eg compatibility or integration of procedures and systems)
- Monitoring 'trade-offs' in objectives, the 'net balance' of benefits accruing to both parties, stakeholder satisfaction and so on over time

6 *Low-value orders*

Purchasing cards

6.1 A problem that has attracted increasing attention in recent years is that of purchasing the numerous small-value items that must be purchased only occasionally, or perhaps just once, so that overall demand is low. The problem is that use of the traditional purchasing process may lead to transaction costs out of all proportion to the value of the items purchased.

6.2 One obvious approach is to consolidate such orders so that the overall value is higher and justifies the trouble and expense involved. Unfortunately, this is not usually feasible. It is difficult to predict when demand will arise for such non-recurring purchases. In many cases the item is only available from one particular supplier, so that there is no flexibility available to the buyer.

6.3 To handle this problem, purchasing specialists have sought ways to reduce the administrative costs of placing such orders. At the same time buyers must bear in mind the conflicting need to exercise appropriate control over expenditure of organisational funds. To reconcile these demands a number of specialised techniques have evolved.

6.4 Simplest of all is the use of petty cash on delivery. This reduces paperwork to a minimum. Another step in the right direction is to allow telephone ordering. Instead of having to generate paperwork with every order, the buyer simply combines his ordering procedure with his enquiry into price and availability: one telephone call deals with both. The supplier is given oral notice of the order number; and no written order is required.

6.5 Many companies now use purchasing cards issued by a credit card company. The system was pioneered in the UK by BOC, who in 1992 approached their corporate chargecard provider, Company Barclaycard, with the suggestion that their cards be used not just for travel and entertainment, but also to purchase goods from other businesses.

6.6   Working in association with Visa, the major banks developed a separate purchasing card which is already making a major impact in the area of small-value purchases. Companies issue a card to everyone who is likely to need to make small one-off purchases. Credit limits on each card, as well as restrictions on the types of goods purchased, are used to impose control over abuse. The scheme has major benefits for suppliers too, particularly in improving their cashflow from customers.

6.7   The aim of using purchasing cards is to cut down administration by dealing with just a single bill for many small purchases, rather than multiplying paperwork. Obviously the card issuer charges a fee (either a flat amount per transaction, or a monthly management fee, or a percentage of the value of transactions). However, this is outweighed by the savings that can accrue.

6.8   To ensure that purchasing companies can exercise control over this kind of spending the card issuers have worked hard on the reports that they offer. The monthly reports follow a 'line item detail' approach, in which each cardholder's transactions with each supplier are listed line by line. Although this can lead to quite a voluminous report it gives the purchasing company comfort that proper control is in operation.

6.9   In addition to this analysis by cardholder, the report can group purchases by supplier. This enables buyers to see easily how much is being spent with each supplier, which may be useful information if bulk purchase discounts are available.

Purchase-to-pay (P2P) methods

6.10   P2P is a broad term, referring to the use of internet technology and electronic networks to effect payment for goods and services. It is by no means confined to low-value orders, but has proved particularly valuable in this area. Buyers and suppliers use technology to make processes more efficient.

6.11   Apart from the use of company purchasing cards (discussed above) P2P frequently makes use of electronic consolidated invoicing. (In fact the use of purchasing cards can be regarded as a special case of this technique.)

6.12   An electronic consolidated invoice is an electronic file containing all information required to enable the finance department to effect payment. The finance department does not need to re-key the information already generated by the supplier(s).

6.13   Another technique is **evaluated receipt settlement** (ERS). This removes the need for a supplier to submit a hardcopy invoice (and hence is sometimes referred to as self billing, or payment on receipt.) On delivery of the goods, or after internet review of consumption of a service, the buying organisation can authorise automated payment to the supplier.

6.14   Some authors interpret P2P as being a shorthand description of the whole purchasing cycle, from requisition through to paying the supplier. If the term is used in this sense, you should refer to the purchasing cycle described earlier in this chapter.

Other methods of dealing with low-value orders

6.15   A brief mention of other methods is worthwhile here.

6.16   **Catalogue sourcing**. Some suppliers offer a catalogue of their products, with facility for the customer to order by phone, fax or email. Stationery companies such as Viking are good examples of this. Provided the buyer is happy that the catalogue represents good value this method of ordering is very cheap and convenient. In many cases the supplier will invoice periodically (say monthly) instead of invoicing with every supply.

6.17   **E-procurement**. Use of electronic methods, as exemplified by P2P methods above, has streamlined many aspects of the buyer's work. Online catalogues offer a further reduction in paperwork, even as compared with the manual catalogue sourcing described in the last paragraph.

6.18   Baily, Farmer, Jessop and Jones refer to one further method: **forward supply**. The supplier makes quantities of his products available on the customer's own premises. The customer pays for them as he uses them, being billed by the supplier on a periodic basis (say monthly).

Chapter summary

- Supply chain management is concerned with the flow of goods from raw materials stage through to the end user. Most supply chains are controlled through contracts between unrelated parties.

- In many cases supply chains are based on tiering of suppliers. This enables buyers to focus more closely on just a small number of first-tier suppliers, who in turn manage a number of second-tier suppliers.

- Managed services is a term to describe the situation where a main contractor is appointed to take charge of an operation, and in turn appoints specialist subcontractors to do much of the detailed work.

- The role of agents in supply chains has been declining. For many firms, it is preferable to adopt more direct contact with their ultimate customers.

- The purchasing cycle comprises a number of stages (shown in Figure 7.4). For the most part, the cycle is transferable: it applies (perhaps in slightly modified form) in just about any business sector.

- A cross-functional team is a group of individuals taken from different organisational functions so as to work together. The purpose is to direct a range of relevant skills to the task in hand.

- There is a spectrum of relationships with suppliers, ranging from spot buying to partnership sourcing.

- Low-value orders give rise to particular problems, because their processing may cost more than the value of the orders. Possible solutions include the use of petty cash, purchasing cards, purchase-to-pay methods, catalogue sourcing, e-procurement and forward supply

Self-test questions

Numbers in brackets refer to the paragraphs where you can check your answers.

1   Draw a diagram to illustrate the supply chain for a purchaser who performs all manufacturing in-house. (Figure 7.1)

2   What are the reasons for a policy of tiering suppliers? (1.14)

3   List characteristics of a typical first-tier supplier. (1.16)

4   What are the advantages of adopting a managed services approach? (2.6)

5   Why is the role of agents in supply chains declining? (2.11)

6   List the main stages in a typical purchasing cycle. (Figure 7.4)

7   What checks must be made to ensure that a purchasing transaction is completed satisfactorily? (3.22)

8   At what three main points in the purchasing cycle would authorisation procedures be necessary? (3.31)

9   What is the purpose of forming a cross-functional team? (4.1)

10   Describe a three-tier structure for the management of a cross-functional team. (4.11)

11   What is a framework agreement? (5.2)

12   In what circumstances should spot buying be used? (5.5)

13   Describe what is meant by blanket ordering. (5.7)

14   What are the benefits of a systems contract? (5.17)

15   What criticisms have been made of the partnership approach to supplier relations? (5.23)

16   List methods of dealing with low-value orders. (6.4ff)

CHAPTER 8

Different Methods of Purchasing (II)

Chapter learning objectives

2.2 Identify and explain different methods of purchasing.

- Projects: how scoped, purchased and paid for
- Merits of competitive tendering: the key stages, appraisal and evaluation of tenders, and merits of e-tendering
- Good practice and its application to purchasing including benchmarking

Chapter headings

1 The pros and cons of competitive tendering

2 Other aspects of competitive tendering

3 Projects

4 Ensuring best practice

Introduction

In this chapter we continue the examination of different purchasing methods (listed in Section 2.2 of your syllabus). In the first two sections we look at the use of competitive tendering. The third section of the chapter is devoted to the special requirements of project work. Finally, we look at methods of ensuring best practice in the purchasing function.

1 The pros and cons of competitive tendering

When to use competitive tendering

1.1 Once a buyer has determined which vendors he is prepared to do business with, taking into account both his market analysis and analysis of specific vendors, an important decision is whether to enter negotiations with one or more vendors, or instead to use a competitive tendering (competitive bidding) procedure.

1.2 Dobler and Burt (in *Purchasing and Supply Management*) have a useful list of five criteria. If these criteria are satisfied then competitive bidding may be an efficient method to use. Otherwise, it will not be. The five criteria are shown in Table 8.1 below.

1.3 Dobler and Burt also identify situations in which competitive bidding should not be used as the main means of source selection. These are also included in Table 8.1.

Table 8.1 *The use of competitive bidding*

Five criteria for the use of competitive bidding	Four situations in which competitive bidding should not be used
The monetary value of the purchase should be high enough to justify the expense of the method	Situations where it is impossible to estimate production costs accurately
The specifications must be clear and the vendors must have a clear idea of the production costs involved	Situations in which price is not the only important variable
There must be an adequate number of vendors in the market	Situations in which changes to specification are likely as the contract progresses
The vendors must be both technically qualified and keen for the business	Situations in which special tooling or set-up costs are major factors
There must be sufficient time for the procedure to be accomplished	

1.4 Notice the importance of technical qualification in the vendors. To use this method effectively the buyer must first screen the potential suppliers to ensure that the tender documents are addressed only to those who are technically capable of meeting the requirements.

1.5 Typically there may be from three to ten suppliers who are invited to bid, and in general the buyer will intend to choose the one submitting the lowest price. This is why prequalification of potential suppliers is so important: once the tendering process is underway it is difficult (and may cause ethical problems) to choose any bid but the lowest. The buyer does not want to become tangled up at that stage in discussions of technical capability.

1.6 The prequalification of potential suppliers should be done on objective criteria. Certainly past experience will help if the buyer has dealt with the supplier before. Even then, a predetermined list of criteria can provide a systematic means of eliminating firms that should not advance to the tendering stage.

1.7 The kind of elimination criteria that could be used include the following.

- Lack of recent experience in the relevant kind of work
- Inadequate financial resources to complete the work
- Inadequate management resources to control the work
- Lack of the required facilities (eg lack of a strong design capability, or lack of production processes of a type to guarantee the required quality).

1.8 Additional regulations (the EU procurement directives) apply to organisations in the public sector.

Planning the tendering procedure

1.9   We have already emphasised the importance of prequalification of potential suppliers. This is part of the process of **selective tendering**. An alternative approach is simply to solicit bids from any supplier who is capable of doing the work: this is called **open tendering**. In this case it is normal to publish the invitation to tender in a way that will ensure widespread circulation. It is usual also to state that the buyer will not be bound to accept the lowest price quoted, though of course he would normally do so.

1.10   Part of the process of planning a tendering exercise must be to decide between these two methods. In the case of public contracts there is sometimes no choice to be made: regulatory provisions may mean that open tendering will be compulsory. But where a free choice exists selective tendering will normally be used. This is because of the following reasons.

- Open tendering is more expensive in terms of administration and evaluation costs.
- Open tendering is usually more time-consuming, which may be a problem if deadlines are tight.
- Vendors too find the procedure expensive. Selective tendering means that only suppliers with a fair chance of succeeding are put to the trouble and expense of tendering.

1.11   Attention must next be given to tight specifications, precisely defined delivery schedules and careful timetabling of steps in the tendering procedure. The importance of this is that once the procedure is in motion the buyer's task is relatively straightforward. Just check that tenders received comply with the requirements, and then choose the lowest bid.

1.12   Of course, this is an over-simplification which takes insufficient note of the importance of purchasing judgement. For example, there will be exceptional cases (at least in the private sector) where the lowest bid is not chosen for various reasons. Nevertheless, despite occasional exceptions the principle is a sound one.

1.13   Table 8.2 sets out a checklist of the main stages in a tendering exercise which need to be planned in advance.

Table 8.2 *A checklist for tendering*

1.	Determine whether a tendering process is to be used, or whether some other process is preferable.
2.	Determine the type of tendering process to be used – open or selective.
3.	Determine a realistic timetable. This should allow reasonable time for all interested parties to prepare their submissions. It should also allow reasonable time for the purchaser to make available any information that is required by the tenderers.
4.	Issue invitations to tender. In the case of open tendering this would be by means of a public advertisement. In the case of selective tendering it would be by means of a formal approach to each supplier on the shortlist, but the preliminary vetting should have excluded any that may not be willing to tender for any reason.
5.	Ensure that full specifications are issued to each potential supplier in identical terms and by the same date. It should be made clear to tenderers that they are to comply strictly with any timetable for submission.
6.	Arrange the opening of tenders on the appointed date. Return unopened any tenders received after the due date.
7.	List the tenders received and enter the main details of each on an analysis sheet for ease of comparison.
8.	Evaluate each tender and select the best offer from suppliers who meet the tender criteria and who are judged capable of completing the contract to the required standards and within the specified deadlines.

The invitation to tender

1.14 Stage 4 in Table 8.2 is the issue of an invitation to tender (ITT). This must be prepared very carefully to ensure that potential suppliers are absolutely clear about what is required of them. Typically, the ITT will cover the following points.

- The scope and objectives of the tender
- A detailed specification of what is required
- The deadline for submitting tenders
- The point of contact in case of queries
- Confidentiality requirements
- Instructions on not colluding with other tenderers
- Administrative details concerned with the process, such as the format in which tenders are to be prepared (often the tender is to be completed on a standard form issued to the potential tenderers along with the ITT)
- An overview of the award process (timetable, what happens after submission of tender, when and on what basis the contract will be awarded)
- Instructions on pricing (details such as price per unit, any scope for price variation, payment terms, period of validity of the quoted price etc)

Appraisal and evaluation of tenders

1.15 The final stage in the checklist of Table 8.2 referred to evaluation of tenders. How is this done in practice? Is there more to it than simply choosing the lowest price? The answer to this last question is 'yes', as we have already hinted. This is obviously the case in an open tendering procedure where an evaluation must be made of the tenderers' capabilities. But in fact it is normal practice also in selective tendering.

1.16 One of the main reasons for this is that frequently the specification prepared by the buyer, and on which the tenders are based, will be a functional specification. When tenders are received it is not a simple matter to decide whether they meet the requirements of the functional specification.

1.17 Even among those tenderers that do meet the minimum requirement there is likely to be variety in the exact nature of the product being offered: the only feature common to all will be that they are capable of performing the function specified. Exactly how the vendors will have met the requirement will differ, and it is likely that some solutions will have greater appeal to the purchaser than others. The attraction of any particular solution may exceed that of another solution, even if the price difference tells against it.

1.18 Once again, a checklist is provided below for convenience. This lists the main points to take account of in evaluating tenders once they are received.

Table 8.3 *A checklist for evaluating tenders*

1.	Establish a routine for receiving and opening tenders, distributing copies as appropriate and ensuring security.
2.	Set out clearly the responsibilities of the departments involved.
3.	Establish objective award criteria. These may have been set out in the initial invitation to tender, particularly if the contract is subject to statutory control.
4.	Establish teams for the appraisal of each tender. It will be necessary to ensure that the required team members will be available during the time they are required.
5.	Establish a standardised format for logging and reporting on tenders.
6.	Check that the tenders received comply with the award criteria.
7.	Check the arithmetical accuracy of each tender.
8.	Eliminate suppliers whose total quoted price is above the lowest quotes by a specified percentage. For example, eliminate any supplier whose quoted price is more than 20 per cent above the average of the lowest two quotes.
9.	Evaluate the tenders in accordance with predetermined checklists for technical, contractual and financial details.
10.	Prepare a report on each tender for submission to the project manager.

Disadvantages of tendering

1.19 Tendering is not an ideal solution to every purchasing situation. Indeed, it carries some quite serious disadvantages. This is especially true, of course, if the process is used in cases where alternative approaches are superior. This issue has already been discussed above; see in particular Table 8.1.

1.20 Even where the situation appears suited to tendering procedures, care is needed to avoid potential pitfalls. One point often made in the literature is that once a contract has been awarded the contractor may have little incentive to perform to the highest possible standards. Since the contract award is a one-off benefit to the vendor, and leaves him with no particular reason to expect further business, he may be less motivated than a supplier who wins a contract by virtue of consistent quality performance during a long-standing business relationship with the buyer.

1.21 This is a particular danger in areas – principally contracts awarded by public sector bodies – where competitive tendering is compulsory. The successful tenderer knows that when the agreed term of the contract comes to an end he is back on level terms with a multitude of other vendors. In effect, he gains no credit for his successful performance, and is therefore not motivated to achieve high standards. Even worse, as the contract nears its end quality of performance may drop off quite noticeably as the contractor has little left to lose by cutting corners and keeping his own costs down.

1.22 Another general criticism of tendering is that it tends to lead to an increase in the number of suppliers. This conflicts with the modern trend towards a narrower supplier base combined with long-term contractual relationships.

1.23 Finally, tendering is a cumbersome procedure and time schedules may be too tight to permit its use.

2 Other aspects of competitive tendering

The merits of e-tendering

2.1 In recent years, purchasing techniques have been greatly affected by technological developments. These have come to a head in the arrival of complete e-sourcing or e-procurement systems. This essentially means the purchase of items using the internet. One possible application is a method of inviting suppliers to bid for supply contracts electronically. This is what is meant by **online auctions**. The basic idea is that a buyer advertises contracts (usually very large contracts) on the internet and solicits bids. The contract is then (usually) awarded to the lowest bidder.

2.2 According to some commentators (especially those with an interest in promoting e-commerce, such as e-auction providers) there are significant benefits in online auctions. Some of them are highlighted in a *Supply Management* article of 15 February 2001.

- They save time for buyers, enabling them to concentrate on more strategic areas. Time used up in conventional negotiation is reduced or eliminated.

- Established suppliers can be benchmarked to find out whether they still represent best value.

- Although savings achievable are proportionate to the size of the purchasing budget, even small companies can participate via consortia auctions.

- By making the true market price for a product or service transparent auctions enable buyers to analyse price differentials properly.

2.3   The technique is not necessarily ideal for all possible purchases. For example, the danger of selecting an unsuitable supplier for a critical component may well outweigh any potential cost saving. On the other hand, the risk involved in putting a stationery contract up for auction is minimal. Risks can in any case be minimised by pre-selecting suppliers.

2.4   A serious danger that buyers must be aware of and must manage is the risk of alienating existing suppliers. A supplier who has invested time and money in servicing a customer is likely to be unhappy if he hears that his efforts are to be undermined by a buyer intent on offering the business by auction. Indeed, in some cases existing suppliers have refused to participate when a buyer decides to take this route.

2.5   An online auction is prepared in advance by the buyer, who advertises contracts and solicits interest from possible suppliers. When the advertised time arrives the participants join each other online, effectively simulating the physical reality of an auction room. In line with this, each participant can see the offers made by others.

2.6   The buyer is hoping to attract as low a price as possible, which means that bidders (ie potential suppliers) must continually come down in price. (For this reason, such auctions are sometimes referred to as **reverse auctions**, because of course in a regular auction it is buyers who are competing upwards rather than suppliers competing downwards.)

2.7   It has been said by a CIPS examiner that this kind of process is used primarily to reduce prices for inputs such as cement, steel, tyres, packaging and other leverage items. To judge from articles in the professional press the process is much more widely adopted than this, and virtually any commodity appears to have a potential market online.

Ethical issues in tendering

2.8   As already explained, lowest quoted price is not the only criterion for choosing between tenders. That is because other factors must also be evaluated and a balance struck between price and non-price factors. Nevertheless, the tendering procedure by its nature implies that where non-price factors even out, preference will be given to the tenderer offering the lowest price.

2.9   This is an important principle to uphold because relations with vendors, and more generally the public perception of the purchasing firm, can be damaged if it is not upheld. Vendors going to the trouble and expense of preparing a tender are entitled to expect fair and unbiased treatment in return. It is a matter of good purchasing ethics to ensure that they are not disappointed.

2.10 Buyers should not solicit bids other than from vendors with whom they are willing to do business. This may seem obvious, but there have been many instances where buyers have breached this rule. In some cases, negligence is to blame. If the buyer had done sufficient vetting at the prequalification stage he would have realised that the vendor was unsuitable, but he did not do so and as a result the vendor is put to trouble and expense with no hope of reward.

2.11 In other cases the fault lies in poor planning of the tender procedures. For example, inadequate specification may lead to a need for post-tender negotiation, which in some cases vitiates the whole decision to use the tendering method in the first place. There is a place for post-tender negotiation, but it must be conducted in the light of ethical guidance published by the Chartered Institute of Purchasing and Supply.

2.12 Other cases are even more reprehensible. Vendors have been invited to submit bids by buyers who have no intention of working with them, but believe their bids may provide a weapon to use against other tenderers. In other cases, buyers have favoured some vendors over others by their conduct in the management of the process; for example, some vendors may be provided with additional information denied to others.

2.13 Ethics is not specifically mentioned at this point of the syllabus, and further discussion would take us too far afield. Nevertheless, as aspirants to a professional qualification you should be continually aware of the ethical standards that the profession demands.

Enquiries and quotations

2.14 Whether or not a formal tendering procedure is being used, it is common for a buyer to contact a number of suppliers in search of quotations. Often the buyer's enquiry will be on a pre-printed form. This makes life simpler for the buyer, ensures that important points of concern are not overlooked, and makes it easier to compare quotations from suppliers when they are eventually received.

2.15 A pre-printed enquiry may include any or all of the following details.

- Quantity and description of items required
- Required delivery date and address for delivery
- Special requirements relating to packaging and/or materials handling (eg must be supplied on pallets)
- Terms and conditions of purchase, usually the buyer's standard terms
- Terms of payment
- Contact details: contact name, address, telephone number, fax/email details, reference number to use in reply, date by which to reply

2.16 In the normal case the various suppliers contacted will reply by quoting their best price for supplying what the buyer wants. However, there is a more exceptional case, namely the possible existence of a supplier **cartel**. This refers to collusion between suppliers, whereby they agree among themselves not to compete on price.

2.17 Such an agreement, being anti-competitive in nature, is illegal. However, buyers need to be aware of the possibility of illegal collusion. Possible signs of this include the following.

- All the prices offered by suppliers are higher than expected.
- One or more suppliers are reluctant to negotiate.
- One or more suppliers have declined to quote.
- The lowest price offered is significantly lower than all the rest. The suggestion here is that all of the other prices have been pitched artificially high.

2.18   Leaving aside this exceptional case, suppliers will usually respond to the enquiry by supplying a quotation. Usually the supplier's quotation will be regarded as constituting an offer which the buyer may or may not wish to accept.

Quotation analysis

2.19   Once the suppliers' quotations have been received, the buyer will need to analyse them to see which one provides the best value to his organisation. If the buyer's requirement is very simple, there will be little difference between the various quotations except in price. Subject to reasonable undertakings on delivery and quality, the buyer will most likely choose the supplier offering the lowest price.

2.20   However, not all transactions are this simple. For example, suppose the buyer is aiming to buy 20 laptop computers for use by senior managers in the organisation.

- There will be differences in the specifications of the machines offered by different suppliers. Presumably all the offerings will at least match the minimum requirements laid down by the buyer, but some machines will exceed that specification. How valuable, if at all, are the additional features?

- There will be differences in the level of support offered by the suppliers (for example, some may offer a one-year warranty at an additional cost, while others may include a three-year warranty in the basic quoted price). How valuable, if at all, is the extra support?

- There may be differences between the buyer's standard terms and conditions and those quoted by the supplier. How amenable is the supplier likely to be in negotiating terms, and how important are the differences anyway?

2.21   This discussion is meant to illustrate that, in the case of even a moderately complex buying requirement, there will be a range of factors (other than basic price) for the buyer to consider in evaluating the supplier quotations. Here are some examples.

- Previous performance of the supplier (including financial stability, reliability etc)
- Delivery lead time
- Add-on costs (freight, insurance, installation and training etc)
- Running costs (including energy efficiency)
- Warranty terms
- Availability of spares
- Availability of maintenance cover
- Ability to upgrade to higher specification
- Risk of obsolescence
- Payment terms
- Residual value and disposal costs
- In the case of overseas suppliers, exchange rates, taxes and import duties

3 *Projects*

Characteristics of projects

3.1   A project is a unique set of co-ordinated activities that has the following characteristics.

- A finite and defined lifespan
- Defined and measurable deliverables or outcomes to meet the specified objectives
- A set of activities to achieve the specified objectives
- A defined amount of resources
- An organisation structure, with defined responsibilities, to manage the project

3.2   There are three main points that are most important to a successful project.

- A project must meet customer requirements.
- A project must be within budget.
- A project must be completed on time.

3.3   Lysons (following Lock) distinguishes four different types of project.

- **Manufacturing projects**: such as prototyping a new product, development work or any discrete application of machinery or equipment to attain a defined end goal.
- **Construction projects**: that are characterised by being based off-site from a headquarters or central location.
- **Management projects**: activities, often utilising cross-functional teams, that have a defined purpose, eg office relocation, simultaneous engineering teams etc.
- **Research projects**: aimed at the expansion of knowledge or the acquisition of new data or information.

3.4   Successful projects have the following features.

- A well-defined scope and agreed understanding of intended outcome.
- Active management of risks, issues and timely decision-making supported by clear and short lines of reporting.
- Ongoing commitment and support from senior management.
- A senior individual with personal accountability and overall responsibility for the successful outcome of the project.
- An appropriately trained and experienced project team and in particular a project manager whose capabilities match the complexity of the project.
- Defined and visibly managed processes that are appropriate for the scale and complexity of the project.

3.5   For cross-company projects, there may be nominated senior owners from each organisation involved in the project and its delivery. Where this is the case, there must be a single owner who is responsible for the whole project.

Scoping the project

3.6 A project requires a clear and unambiguous statement that encompasses three aspects.

- **Its objectives**: the end result that the project is trying to achieve. The objectives provide a focus to the project team. Good objectives will be clear, measurable and quantifiable. This may be made easier if they are broken into smaller staged sets of objectives that will come together to meet the overall objective at the end. Common objectives would be cost, time and quality.

- **Its scope**: the exact range and responsibilities covered by project management. The scope of the project serves to identify the work content and outcomes. This helps to set boundaries and will be set out in a specification. The scope of the project helps to define contractors or part of the organisation involved, time periods including start and end dates, commercial and legal responsibilities of those involved and the resources to be employed.

- **Its strategy**: how the project management role will ensure that the objectives will be met. The strategy enables an overview of the project and allows for phases of the project to be identified which then allows for milestones to be set. These can then be conveyed to those involved so as to provide a common understanding.

3.7 A **specification** is the definition of the project. The specification will initially contain errors, ambiguities and misunderstandings. In consequence, the specification will usually need clarification with everyone concerned with the project (from originator, through the workers, to the end-customer) to ensure everyone is working with the same understanding. The outcome of this deliberation should be a **written** definition of what is required, by when; and this must be **agreed** by all involved.

3.8 The agreement upon a written specification has several benefits.

- The clarity will reveal misunderstandings.
- The completeness will remove contradictory assumptions.
- The rigour of the analysis will expose technical and practical details which may otherwise be overlooked.
- The agreement forces all concerned to read and think about the details.

3.9 The work on the specification can be seen as the first stage of quality assurance since you are looking for and countering problems in the very foundation of the project. From this perspective the creation of the specification clearly merits a large investment of time. The specification will change as the project progresses but deviations will be agreed rather than imposed.

3.10 The project management plan is a document that embodies the project. It is the most important document in the overall planning, monitoring, and implementation of the project and should be 'owned' by the project manager and his team.

3.11 The plan should include the following elements.

- A definition of the objectives
- Statements as to how these will be achieved and verified

- Estimates of the time required
- Financial budget
- Safety, health and environmental policies
- Quality policy
- Risk management strategy
- Related items concerning technical, commercial or organisational aspects

Contracts in project work

3.12 Forms of contracts used in projects vary according to the complexity, nature and risk involved. The project plan and the agreements on specifications will provide the basis for the contract but areas of risk and contingency may need to be considered and incorporated.

3.13 The choice of contract can be between a tailor-made one to fit individual circumstances or a standard form contract, which will usually relate to a specific business sector. Standard form contracts have usually been agreed by the industry and its professional body and are designed to be balanced contracts. The principal is often in a dominant position when it comes to the awarding of contracts and it is often a case of the contractor accepting the contract offered with little negotiation.

3.14 There are three main categories of contract: lump sum contracts, measured form contracts, and turnkey contracts.

3.15 In a **lump sum contract**, the principal and contractor agree a fixed sum for completing a specified programme of work by a given date. This type of contract may include a contract price adjustment clause (CPA), usually based on agreed cost indices to take account of price fluctuations outside an agreed limit through factors such as exchange rate movements, fluctuations in commodity prices or high levels of inflation etc.

3.16 The role and accuracy of the specification is paramount in awarding lump sum contracts as it forms the basis for the contract. The lump sum approach ensures a high degree of contractor motivation but can lead to quality concerns if attempts are made to cut corners or if time becomes an issue toward the contract end. The contractor carries the greatest risk during the operational phase. The project manager needs to monitor progress carefully (particularly on quality issues) but is freed from the daily work scheduling and costing task.

3.17 **Measured form contracts**. If the contractor is unable to draw up a detailed enough specification to base the contract on then he can agree rates associated with aspects of the anticipated work. Payment is then made against actual quantities (hours or volumes used) applying the agreed rates.

3.18 **Turnkey contracts**: by definition 'turn the key and it works'. When using this style of contract the entire project is placed in the hands of one contractor who will carry the project through to conclusion. The contractor (who may be a consortium in the case of a large infrastructure project) will then organise and operate the project. Quality issues can be a concern as can after-project support and these considerations require both monitoring and specifics included in the contract.

Project variation

3.19 Projects by their nature tend to be large-scale and to extend over long periods of time. This makes it difficult to predict all possible eventualities at the time of contracting. For this reason, it is common to lay down defined procedures for varying the terms of the contract as the project progresses.

3.20 It is sometimes felt that this recognises failure to plan properly, but this is a shortsighted view. Over the course of a large project any or all of the following unpredictable outcomes may occur.

- Changes in the buyer's requirements
- Changes in the supplier's resources, processes and procedures
- Changes in key personnel
- Changes in markets
- Changes in economic conditions

3.21 To cope with this, the project contract should incorporate mechanisms whereby buyer and supplier can negotiate changes to what was originally agreed, and corresponding changes to the contract price.

3.22 The lengthy lifecycle of a project also gives rise to a need for agreed payment terms. Often payment will be made in instalments, each instalment being linked to a defined 'milestone' in the project. Alternatively, there may be a scheme of payments at defined intervals, eg monthly or quarterly. The buyer must ensure that such payments are made according to the agreed terms, provided he is satisfied that the supplier has performed to standard.

The role of purchasing in projects

3.23 Lysons has a helpful analysis of the various tasks to which purchasing can contribute in projects. These are summarised in Table 8.4

Table 8.4 *Purchasing's contribution to project work*

- Liaising with members of the project organisation (project manager, consultants, site engineers etc)
- Agreeing where and by whom purchasing will be undertaken (eg an independent purchasing organisation)
- Advising on lease or buy decisions, especially in relation to capital equipment
- Assisting with tender specifications and negotiations with subcontractors
- Evaluating tenders and post-tender negotiations
- Placing of orders and subcontracts
- Expediting orders
- Inspection and quality control
- Certifying payment of invoices for goods and services provided by external suppliers and subcontractors

4 Ensuring best practice

What is meant by best practice?

4.1 There is debate in academic circles about the possibility of defining procedures and approaches that represent 'best practice'. Academics and practitioners alike have greeted successive new developments as breakthroughs that will transform the way that business is conducted. In the sphere of purchasing, such developments in recent years have included just-in-time techniques, partnership relationships, supply chain management, network sourcing, manufacturing resources planning and others.

4.2 Other academics have queried whether it is possible to think of one single approach as representing 'best practice'. If tomorrow's new technique will be hailed as best practice, then presumably what we are doing today must be inferior in some way. And in any case, what is good for one organisation may not be good for another.

4.3 Despite this debate, most organisations feel compelled to respond to competitive pressures. To do so, they try to ensure that their operating systems are of the highest quality. One approach to doing this is to adopt a formal benchmarking procedure; we look at benchmarking later in this chapter.

Using technology to achieve best practice

4.4 A feature of modern purchasing that would almost universally be regarded as contributing to best practice is automation. The use of information technology to streamline operating procedures has been a dramatic feature of procurement in the last two decades.

4.5 Technology can improve efficiency of processes, increase the volume of transactions handled, reduce delays in cycle time, and vastly improve the spread of communication within an organisation and between organisations. This can in turn lead to savings in costs and time, greater accuracy and reliability, and improved business relationships.

4.6 We will look at just four aspects of technology that have impacted on purchasing: electronic data interchange, e-procurement, electronic point of sale systems, and barcoding.

4.7 A significant advance from the purchasing viewpoint has been the increased use of **electronic data interchange** or EDI. This has been defined as 'the exchange of structured data between computer applications without manual intervention'. For a buyer, what this means is communication of purchase orders, delivery instructions and other messages direct from his organisation's computer to that of his supplier. And the process is two-way: the supplier can communicate back to the buying organisation, including automatic transmission of invoices for payment.

4.8 The word 'structured' in the definition is important. The data transferred between buyer and seller must be in a mutually agreed standard format. Often a translation process is necessary, which may be carried out by a specialist third-party provider.

4.9 The use of EDI techniques is now widespread in industrial, commercial and public sector organisations. For the most part the data transferred is standard documentation such as purchase orders (or call-offs against a blanket order) and invoices. The speed of transaction processing and completion is greatly enhanced by the use of electronic communication.

4.10 Reasons for the increased use of EDI spring from both internal and external sources. A company may be seeking reductions in the cost of transaction processing and in lead times, both of which are assisted by EDI. This is an example of internal pressure. Often the impetus in these cases comes from a move to world class manufacturing techniques such as just in time or MRP. With conventional transaction processing times such systems would hardly be feasible, and EDI is a great boost to their chances of success.

4.11 External pressures arise from customers and competitors. The consequence of a buyer's wish to use EDI is that his suppliers must take steps to comply or face the possibility of losing business. Often buyers are insisting on EDI as a condition of awarding contracts. This is how customers provide an external impetus for adoption of EDI. Competitors are the other external impetus: to keep pace with competing businesses it is necessary to adopt the latest means of improving efficiency.

4.12 Once EDI is in place it can lead to immediate cost savings, for example on stationery, postage, mail handling, and data entry and correction. Other savings arise from the reductions in stock that improved lead times make possible.

4.13 Successful implementation of EDI depends crucially on adequate training. This is a management task which is often overlooked, but the best companies take it seriously. Indeed, it is common for leading companies to encourage EDI adoption among their suppliers by assisting in their training needs in addition, of course, to providing training to their own buying staff.

4.14 The implications for purchasing staff are far-reaching.

- The speed of transactions increases, permitting greater use of modern world class techniques such as just in time purchasing and production.

- Bottlenecks in the purchasing system are highlighted and must be removed. In particular, attention must be paid to approval and authorisation procedures which do not add value but do add to lead times.

- Relations with suppliers must become much closer, implying almost certainly a need to reduce the supplier base. This is in line with modern thinking on supplier relations.

- Service levels to internal 'customers' of the purchasing department will improve.

- The amount of administrative and clerical work required from purchasing staff is reduced, leading to more effective use of time on creative and strategic activities.

4.15 In recent years, many of these developments have come to a head in complete **e-procurement** systems. E-procurement essentially means the purchase of items over the internet. One possible application is a method of inviting suppliers to bid for supply contracts electronically. This is what is meant by **online auctions** (see earlier in this chapter).

4.16 There are opportunities for using e-procurement to enhance the customer-supplier relationship and to add value for all participants in the supply chain. The potential benefit comes from feeding real-time information about customer demand to suppliers over the internet.

4.17 Nowadays, purchasers routinely use the internet for a variety of purposes.

- Using web browsers to search suppliers' catalogues. This permits immediate access to information on product features, availability, prices, delivery methods etc.

- Electronic ordering. This takes the process one step further: once the buyer is satisfied, he can place his purchase order online.

- A further step still is payment by electronic funds transfer or by purchasing cards.

- Buying departments can track shipments and receive delivery information by directly accessing the websites of transportation companies.

4.18 Apart from accessing information from suppliers, buyers can also use the internet to publicise information about themselves: their mission statement, their environmental policy, details of how the purchasing system operates etc.

4.19 The beauty of this approach is the reduction in transaction costs. Instead of sending out a copy of, say, an environmental policy to every supplier on the list, it is sufficient to post the document onto a website and the job is done in a single hit. The use of online auctions is another example where traditional processes can be extremely streamlined by electronic means. Overall, this means that information technology can make a vital contribution to the ideal of lean supply.

4.20 Even in highly automated systems there is usually at least some manual work involved. Efforts to streamline such systems often focus on reducing the manual element. One area where human intervention is still necessary and costly is that of capturing the data that the computer will work on.

4.21 **Electronic point of sale (EPOS) systems** include a variety of devices used in retailing. One example is the familiar kind of cash register in which each key is labelled with the name of a product, rather than with an amount of money. For example, when a customer orders a hamburger in a fast food restaurant the operator presses a key marked 'hamburger'. This is then interpreted by the computer within the till and a receipt is produced showing the item and its price.

4.22 Most POS systems are based on the use of **barcodes**. The code is written onto a data carrier, which may be a label, a tag, a plastic card or something similar. This is attached to the product. The barcode is in effect a code number represented in the form of optical bars. Each digit in the number is identified by the spacing and thickness of each bar.

4.23 Barcoding is used widely in retailing, both for stock control purposes and for improving speed and efficiency at checkouts and cash registers. Usually, the code is read by a scanner and the sale is automatically recorded. The price and description of the item are retrieved from the computer stored in the till and displayed on the customer's receipt. Stock records are automatically updated to reflect the sale.

4.24 The use of barcoding is important for purchasing specialists because of its applications in various materials management areas. For example, goods received may be barcoded either by the supplier (in liaison with the buyer) or by the buying organisation. Either way, the receiving staff can simply scan the barcode in order to transmit updating information to the computerised stock system. If incoming materials are packaged in standard quantities the process can be streamlined even further.

4.25 It is not just receipts of goods that can be tracked and recorded in this way. The location of stock items, issues to production, tracking of work in progress, and eventually sales to customers are all amenable to barcoding techniques. It is common for stores staff to use portable decoders capable of reading the barcodes and transmitting data to a central computer. Equally, the computer can pass back information through the decoder: requisitions, picking lists and so on.

Benchmarking

4.26 To ensure that purchasing disciplines comply with best practice many organisations use the technique of benchmarking. This has been defined as 'the continuous process of measuring products, services and practices against the toughest competitors or those companies recognised as industry leaders'.

4.27 The process was pioneered by the Xerox corporation in 1979. Finding that their competitors were able to sell products more cheaply than Xerox could even manufacture them, they embarked on a systematic pursuit of improved business processes. This applied not just to manufacturing, but to all areas of their business.

4.28 The basic idea of benchmarking is that a comparison of existing processes against some form of standard may identify areas where improvements are possible.

4.29 It is common to distinguish four types of benchmarking; for example, this is the analysis adopted by Bendell, Boulter and Kelly in *Benchmarking for Competitive Advantage*.

- In **internal benchmarking** the comparison is with other parts of the same organisation. For example, a divisional purchasing function might be benchmarked against the purchasing function in another division.
- **Competitor benchmarking**, as the name suggests, involves comparison with a competitor. This is obviously difficult to achieve because of confidentiality.
- In **functional benchmarking** the comparison is with a similar function in another organisation, not a competitor. For example, an electronics manufacturer might benchmark its purchasing function against that of a construction company. Clearly the aim is to identify an organisation which has special strengths in the function to be benchmarked.
- **Generic benchmarking** is the most generalised form of the technique. Comparison involves business processes which may cut across functional boundaries and operate in different industries.

4.30 Alternative analyses are possible. For example, a simpler categorisation distinguishes simply between competitor benchmarking (using publicly available information on competitors) and process benchmarking (in which the comparison is with anyone other than a competitor). As suggested above, this will be particularly valuable if the chosen benchmark partner is especially strong ('best in class') in the function concerned.

4.31 Within a purchasing function it is clear that various different activities could benefit from a benchmarking approach. Possibilities include the following.

- Purchasing training
- Structures
- Performance measurement
- Supplier development
- Co-makerships and partnerships
- Interface developments
- EDI and systems developments

Benefits of benchmarking

4.32 There are several potential benefits of benchmarking.

- It moves the organisation from 'compliance'-based quality systems (conformance to specification and standards) to performance-based evaluations, reflecting the pursuit of competitive survival and advantage.
- It replaces an ad hoc or subjective approach to improvement and competition with a set of objective, systematic criteria.
- It sets performance targets and quality standards which are realistic (since other organisations have achieved them) yet challenging (since the benchmarking organisation has not yet achieved them). This is the most effective combination for maintaining motivation.
- It stimulates more research and feedback-seeking into customer needs and wants. Even if no specific areas for improvement are identified from the direct comparison, this may lead to useful insights for learning and innovation.
- It generates new ideas and insights 'outside the box' of the organisation's accustomed ways of thinking and doing things. Proponents of the learning organisation identify benchmarking as an important technique which they identify as SIS: 'steal ideas shamelessly!'
- Specific improvements may be identified and implemented, leading to improved customer service, lead times for delivery, time-to-market for new product development, and so on.

The process of benchmarking

4.33 The process of benchmarking has not always been easy, because of the restricted information available about organisational processes and practices (particularly among competitors). However, considerable resources have developed to support benchmarking, including online clubs and networks.

4.34 A 15-step model of competitive benchmarking has been suggested by Oakland (*Total Quality Management: the Route to Improving Performance*): Table 8.5.

Table 8.5 *A systematic approach to benchmarking*

Stage 1: Plan	1	Select the function, unit or process to be benchmarked
	2	Identify the exemplar of best practice or key competitor (using industry analysis, customer feedback, benchmark consultants)
	3	Identify the criteria to be benchmarked (delivery times, customer service, innovation, invoicing efficiency or whatever)
	4	Establish a benchmarking project team
	5	Determine methods for data collection (customer questionnaires, benchmark networks, published reports, site visits, etc)
	6	Apply data-collection methods: conduct research
	7	Plan and manage direct contacts with target organisations (interviews, visits, etc)
Stage 2: Analyse	8	Collate and analyse benchmark data to compare organisational performance with that of the target organisation in key criteria
	9	Create a 'competence centre' and knowledge bank: a catalogue of the information gained, for future reference, training and development planning, etc
	10	Analyse the underlying cultural, structural and managerial factors that enable performance to benchmarked standards – not just the performance measures themselves
Stage 3: Develop	11	Develop new performance standards, targets and measures, to reflect desired improvements
	12	Develop systematic action plans to achieve performance standards, including change management programmes, human (and other) resource plans, realistic timescales, accountabilities and monitoring-and-review procedures
Stage 4: Improve	13	Implement the action plans
Stage 5: Review	14	Continuously monitor and/or periodically review progress and results against key performance criteria (as planned)
	15	Review the benchmark data for further areas for improvement and start the cycle again

Purchasing benchmarks

4.35 Interfirm comparison schemes have been developed to produce benchmarks for numerous purchasing activities. Some of these are listed in Table 8.6, which is based on the findings of the Centre for Advanced Purchasing Studies in Arizona.

Table 8.6 *Purchasing benchmarks*

1	Total purchasing spend as a percentage of sales revenue
2	Purchasing operating expense as a percentage of sales revenue
3	Purchasing operating expense as a percentage of total purchasing spend
4	Number of purchasing staff as a percentage of organisation's total staff
5	Sales revenue per purchasing employee
6	Total purchasing spend per purchasing employee
7	Total purchasing spend per professional purchasing employee
8	Number of active suppliers per purchasing employee
9	Number of active suppliers per professional purchasing employee
10	Purchasing spend per active supplier
11	Cost of operating the purchasing function per active supplier
12	Percentage of active suppliers accounting for 50 per cent, 75 per cent, and 90 per cent of total purchasing spend
13	Percentage change in number of active suppliers during the reporting period
14	Percentage of total purchasing spend spent with minority-owned businesses
15	Percentage of total purchasing spend spent with women-owned suppliers
16	Percentage of total purchasing transactions processed through EDI
17	Percentage of total goods purchases handled by the purchasing department
18	Percentage of total services purchases handled by the purchasing department
19	Percentage of total company purchases handled by the purchasing department

Externally accredited performance measures

4.36 Because there can be difficulties in obtaining information for comparison direct from competitors – and, indeed, any other organisations – performance measures which have been designed by third parties and accredited by reputable organisations are very useful and cost-effective. Three important ones to note are ISO 9000, Investors in People and Charter Mark.

ISO 9000 accreditation

4.37 ISO 9000 is an international standard that describes how an organisation can set up 'quality management systems' to ensure that quality and customer focus are at the heart of everything the organisation does.

4.38 Simply put, the key principles of ISO 9000 are as follows.

- Focus on your customers' needs, requirements and expectations.
- Provide leadership (unity of purpose and encouragement).
- Involve your people at all levels, and use their abilities.
- Use a process approach to manage activities and related resources.

- Take a systems approach (identify interrelated processes and manage them as a system).
- Encourage continuous improvement.
- Get the facts and analyse them before you decide.
- Work with your suppliers in a mutually beneficial relationship to create value.

Quality circles

4.39 Once best practice has been established, it is important to ensure its spread throughout the organisation. One technique for achieving this is the use of quality circles. These aim to harness the expertise and commitment of staff in all areas of the organisation by involving them in exploring quality issues and sharing best practice.

4.40 A quality circle consists of a voluntary group of about eight employees, which meets regularly (during working hours) to discuss problems of quality and quality control in their area of work, and to suggest quality improvements. The circle is facilitated by a leader who directs the discussion and helps to orient and develop members of the circle (as required) in quality control and problem-solving techniques, presentation and meetings skills.

4.41 It is important that the group is made up of volunteers, since it harnesses genuine commitment and enthusiasm. Management should not impose agendas on the meetings, in order to permit openness about problems and conflicts and to encourage thinking 'outside the box'. Feedback on suggestions offered and problems raised, however, should be swift and constructive, in order to demonstrate that they are taken seriously.

4.42 In practice, quality circles may or may not have genuine responsibility for making, implementing and monitoring the progress of their recommendations. Even as discussion groups, however, they may have significant benefits, especially if members return to their departments as 'ambassadors' for quality, having been involved in the circle. Benefits claimed for quality circles include:

- greater motivation, satisfaction and commitment of employees, through involvement in key organisational values and processes.
- improved productivity and quality of output, through involving operational staff and generating new ideas.
- more multidirectional communication and the establishment of informal networking.
- development of employees in teamworking, project management, presentation and problem-solving skills.
- greater awareness of quality and service issues and the need to satisfy customer demands.

Teamworking

4.43 Even if an organisation does not formally set up quality circles, most firms that are interested in quality management will ensure that they make use of teamworking as part of their strategy. The ways in which teams function lend them to the sharing of best practice (although a poorly functioning team can also ensure the spread of worst practice!).

4.44   In the context of quality and in particular of continuous improvement, working in teams generates the following two types of advantage.

- Motivational advantage: they fulfil the individual's social need to be accepted by a group; they encourage participation; interlocking supportive relationships give strength to the organisational structure.

- Business advantage: they bring together complementary skills beyond the capability of one person alone; they allow information to be shared; they help reduce costs; they can improve performance quickly; they improve flexibility and responsiveness; they give the benefit of the insights and knowledge of many people.

Chapter summary

- Dobler and Burt list useful criteria for the use of competitive bidding, and also situations in which competitive bidding should not be used.

- It is important to prequalify potential suppliers using carefully chosen elimination criteria. This is a step in selective tendering. In open tendering this step is not used.

- An invitation to tender should contain details designed to simplify the overall process. Suggested details are given in paragraph 1.14.

- Appraisal of tenders is more complicated than simply choosing the lowest price.

- There are important drawbacks to the use of tendering; for example, in some cases it is not the best way of motivating suppliers to perform well. It is also cumbersome in administrative terms.

- E-tendering (the use of online auctions) has been an important development in recent years. But buyers must beware of alienating existing suppliers.

- When a buyer seeks quotations from a number of suppliers it is important to watch for signs that a cartel may be operating.

- In project work, there are three major requirements: completion to customer requirements, completion within budget, and completion on time.

- When planning a project, three key aspects must be defined: objectives, scope, strategy.

- Different types of project include lump sum contracts, measured form contracts, and turnkey contracts.

- Buyers must always seek to observe best practice in their purchasing activities. Using electronic techniques (such as EDI) can help with this. Benchmarking is another important technique. Finally, buyers should be aware of international standards such as ISO 9000.

- Quality circles and teamworking are methods of widening involvement in the process of achieving best practice.

Self-test questions

Numbers in brackets refer to the paragraphs where you can check your answers.

1   List criteria to determine when competitive bidding should be adopted. (Table 8.1)

2   What elimination criteria could be used in the process of prequalifying potential suppliers? (1.7)

3   List the main stages in a tendering exercise. (Table 8.2)

4   What are the disadvantages of tendering? (1.19ff)

5   What are the benefits of online auctions? (2.2)

6   What signs of a possible cartel should a buyer look out for? (2.17)

7   What factors should a buyer consider when evaluating a supplier's quotation? (2.21)

8   What are the characteristics distinguishing project work from other operations? (3.1)

9   List features of successful projects. (3.4)

10   Describe what is meant by a lump sum contract. (3.15)

11   What factors may make it necessary to vary the terms of a project? (3.20)

12   What contributions can buyers make towards a successful project? (Table 8.4)

13   How has EDI contributed to best practice in purchasing? (4.7ff)

14   What are the implications of EDI for purchasing staff? (4.14)

15   For what purposes might buyers use the internet? (4.17)

16   Describe four different types of benchmarking. (4.29)

17   What are the key principles of ISO 9000? (4.38)

18   What are the benefits of quality circles? (4.42)

CHAPTER 9

Purchasing Raw Materials and Commodities

Chapter learning objectives

2.3   Analyse and explain different ways of purchasing raw materials and commodities.

- The key differences between direct and indirect purchasing
- Methods of purchasing raw materials and commodity items and key considerations; finance and the futures markets
- Contribution of purchasing to the bottom line
- Purchasing for stock
- Purchasing for production
- Key considerations when purchasing perishable items

Chapter headings

1   The contribution of purchasing to bottom-line profit

2   Direct and indirect purchasing

3   Maintenance, repair and operating (MRO) supplies

4   Purchasing commodities

Introduction

This chapter, as its title suggests, is primarily concerned with the purchase of raw materials and commodities. However, there is also a syllabus caption in this area about the contribution of purchasing to the bottom line, so we begin with a general section to illustrate this idea. We then move on to discuss direct purchasing (the purchase of goods for resale, or for incorporation into goods for sale) and indirect purchasing (the purchase of operating supplies). Finally, we look at the specialised issues concerned with the purchase of commodities.

1   The contribution of purchasing to bottom-line profit

Changes in the cost base of business

1.1   In recent decades, the cost structure of manufacturing firms has been transformed. Previously, the largest expense borne by a typical manufacturer, by far, was the cost of wages. Most manufacturing industry was heavily labour intensive; most manufacturing processes were carried out manually by skilled and unskilled workers. The result was a large workforce and a large wages bill. In this area of expenditure of course purchasing staff had little or no role to play.

1.2 Today the situation is very different. Many industries have seen a huge investment in automated production processes. In many cases this has been accompanied by painful cuts in manufacturing personnel. From being labour intensive, such industries have become capital intensive. The sums invested in plant and equipment, often computer controlled, are high in relation to the sums paid out to employees.

1.3 A related trend is a new focus on core activities – what Peters and Waterman in their management classic *In Search of Excellence* call a 'stick to the knitting' approach. Many businesses now see their strategic direction as being a concentration on certain core activities where they believe they hold competitive advantage. Many support activities, which previously would have been provided by in-house departments, are now outsourced – handed over to specialist external suppliers who provide the required service in exchange for a fee. In some cases this trend has been accentuated by regulatory pressures; for example, in many public sector concerns a regime of market testing and compulsory competitive tendering has been imposed.

1.4 This trend applies not just to the provision of services; manufacturing businesses have been increasingly ready to focus on just one part of the manufacturing process. Where previously they might have made Product X entirely from scratch, nowadays they buy the parts for Product X externally and confine themselves to the assembly process. Another organisation in the supply chain specialises in manufacturing the parts required for Product X.

1.5 Both of these trends point to the same outcome: organisations spend a much greater proportion of their income on buying in goods and services than they used to do. The impact for purchasing departments is obvious. Where previously the purchasing responsibility extended only to a small proportion of the organisation's total income, the proportion has now increased dramatically.

The financial impact of purchasing

1.6 Crucially, the financial impact of purchasing effectiveness and efficiency is a very direct one. Every pound saved by purchasing activities is a pound added to bottom line profit. On the other hand every pound wasted by purchasing is a pound lost to profit. Contrast this with the efforts of, say, a selling department, where every pound gained in extra sales brings with it perhaps 90 pence of extra costs; the net impact on profit in that case is only a 10p boost.

1.7 This is not to say that selling departments are in any sense less important than purchasing departments. The purpose is merely to explain why the attention of senior managers has increasingly focused on the effective management of purchasing activities. This has been part of the reason for the increased status accorded to the purchasing function in recent years.

1.8 These ideas can be illustrated in a number of ways. One approach is to show the total organisational revenue as a 'cake' which has to be sliced up: one portion to satisfy external costs, one to pay internal costs (such as wages), and one (usually small!) slice left over for profit. For a typical manufacturing business the cake might be divided as shown in Figure 9.1.

Figure 9.1 *How income is spent*

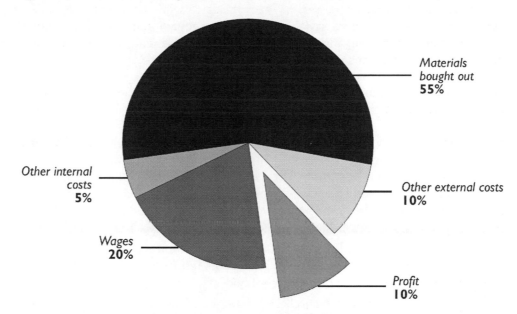

1.9 It should be easy to see from this that external costs typically consume a large part of the cake, and that if they are not checked they could easily expand to eliminate the thin slice left for profit.

1.10 Another way of illustrating the impact of purchasing on organisational profitability is to compute some figures. Suppose that annual sales are £50m, with variable materials costs equal to 60 per cent of sales and 'internal' costs of £15m. Profit is therefore £5m (50 – 30 – 15 = £5m). Now look what happens if:

(a) sales volumes rise by 5%; or alternatively

(b) materials costs fall by 5%.

	(a)		(b)	
	£m	£m	£m	£m
Sales		52.5		50.0
Materials costs	31.5		28.5	
Internal costs	15.0		15.0	
Total costs		46.5		43.5
Net profit		6.0		6.5

1.11 The profit increase achieved by increasing sales volume is not as great as that achieved by reducing costs. (A 5% saving in costs has led to a 30% increase in profit.) Of course, the figures have been chosen to illustrate the point, but you will find that if anything this example understates the effect of purchasing economies as compared with other means of increasing profitability. And the example does not even mention the other saving achieved by alternative (b): If materials costs are lower, then so too is the cost of inventory. A lower inventory value saves costs, and this saving ought to be added to the benefits already apparent from the figures above.

Cost reduction and cost avoidance

1.12 Purchasing's contribution to saving costs should be very apparent. However, this does not always affect the organisation's bottom-line profit. This is because we have not investigated what happens to the money saved.

1.13 In the financial (and purchasing) literature, three main possibilities are identified. The first two are cost reductions; the last is cost avoidance.

- The money saved is simply retained within the business. In effect, the finance department say that the saving will become an amount removed from the control of the relevant budget holder, who consequently spends less than originally budgeted. In this case, the saving is indeed reflected immediately in an improvement in bottom-line profit.

- The money saved remains in the control of the budget holder, who is now free to spend it elsewhere. If he does, there will be no direct impact on the bottom line profit, but the organisation will have benefited from a greater level of resources than was expected from the original budget.

- The third case is where purchasing manages to avoid an additional cost that would have been incurred. For example, by careful negotiation with a key supplier, purchasing manage to defer an intended price increase. In this case there is no immediate effect on bottom line profit (at least for the current year – it may well be a boost to the profit of subsequent years, when the intended price rise would have taken effect).

Purchasing on price alone

1.14 This section has concerned the impact of purchasing on profitability measured in pure financial terms, and specifically in terms of reducing costs. However, this should not be taken to imply that the sole or principal function of purchasing is to achieve cost reductions. On the contrary, there is a delicate balance between cost considerations and other factors which purchasing professionals must be adept in managing.

1.15 The overall objective can still be stated in terms of improving profitability, but 'profit' in this sense means any benefit, and particularly long-term benefits, accruing to the organisation; and this may go far beyond short-term cost considerations. Even when we fix our attention on actual costs the modern view is that cost is a far broader concept than simple purchase price. Current thinking emphasises a 'total cost of ownership' or 'total acquisition cost' which includes a basket of costs not immediately apparent from the purchase price.

1.16 These ideas are neatly captured by Baily, Farmer, Jessop and Jones in the form of a 'price/cost iceberg': see Figure 9.2.

Figure 9.2 *The price/cost iceberg*

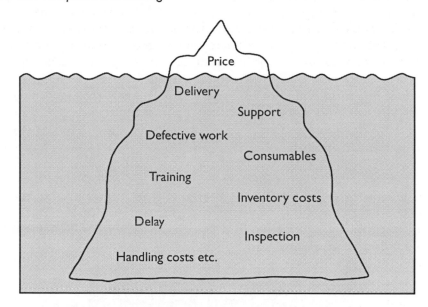

1.17   The diagram illustrates the important point that there is much more to purchasing than the basic price charged by the supplier. The total costs of ownership include a wide range of other costs which must also be considered by the buyer. As the authors state, 'it is an obvious fact, yet a commonly ignored one, that a low price may lead to a high total acquisition cost'. **Total acquisition cost** (TAC), otherwise referred to as **total cost of ownership** (TCO), is an important concept in modern approaches to purchasing.

1.18   Even when buyers consider the broader concept of TAC or TCO, rather than just purchase price, they do not necessarily go far enough. There are many factors to consider other than the purely financial ones. Failure to take these into account can lead to bad decisions.

1.19   As an example of this, a buyer may sacrifice quality by favouring a cheaper product. The added waste and costs associated with rework and rejections may outweigh the saving on basic price. There may also be an impact on sales if customers perceive the resulting finished product to be of inferior quality.

2   Direct and indirect purchasing

The distinction between direct and indirect purchasing

2.1   A manufacturing business generates a constant requirement for production materials. These may take various forms: raw materials, parts and components, subassemblies and so on. Without adequate supplies of these materials when they are needed production operations may be disrupted with expensive consequences. The purchase of these items is often referred to as **direct purchasing**.

2.2   Manufacturing businesses also require consumable supplies, sometimes referred to as maintenance, repair and operating (MRO) supplies. And all businesses spend money on general 'running' expenses: travel, stationery, telecommunications etc. The purchase of these items is often referred to as **indirect purchasing**.

2.3   In the purchasing literature, this distinction is often made in the context of manufacturing businesses alone. However, as purchasing disciplines develop and spread more widely in the non-manufacturing sector the distinction is broadened. Nowadays, it is usual to speak of direct purchasing when the items purchased are either for resale (eg the goods purchased by a retailer), or for incorporation in goods for sale (eg raw materials purchased by a manufacturer). Indirect purchasing then refers to the purchase of any other items. In general, indirect purchasing is more likely than direct purchasing to be carried out by end users rather than specialist purchasing staff.

Porter's value chain model

2.4   A slightly different (but overlapping) way of looking at the distinction between direct and indirect purchasing is provided by Professor Michael Porter's value chain model. See Figure 9.3.

Figure 9.3 *Porter's value chain*

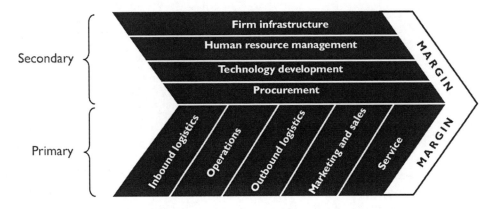

2.5   This model distinguishes between the primary activities of an organisation and the secondary or support activities.

- Primary activities are concerned with bringing resources into the organisation, transforming them by means of a 'production' process, moving finished products to customers, and marketing them.
- Secondary activities are concerned with supporting the primary business functions.

2.6   On this analysis, we use the term direct purchasing when we refer to purchases for the primary activities. We use the term indirect purchasing to refer to purchases for the support activities. In effect, we are distinguishing between two supply chains: a primary one and a secondary one.

The impact of direct purchasing

2.7   We can distinguish certain characteristics that apply to direct purchasing.

2.8   The cost of direct purchases is part of the organisation's cost of goods sold. If this can be reduced, the company's gross profit (and as a consequence net profit) will be improved. By contrast, the cost of indirect purchases affects the organisation's overheads. If this can be reduced, net profit will be improved, but there will not be any effect on gross profit.

2.9 The quality of direct purchases has a direct impact on the quality of goods produced. Poor quality will lead to increased quality costs, increased waste, scrap and rejects, and possibly reduced customer satisfaction. By contrast, the quality of indirect purchases does not impact on the production process.

2.10 Direct purchases frequently need to be stocked, so as to ensure there is no disruption to production operations. By contrast, indirect purchases are usually made when required, without holding stocks.

2.11 In terms of supplier relations, direct purchases are more likely to be covered by long-term relationships. By contrast, indirect purchases are frequently made on the basis of one-off, transactional relationships.

2.12 In many organisations, and especially manufacturers, the cost of direct purchases is a very high proportion of total external spend. Opportunities for the purchasing function to improve the bottom-line profit are that much greater.

2.13 For example, if a manufacturing company's cost of sales is 60% of its sales revenue (ie it makes a gross profit of 40%), and purchasing can trim 2% from the cost of direct purchases, this translates into a 1.2% increase in gross and net profit. The same organisation might typically spend perhaps 10% of its revenue on indirect purchases; the opportunity for purchasing to improve bottom-line profit in this area is only one-sixth of what it is in the case of direct purchases.

Purchasing for stock and purchasing for production

2.14 Most organisations need to hold a level of stock to meet customer needs and production requirements. Buyers will purchase such items on the basis of their past experience and any forecasts that may be available. However, there are costs associated with holding stocks (eg the cost of storage space and the cost of insurance). Modern thinking therefore emphasises the need to minimise stock levels.

2.15 This has led to a trend of purchasing for production. This means that materials are purchased with a view to immediate incorporation into the manufacturing process.

2.16 This form of purchasing will invariably prevail in sectors such as construction, where most of the organisation's outputs consist of 'products' made to customer orders. The products, in this case, may be a hospital, a bridge, a housing development etc. The major supplies required by such a business are devoted to a particular project, and are therefore purchased when the project requires them rather than being purchased for stock.

2.17 Purchasing for production is also a feature of just in time (JIT) environments. JIT is a philosophy that has won many adherents in recent years. It is based on the idea of minimising or eliminating 'buffer' stock: materials are purchased only at the moment they are required in the production process. JIT purchasing is a technique that is only feasible with the closest possible collaboration between buyer and suppliers.

2.18 Few companies take just in time principles to their ultimate conclusion; in other words, few companies dispense with production stocks altogether. But to minimise the ill effects of stockholding, described above, a number of techniques have emerged.

- The use of economic order quantities (ie calculating the optimum size of order for each material so as to minimise the combined cost of acquiring and holding stocks)

- Improving the process of forecasting production so that stockholdings are not excess to requirements

- The use of **vendor managed inventory**, which means that suppliers are asked to hold stock instead

- The use of management information systems, perhaps based on EPOS systems, to exercise tight control over stock

2.19 Where an organisation is prepared to purchase for stock, issues of forecasting become much less critical. But with an objective of minimising production stocks, demand forecasting must be taken very seriously so as to avoid causing disruption to production.

Stocking for inventory

2.20 Under a 'stocking for inventory' (or purchasing for stock) policy, inventory is purchased and placed into storage in advance/anticipation of need or demand.

2.21 There are many circumstances where this policy would be appropriate.

- In situations of **independent demand**: where the demand for a stock item exists *independent* of, or in isolation from, the demand for any other item. Examples include consumables and maintenance items, and finished goods sold in the retail sector

- In situations of **stable/predictable demand** for **low-value, non-perishable** items (especially if these do not take up too much warehouse space)

- Where there is a **long lead time** for obtaining stock from suppliers: the buyer may need to keep sufficient stock to meet customer orders

- Where items are **critical for operations**, and running out of them (or not obtaining them in time) would cause disruption to production

- Where there is a **legal requirement** to hold stocks (eg of health and safety equipment)

- Where inventory **appreciates in value** over time (eg wine or timber)

- Where **prices are expected to rise**, and it will be more cost-effective for the organisation to buy or stockpile items while prices are still low

- Where **demand is seasonal**, and the organisation lacks the capacity to cope with peaks of demand: finished stocks will have to be made in advance

2.22 The benefits of such a policy include: the ability to respond to seasonal or unexpected peaks in customer demand; the availability of buffer/safety stock to maintain customer service and operations (in the event of supply disruptions); cost efficiencies from bulk ordering and transport (rather than multiple smaller deliveries); the securing of low prices while available; legal compliance (where relevant); and potentially, appreciation in the value of stock over time.

Stock to order

2.23 Stock to order (or 'purchasing for production') is a stockholding policy whereby a company only purchases materials as required to fulfil orders received from customers. Examples of industries where this might be the case include 'jobbing' manufacturers, construction companies, bespoke tailors and providers of services that require materials to support the service (eg caterers).

2.24 A major challenge with this approach is the need to ensure good performance from suppliers against tight delivery schedules.

Stock to forecast

2.25 A stock to forecast policy is based on forecasting or estimating demand for finished products (for sale to customers) and for supplies (for operations), and planning inventory quantities and timing on this basis. Forecasting is particularly important in the retail sector where there may be wide seasonal variations in demand.

2.26 Although future demand may not be exactly known for purchased inputs, estimates can be made based upon past experience, statistical techniques or computer simulations and modelling.

Perishable goods

2.27 Finally in this section we make brief mention of perishable goods, which are specified on your syllabus at this point. Perishable goods are those that are subject to deterioration over time. Once they have deteriorated, they are no longer fit for their intended purpose. A simple example is food products.

2.28 It is critical that such products are studied carefully so as to determine their useful life. In the case of food products it is usual to display this information in the form of 'sell-by dates' or 'use-by dates'. Quality control of goods inwards is also critical.

2.29 This kind of product creates a need for careful transportation and storage. If these areas are handled badly, the process of deterioration may be accelerated. Buyers must guard against this not only by careful planning of the transportation and storage activities, but also by rigorous testing to ensure product quality at the time of receiving the goods and afterwards.

2.30 In some cases the process of deterioration carries actual physical dangers. For example, this is the case with certain chemicals. In such cases the storage and control of materials is tightly regulated, in particular by the Control of Substances Hazardous to Health Regulations (COSHH).

3 *Maintenance, repair and operating (MRO) supplies*

The nature of MRO supplies

3.1   MRO supplies have been defined as 'all goods and services (other than capital equipment) necessary to transform raw materials and components into end products'. They include such items as paint, lubricants, packing materials, cleaning products and industrial clothing. As a part of the production process, these materials can be regarded as a direct purchase. But in some respects they straddle the categories of direct and indirect purchase because they are not materials incorporated into the end products.

3.2   All manufacturing plants use MRO supplies regularly. The number of MRO items may be very large; some estimates suggest that a reasonably large manufacturing plant will carry in excess of 10,000 MRO stock lines. Although usage of any particular part may be relatively slight, the potential for incurring high purchase and stocking costs is clearly high.

3.3   For this reason it is important that purchasing staff exercise as disciplined an approach to MRO supplies as to any other area of their responsibilities. This is not always easy to do. One problem is that some firms, failing to recognise the importance of this area, have no defined policy on the issue. Often it is open to user departments to order MRO items without recourse to purchasing specialists and with little control over their expenditure.

3.4   The problems associated with MRO items are not all to do with expenditure. Potential disruption to production is an equally important concern. The value of an item may not be fully reflected in its purchase price. If its absence means a production hold-up then it would be more appropriate to measure its value in terms of the additional costs or lost revenue that might result.

Determining stock levels for MRO items

3.5   There are peculiar difficulties in establishing an appropriate stock level for an MRO item.

- In many cases the actual usage of the item will be very low, or even zero in some periods. This is because the purpose of stocking it is to obtain relatively cheap insurance against a hazard that is unlikely to occur, for example a fault in a particular machine.

- In other cases, the purpose of stocking the part may be to compensate for unwillingness of distributors to do so. Again, the aim is insurance against expensive disruption.

- The numerous items of MRO supplies are subject to very wide patterns of demand. Determining a stock level separately for each is a daunting prospect, and may not seem cost-effective if the total cost of such items is not fully appreciated.

3.6   To get the right results a systematic approach is essential. Each item of MRO supplies must be accurately described and a comprehensive catalogue developed. At this stage, opportunities for **rationalisation** – reducing duplication – should be investigated. Earlier we mentioned the case of a company that reduced the number of lubricating greases used in plant maintenance from 27 down to 6.

3.7 As with other stock items, stock movements must be recorded accurately, preferably on a computerised system. Slow moving stock should be monitored with particular care as this problem is common with MRO items. Clearly items that remain on storage shelves for long periods are prone to deterioration.

Maintenance policies

3.8 Buyers face a particular difficulty in respect of MRO supplies used in maintaining equipment and especially in relation to spare parts. The difficulty is that manufacturers of capital equipment have an obvious interest in binding the purchaser to their own products. They can do so by specifying a list of recommended spares, all manufactured by themselves and bearing their own item codes and descriptions.

3.9 Purchasers should resist this attempt to restrict their options. While the spares offered by the equipment manufacturer may indeed be the best buy, it does not make commercial sense to accept this without looking at alternatives. This is particularly so in the case of spares which may be needed for several different machines, purchased from different manufacturers. The buyer may clearly be able to benefit in such cases if he can purchase spares for all the machines in question from a single source. Purchasing similar items in small quantities from a wide range of different sources is unlikely to be economic.

3.10 Ideally, this problem should be addressed at the earliest stages, namely at the point when the machine is being purchased. While the deal is being negotiated the buyer is in a strong position to insist on seeing drawings of equipment and designation of parts. This can be a great help in designing policies of preventive maintenance, and also in planning replacement parts. In some cases it may be possible for the buyer to go further and require the manufacturer to use certain parts that fit the buyer's own requirements for standardisation.

3.11 A useful checklist for the buyer to use in these circumstances is given by Louis Jacobs ('Purchasing Maintenance, Repairs and Operating Supplies', in the Gower *Handbook of Purchasing Management*. This is briefly summarised in Table 9.1 below.

Table 9.1 *MRO checklist for purchasing capital equipment*

1.	Ask for all relevant engineering drawings.
2.	Request a list of all parts plus a recommended schedule of spares with expected life spans and other details.
3.	Consider linking the price paid to performance levels actually achieved; shortfalls in performance lead to reductions in price.
4.	Plan a first purchase of spares at the time of purchasing the equipment. Consider carefully whether the recommendations of the supplier are more than is likely to be required: avoid overstocking.
5.	Agree guaranteed lead times for spares if these are to be purchased from the manufacturer.
6.	Consider a maintenance agreement with a third party contractor, possibly with the contractor holding stocks of spares.

4 *Purchasing commodities*

The nature of commodities

4.1 Primary commodities are items that occur in nature and provide raw materials for businesses to incorporate in their products. They include crops such as cotton, coffee, tea, wheat and soya; and also minerals such as coal, iron ore and bauxite. In many cases such items are sold locally much as any other product might be, but there is also an international demand from companies worldwide who need such raw materials. To satisfy such demand a complex market has grown up in the form of commodity exchanges.

4.2 A key feature of primary commodities is a geographical one: supplies of a particular commodity may be plentiful in one part of the world, while they are very scarce or non-existent in other regions. Firms wishing to use such items in their products are dependent on some form of international trade.

4.3 From the purchaser's viewpoint, the main difficulty with commodities is that they are subject to significant and unexpected fluctuations in price. For example, if the Brazilian coffee crop is unusually bad because of weather conditions, coffee will be scarce on the world markets, and prices will rise for the limited supplies that are available. Similarly, wars, revolutions, changes in government and simply strikes have often interrupted the supply of minerals from third world countries, again pushing up prices.

4.4 These effects are made worse by the difficulty of taking compensating measures. If the rubber crop fails, a planter might consider increasing the number of his trees to make up the deficit. However, it will be years before newly planted trees are productive and in the meantime the price may remain unusually high. The purchaser is rarely able to pass on such increases to his customers and risks paying more for his raw materials than he can recover in his selling prices.

4.5 The commodity markets come to the aid of purchasers (and of producers) by offering a number of methods that can dampen price fluctuations and enable sensible forecasting and budgeting. In particular, buyers can take advantage of futures contracts (discussed later in this section).

The main commodity markets

4.6 The main markets in which commodities are traded are in the United States. They include the market for precious metals (Comex) in New York, the New York Mineral Exchange (Nymex) and the Chicago Board of Trade, where grain, rice and soya are traded. Major markets in the UK include the London Metal Exchange, with dealings in metals such as copper, zinc, tin and aluminium, and the International Petroleum Exchange.

4.7 Frans J Vanhorick ('Purchasing Raw Materials', in the *Gower Handbook of Purchasing Management*) identifies the features that must be present for effective functioning of a commodities market. These are described in Table 9.2.

Table 9.2 *Features of an effective commodities market*

Feature	Explanation
Logical geographical location	The site must be an export harbour, and a financial centre, and must possess first class communication facilities. Time zone is also important.
Liquidity of the product	The commodity must be available in sufficient quantity, but the quantities must also be manageable.
Liquidity of the market	There must be sufficient interested parties, both buyers and sellers. This is usually not the case in local markets.
Financial liquidity	There must be unrestricted currency movements.
Political stability	The huge sums involved mean that participants shun any danger of instability.

4.8   Four groups participate in these markets: producers, buyers, traders, and speculators.

- Producers – eg farmers with a crop to sell – are interested in securing a good price for their produce.

- Buyers are interested in guaranteeing the price they will pay for commodities to be used in their businesses.

- Traders make the wheels go round. They are both buyers and sellers, and make a small commission on trades in either direction.

- Speculators are also both buyers and sellers, but their aim is usually to make a substantial profit from their expertise in forecasting price movements. Speculators play a valuable role in that they foster the liquidity of the market by, in effect, introducing a greater number of both buyers and sellers.

Futures contracts

4.9   Futures contracts are a form of forward buying. Forward buying in itself is a fairly simple concept. Rather than wait until stocks are actually needed, a buyer will sometimes see advantage in buying ahead of demand. This may be because a large order will trigger a discount, or because the buyer wishes to use an economic order quantity. More speculatively, a buyer may buy today because he foresees that prices are likely to rise tomorrow. In all these cases the buyer has to reckon with the usual disadvantages of holding stock, but on balance it may still pay him to buy forward if the circumstances are right.

4.10   It is this last issue of price fluctuations which is central to the specialised form of forward buying known as futures contracts. Both producer and buyer can benefit if the effects of such fluctuations can be ironed out in advance. In particular, both can budget with confidence. The detailed workings of such contracts are the province of specialists and would take us outside the scope of the examination syllabus. However, a broad knowledge is useful as most buyers, even if they do not specialise in commodity buying, are likely to be faced with this kind of transaction on occasion.

4.11   To begin with it is worth asking why futures contracts are needed at all. Surely an ordinary commercial insurance contract could be taken out to cover the risk of price fluctuation? Unfortunately this is not so. The reason is that an insurer makes his money from the people who do **not** make claims; their premiums enable the insurer to pay out the unfortunate minority who suffer loss. But in a commodity market **all** parties stand to lose if, for example, supply suffers through a crop failure. There are no winners in this situation and no fund from which to pay the losers.

4.12   Futures contracts provide an alternative to insurance. The subject of a futures contract is not a quantity of a physical commodity such as wheat or iron ore; it is the right to purchase or sell a quantity of such a commodity. It is used by a buyer or a seller to 'hedge' a contract in the physical commodity by making sure that any movement in price has self-cancelling effects on his financial position.

4.13   To see how it works, note that a buyer of a commodity today fears a price **fall** in the future. This is because when he later comes to sell the product in which the commodity is incorporated his customers will expect a low selling price. Conversely, a seller of coffee today fears a price **rise** in the future – 'If only I had delayed selling!'.

4.14   The fact that buyers and sellers have opposite fears is what makes futures contracts work. The idea is that a buyer of the physical commodity should make himself also a seller of that commodity by means of a futures contract. Then if the price falls, he loses as a buyer but gains as a seller. In a perfect hedge these effects would cancel out exactly and the buyer would make neither profit or loss as a result of the price change. His profitability would reflect his trading ability, and would not depend on price fluctuations beyond his control.

4.15   To illustrate this, suppose a buyer needs 5,000 bushels of wheat on 1 January, when the price stands at £3 per bushel. This will be incorporated in products for sale two months later on 1 March. Clearly the price the buyer will be able to charge his customers will depend crucially on the price of wheat on that date. Suppose that by then the price of wheat has fallen to £2 per bushel. In broad terms, the buyer will only be able to sell his products for £5,000 less than expected.

4.16   To protect against this disaster the buyer could enter a futures contract on 1 January under which he agrees to **sell** 5,000 bushels of wheat on 1 March. The 'forward price' of wheat for delivery in two months time will not in practice be exactly the same as the 'spot price', but to illustrate the perfect hedge we will assume it is.

4.17   Now what happens on 1 March? First, the buying company sells its finished products for £5,000 less than expected – bad news. However, the company can also purchase 5,000 bushels of wheat at the March price of £2, knowing that under his futures contract he has a guaranteed customer for this quantity at a price of £3 – good news. Result: he gains £5,000 on the futures contract, which exactly offsets his loss on the physical purchase of wheat.

4.18   The detail of these computations is not so important as the general principle. A buyer of a physical commodity can protect himself against price fluctuations in the commodity. He does so by entering a futures contract under which, in effect, he becomes a seller as well as a buyer. Any price fluctuation then has equal and opposite effects on his financial position.

4.19 This is a complex area of the purchasing profession and the discussion has inevitably glossed over many practical points. However, this is likely to be sufficient for any question you are likely to meet in the exam.

Pound cost averaging

4.20 Another method of protecting against price fluctuations in commodity purchases is in effect to spread the risk over a large number of purchases. In very simple terms, suppose that we intend to spend approximately £12 million on a particular commodity over a period of a year.

- If we go out today and buy our whole year's supply we may soon regret it. If the price falls we will have paid more than we needed to.

- We may instead decide to spend £1 million each month. In some months (when the price happens to be low) we will acquire a relatively large quantity of the commodity. In other months (when the price happens to be high) our £1 million will not stretch so far.

4.21 Over the year this method ensures that the total price we pay is (roughly) the average of the various prices prevailing during the year. For this reason the technique is referred to as **pound cost averaging**.

Other methods of cost control

4.22 **Time budgeting** or **averaging** means that supplies are purchased as they are required. No stocks are held. Each purchase is at the prevailing market price, which means that windfall gains will not arise, but by the same token losses due to price fluctuations are avoided. This is obviously not a practical solution if it is necessary to hold stocks.

4.23 **Volume timing** means that supplies are purchased by means of forward buying if prices are expected to fall. If price **increases** are expected, a policy of hand-to-mouth buying is adopted instead. To apply this method successfully demands skill and good fortune in predicting price movements.

Chapter summary

- Recent trends in the cost base of manufacturing businesses have led to increasing scope for purchasing to contribute to bottom-line profit. But note that not every cost saving translates into an increase in profit.

- There is much more to purchasing than the basic prices charged by suppliers. Buyers must be aware of the 'price/cost iceberg'.

- Porter's value chain suggests that buyers must deal with two separate supply chains, one representing direct purchasing and the other indirect purchasing.

- The costs of holding stock have led to an increasing trend of purchasing for production rather than for stock.

- Perishable goods give rise to special problems of transportation and storage. It is important to maximise their useful lives.

- The large number of MRO items means that buyers must exercise special care in purchasing and in determining stock levels. There is a particular problem relating to MRO items used in maintenance of capital equipment.

- Commodities include crops, minerals etc. They are subject to extreme price fluctuations, which buyers may guard against by means of specialised techniques such as futures contracts.

Self-test questions

Numbers in brackets refer to the paragraphs where you can check your answers.

1. What do Peters and Waterman mean by 'stick to the knitting', and what has been the effect of this policy on purchasing? (1.3)

2. The sole purpose of the purchasing function is to achieve cost reductions. True or false? (1.14)

3. Distinguish between direct and indirect purchasing. (2.1, 2.2)

4. What factors have led to a trend towards purchasing for production rather than for stock? (2.14, 2.15)

5. Define MRO supplies. (3.1)

6. Why is it difficult to establish an appropriate stock level for an MRO item? (3.5)

7. What is meant by forward buying? (4.9)

8. Describe pound cost averaging. (4.20)

CHAPTER 10

Purchasing Services

Chapter learning objectives

1.5   Evaluate the context of the purchasing function and different purchasing situations.

- Merits of internal versus external outsourcing of supply

2.4   Analyse the differences between purchasing services as opposed to purchasing goods.

- Key differences between a product and a service
- A range of services: legal, professional, human resources, advertising and media, facilities management, IT, maintenance repair and operations (MRO) and finance
- Key requirements when specifying a service to be purchased
- Operation and merits of managed services
- Managing service level agreements

Chapter headings

1   Services distinguished from products

2   Specifying a service to be purchased

3   Managed services

Introduction

Services differ from tangible products in ways that have important implications for buyers. In the first section we look at the characteristics of services to see how they are distinct from tangible products. We then examine the problem of drawing up specifications for the purchase of a service. Finally, we look at the increasing trend to outsource services that previously might have been provided by in-house staff.

1   Services distinguished from products

The increasing importance of service purchases

1.1   As with many advanced economies, the UK's wealth generation depends very largely on the activities of service companies. The range of services provided to consumers and industrial organisations is very wide. Examples of such services are specified in your syllabus: legal and professional services, human resource services, advertising and media services, facilities management, IT services, MRO services, and financial services.

1.2   In the past decade the importance of the service sector has outstripped that of manufacturing in terms of contribution to gross domestic product. This is good news for service companies, but also has important implications for purchasing functions.

1.3   One indication of this importance is the growth in 'outsourcing'. This is the practice of buying services from specialist external suppliers instead of taking on internal employees to perform them. For example, many companies that used to employ their own cleaning staff now pay specialist cleaning companies to perform these tasks.

1.4   Another influence in this direction has been the European Union procurement directives that apply to most public sector bodies in the UK. The effect has been to increase the amount of work done for such bodies by external organisations, while reducing the work provided by in-house services.

1.5   In this section our objective is to focus on a more general theme. What features of services distinguish them from tangible products in terms of purchasing disciplines and procedures?

Differences between a product and a service

1.6   The peculiar characteristics of services have been much discussed, in the marketing literature as much as in standard purchasing texts. For example, Adcock *et al* in *Marketing Principles and Practice* refer to intangibility, perishability, and the personal element as features which distinguish services from physical products. Mirroring this from the purchasing viewpoint, Baily, Farmer, Jessop and Jones in *Purchasing Principles and Management* refer to impracticability of storage, lack of 'inspectability', uncertainties in contractual arrangements, and sheer complexity. These factors are discussed below.

1.7   **Impracticability of storage**. This can give rise to scheduling problems, and the effect of this is that the purchase of services is typically the subject of detailed forward planning between buyer and supplier. Of course, the difficulty does not apply to all services: Baily et al cite cleaning services, which are usually not time-critical, and insurance, which is usually provided continuously in return for an annual premium.

1.8   **Lack of inspectability**. A service cannot be measured, weighed or chemically analysed to check compliance with specification. Indeed the whole issue of specifying service levels is fraught with difficulty, and many of the problems that commonly arise spring from disagreement between buyer and supplier as to what was agreed.

1.9   **Uncertainties in contractual agreements**. This is another aspect of the specification problem. Baily et al cite the case of an architect who submits a design meeting the criteria of the client in terms of budget, required accommodation etc; and yet the client finds the design unsatisfying on aesthetic grounds. Who, if anyone, is at fault and who pays for the architect's second attempt?

1.10   **Complexity**. The purchase of a tangible asset **sometimes** involves the purchase of a service; for example, if you purchase a large item of machinery, the manufacturer may provide your staff with training on its use. But the converse is **nearly always** true: most service providers will also have to supply tangible product along with the service. For example, a training organisation will invariably provide delegates to its courses with course handouts. This mix of product and service elements adds to the complexity facing the purchaser.

1.11   Note that in the above analysis we are looking at services as an item to be purchased, and distinguishing it from a tangible product by reference to the **buyer** of a service. Don't be confused by our earlier distinction (in Chapter 3) between buyers who work in the services sector (ie who work for firms that **sell** services) and buyers who work in the manufacturing sector.

Purchasing procedures for services

1.12   The above problems make it all the more important to observe traditional purchasing disciplines in order to achieve a satisfactory result. A few of the particular points that buyers should watch out for are spelled out below.

1.13   Firstly, the more work that can be done at the pre-contract stage the better. This means agreeing service levels, schedules, and the basis for charges in as much detail as possible before the final agreement is signed. Often, the difficulties which arise subsequently turn out to stem from different expectations held by buyer and supplier.

1.14   This point is particularly vital if the decision relates to outsourcing a function currently performed by in-house staff. The point is that once the decision to outsource is taken the buyer will typically close down its own internal service provision, disposing of equipment, making staff redundant and using office space for alternative purposes. Once this has been done, the supplier is in an extremely strong position and he must not have the opportunity at that stage to renegotiate on the basis that the original agreement embodied misunderstandings.

1.15   One possible precaution in this respect is to insist that the external contractor should 'audit' the service currently being carried out. His quotation must then be on the basis of providing at least an equal level of service in future. In the event of dispute as to what is included in this, it should be easy for the buyer to demonstrate that such and such a task was always carried out in the past and is therefore part of the contract.

1.16   Another basic point to look out for is the tendency for services to be bought without professional purchasing involvement. Often a user department will commission a consultancy assignment, or a finance officer will organise vehicle leasing. Too often, the role of purchasing is perceived too narrowly as being concerned with the purchase of manufacturing materials, and this perception should be opposed.

1.17   This concern leads on to an important point about the specification of the service. As suggested above, the drafting of the specification is a difficult but highly important task, in which it is essential to involve purchasing staff. However, it is equally important to involve user departments. For one thing, they are ideally placed to help determine the level of service required; for another, it is important for behavioural reasons to win the commitment of user departments. This is more likely to be achieved if they have participated in the project.

1.18   Supplier management is an important ingredient in successful service buying. Often the level of service agreed upon is expressed in terms which are difficult to measure (it is not like purchasing steel rods which definitely are, or definitely are not, of the diameter specified). It is vital that from the earliest stages the supplier is made aware of what the buyer regards as satisfactory performance, and what is unsatisfactory.

1.19 Certain legal and technical considerations must also be addressed. One example concerns staff employed by the contractor but working on the buyer's premises. Indemnity insurance may be appropriate.

1.20 Another point is the issue of confidentiality. The contractor may by the nature of his work, or in the course of the negotiations, gain access to information which is commercially sensitive. It must be made clear very early that confidentiality is essential, and the contractor should usually be made to sign a confirmation that this will be observed.

Similarities between a product and a service

1.21 Among all this discussion of the distinctive nature of services it is easy to forget that there are also essential similarities between services and tangible products.

- Services can be specified and costed.
- Services can be measured and assessed.
- Service suppliers can be rated and assessed.
- Services can be segmented in ways that help purchasers to analyse them.

1.22 In relation to this last point, Lysons and Farrington (following the work of JE Hadfield) cite the example of services typically purchased by a bank and also a categorisation of services due to CS Lallatin. See Figures 10.1 and 10.2 below.

Figure 10.1 *Matrix of services typically purchased by a bank*

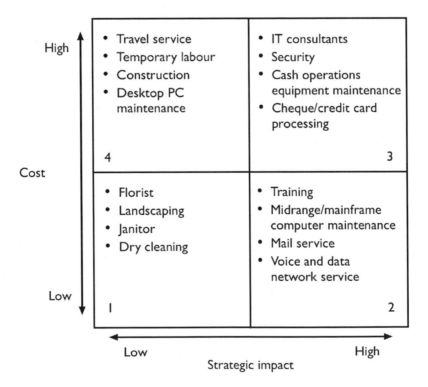

Figure 10.2 *Lallatin's categorisation of services*

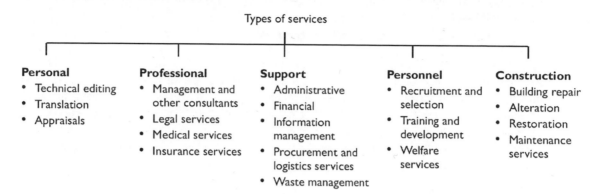

Types of services

Personal
- Technical editing
- Translation
- Appraisals

Professional
- Management and other consultants
- Legal services
- Medical services
- Insurance services

Support
- Administrative
- Financial
- Information management
- Procurement and logistics services
- Waste management

Personnel
- Recruitment and selection
- Training and development
- Welfare services

Construction
- Building repair
- Alteration
- Restoration
- Maintenance services

2 Specifying a service to be purchased

Service level agreements

2.1 A good specification is a vital step in assuring the quality of the eventual service delivery. A Parasuraman lists the following quality characteristics of services.

- Reliability, ie how consistently and dependably the supplier provides the service
- Responsiveness, ie how promptly and willingly supplier staff provide the service
- Competence, ie how skilfully and knowledgeably supplier staff provide the service
- Access, ie how easy it is to access the supplier
- Courtesy, ie how polite the supplier staff are
- Communication, ie how often and how understandably the supplier keeps the customer informed
- Credibility, ie how trustworthy the supplier is
- Security, ie how safe the customer can feel in terms of avoiding risk or danger
- Understanding, ie how hard the supplier works to understand his customer's requirements
- Tangibles, ie the physical goods supplied as part of the service

2.2 A crucial element in the success of external service provision is to reach clear agreement on the level of service to be provided, by means of a service-level agreement (SLA). For example, suppose a company decides to hire external contractors to provide office cleaning services. Among the many points to discuss the following basic service-level issues should be considered.

- How often is the service to be provided?
- During what hours will the service be carried out, and in particular will there be any disruption to office activities?
- How many staff (and, if relevant, what grades of staff) will be involved in providing the service?
- How far will the service extend (eg does it include cleaning of computer monitors, telephone equipment, etc)?

- What qualifications are needed by staff members providing the service?
- What speed of response is expected from the supplier when the customer makes a request?
- What dispute procedures will be required?

2.3 Speed of response is a major consideration in many types of service provision. This must be carefully considered and agreed when service levels are discussed. It is easy for the purchasing organisation to complain that the service provider is not reacting quickly enough, but the supplier may retort that constant calls for 'urgent' attention suggest lack of forward planning by the purchaser. To avoid this kind of argument both sides must accept a responsibility for planning and communication, as well as agreeing the extent to which the supplier will be required to respond within a particular timescale.

2.4 The buyer needs to investigate the supplier's plans with some care. For example, he should enquire about the rates that the supplier intends to pay his staff. If these appear to be below average there is a potential impact on the quality of service likely to be delivered. This is particularly the case when the service is high on labour content.

2.5 Where services are currently provided by in-house staff it is important to determine whether existing service levels are adequate. If they are not, it is not sufficient to require a similar level of service from the new supplier. Instead, defined improvements to the current level of service must be agreed in advance.

2.6 We have emphasised the importance of a professional purchasing input in this kind of decision. However, it is equally vital to ensure the full co-operation of user departments. They are uniquely well placed to determine the level of service that should be required. In addition, their support will be essential when the service goes live; they are unlikely to be supportive if they have not been consulted.

The process of preparing a specification

2.7 The process of preparing specifications is unlikely to be uniform in every case. This is true even within a single organisation, and even more so if one organisation is compared with another. One key element of variety is who is responsible for preparation.

2.8 In most cases, the lead role is taken by users. In this case the process of preparing a specification is a difficult management task, not least because of the sensitivities of the different departments that may need to contribute.

2.9 Whatever approach is used in preparing the specification, it is advisable to ensure controlled **signing-off procedures**. Before a specification is released to a supplier it must have the formal approval of the purchasing department and ideally the prior certification of the supplier. This reduces the common risk of changes being made in order to solve problems not envisaged at the time the specification was finalised.

2.10 This precaution should then be followed up by ensuring that any changes which **are** deemed necessary are subjected to appropriate approval procedures – in writing!

3   *Managed services*

Terminology

3.1   The term 'managed services' is increasingly used to refer to outsourcing – the practice of delegating a task to an outside supplier rather than performing it in-house. 'Outsourcing' usually refers to the delegation of a service (though it could equally refer to farming out a part of the production process); 'managed services', of course, always refers to delegation of a service. We discussed the concept of managed services, in general terms, in Chapter 7. Here, we look in more detail, both at the general concept, and at specific functions that may be suitable for this kind of treatment.

3.2   The problems of buying services have become increasingly important for purchasing professionals as the general expenditure on services throughout the economy has risen. This presents buyers with problems additional to those that arise in purchasing manufactured goods.

- Manufactured goods are tangible: they can be inspected and tested before purchase. Services are intangible.

- Goods emerging from a manufacturing process almost certainly have a high degree of uniformity which simplifies their evaluation. Every separate instance of service provision is unique and may or may not be equivalent to previous instances.

- The exact purpose for which a manufactured good is used will usually be known and its suitability can therefore be assessed objectively. It is harder to assess the many factors comprised in provision of a service: for example, what weight should be placed on the friendliness or smart appearance of the supplier's staff, compared with their basic efficiency in doing the job?

- A manufactured good is usually purchased for immediate use in some well defined way, such as incorporation in a larger product or onward sale. A service may be purchased for a long period, during which requirements may change subtly from the original specification.

- When purchasing a manufactured good a buyer can usually identify a number of suppliers offering products with essentially similar features (including price). Services are different: the offering from one supplier will inevitably differ from those of other suppliers in a whole range of mostly intangible ways.

The nature of outsourcing

3.3   Outsourcing is the ultimate expression of a buyer's attitude to a supplier as an extension of in-house resources. Facilities or functions that were produced in-house are instead performed by external contractors working very closely with the buying organisation.

3.4   In many cases the same personnel carry out the outsourced tasks, only instead of being employed by the buyer they work for the contractor. There are instances where the original staff remain *in situ*, and even work on the same equipment; the only difference is in the status of the staff (they now work for the contractor, not for the buyer) and the ownership of the equipment (transferred from buyer to contractor).

3.5   Outsourcing has been used in respect of many different functions. Organisations have contracted with external suppliers to provide cleaning or catering services previously performed by internal staff; banks have outsourced their information systems development to specialist external consultancies; major international businesses have outsourced their accounting and tax planning functions to firms of chartered accountants.

3.6   'The problem with outsourcing is that while a series of incremental outsourcing decisions, taken individually, make economic sense, collectively they represent the surrender of the business's competitive advantage.' (Zenz)

Value for money

3.7   Clearly a major reason for outsourcing is the possibility that it will be cheaper to buy the services than to provide them in-house. This is not necessarily an easy matter to establish, and assessing value for money in outsourced services is a delicate process.

3.8   The first step is to learn as much as the supplier is willing to disclose of his cost and profit structure. This will facilitate comparison with alternatives.

3.9   The overall cost of the service would obviously be compared with prices offered by alternative suppliers, and possibly with the costs of in-house operation if these are known. (They may not be if it is a new type of service that is being bought.)

3.10   More crucially, the effectiveness of the supplier must be evaluated by a comparison of actual outputs achieved with the original objectives specified. This of course implies that the buying organisation starts with a clear idea of what it needs and what it expects to get. The involvement of purchasing professionals in the early stages can be of great assistance here.

Which activities should be outsourced?

3.11   Ray Carter has suggested a helpful matrix for determining whether an activity should be outsourced. This is based on analysis of two factors.

  •   The extent to which the activity is core to the organisation's main functions.
  •   The competence of contractors available to carry out the outsourced activity.

3.12   This analysis leads to the following matrix.

Figure 10.3 *Outsourcing matrix*

Competence of contractors

	High	Low
Low	Outsource/buy in	Develop contracting
High	Collaboration	In-house

Core importance (Low at top, High at bottom)

3.13 The conclusion from this is that an activity is a candidate for outsourcing if it is not core to the organisation's main functions, and if there are competent contractors able to carry out the activity. The idea of outsourcing non-core activities has been a key argument of Prahalad and Hamel, who believe that organisations should manage and leverage their **core competencies** to achieve competitive advantage, while leaving others to provide non-core services.

3.14 Prahalad and Hamel identified three characteristics of core competencies.

- They are activities that add value in the eyes of the customer.
- They are scarce and difficult for competitors to imitate.
- They are flexible in light of the organisation's future needs.

Third-party logistics and distribution services

3.15 An important strand in modern management thinking (as seen in the work of Prahalad and Hamel) is the need to concentrate on core activities in order to secure competitive advantage. The consequence of this philosophy is that more use is made of external suppliers for activities previously provided in-house.

3.16 Most manufacturers regard logistics as a support function rather than as a core activity. Even those who still maintain an 'own-account' operation are willing to make use of contractors to a greater or lesser extent.

3.17 The potential benefits that may be realised by manufacturers include the following.

- Contracting out frees up resources – above all, financial capital and management time – which can more profitably be devoted to core activities.
- Logistics specialists are well placed to recognise and respond to rising customer expectations. This would be a serious management burden if distribution remained in-house.
- Contracting out gives greater flexibility in times of difficulty. Firms with their own operation may suffer if employees go on strike, or if demand is very variable during the year. Access to outside specialists enables these risks to be spread.
- Buying firms gain access to specialist expertise which may enable them to develop improved distribution systems, offering better service than customers would otherwise have received.

3.18   All of these benefits presuppose that the external contracting is conducted on the basis of long-term relationships with a small number of suppliers. For example, any saving in management time would quickly be dissipated if negotiations with new suppliers, and the process of familiarisation, were on-going; ideally, this should be a one-off exercise.

3.19   Despite the benefits outlined above, not all manufacturers are willing to outsource the logistics function. Several reasons may be suggested for this.

•   Most fundamentally, a firm may be concerned that outside contractors will not give the required level of service. There has been some justification for such a view in the historical development of specialist logistics suppliers. Nowadays, however, the range of services offered has increased, standards are high, and advances in information technology have enabled buying firms to monitor the service provided very closely.

•   A firm may fear that a large number of separate outside contractors – for storage, materials handling, haulage etc – would complicate matters. This too has been a justified worry in the past, but can now be overcome by making use of one of the various contractors that offer an integrated service covering all logistics areas.

•   Finally, reluctance may stem from a general policy of wishing to retain control. Handing over major functional areas lock, stock and barrel to external suppliers runs counter to this natural instinct. Again, the solution lies within the varied offerings available from logistics providers. These range from management-only contracts (in which the buyer retains ownership of logistics assets, but contracts out their management), through various forms of joint venture, to full system takeover by the outside specialist.

Outsourcing information systems

3.20   An area where outsourcing has become particularly prevalent in recent years is that of information systems (IS). Many organisations have handed over their data processing functions, and in some cases their systems development functions as well, to external specialists.

3.21   The technical complexity of this area makes it an attractive candidate for outsourcing. The cost of maintaining IS expertise in house is high. But in some cases the move to outsourcing has been made for the wrong reasons. In particular, some organisations despaired of solving the so-called 'millennium bug' – the problem of computer systems that might have failed when the year 99 gave way to the year 00.

3.22   Outsourcing consultants are unanimous in condemning this approach. As with all outsourcing, the objective should be to draw on specialist expertise, not to abandon all responsibility for the outsourced activity. A consultant quoted in *Supply Management* summed it up as follows: 'The management that wants to outsource problems in order to get rid of them is a disaster waiting to happen. You've got to solve the problems first before you outsource'.

3.23   Even assuming that management are outsourcing for the right reasons, it remains difficult to measure the success of the project. The main problem is in defining the level of service. It is highly unlikely that one outsourcing supplier will offer exactly the same level of service as another, which means that the costs they quote are not strictly comparable. At the level of detail, what one supplier is offering to do will differ from the other's offering.

3.24   In practice this will lead to serious problems of evaluation, but once again it is clear that a proactive purchasing function has an important role to play. Essentially, the problem is one of specification: the buyer must know in advance, and in detail, exactly what he requires the supplier to provide. In the light of a detailed specification it will be much easier to monitor performance and to assess value for money.

Outsourcing facilities management

3.25   We have looked above at some specific services that may be outsourced, such as logistics services or IT services. A more radical approach to this general issue goes by the name of facilities management. Under this kind of agreement a specialist facilities management company is contracted to run services such as buildings maintenance, catering, heating and lighting, security and waste disposal.

3.26   At its extreme this approach is summed up in the words of a car manufacturer wishing to open an overseas manufacturing facility. 'Provide everything I need in support services: that's what I pay you for. All I want to do is make cars.' In a case like this the facilities management company will take on a very wide range of responsibilities, and the manufacturer must be certain that service provision will be up to the appropriate standard and at the right cost.

3.27   Experts in the field believe that the impulse towards outsourcing comes not from cost considerations (though of course value for money is important), but from a wish for greater efficiency. Buyers want to tap in to specialist expertise so as to increase the quality of service.

3.28   Another stimulus to this kind of agreement has undoubtedly been a desire to share risks. Buyers have sometimes welcomed the idea that if things go wrong it is an outside contractor that is to blame. While this may be regarded as a somewhat negative attitude – it would be better to concentrate on ensuring that things **don't** go wrong – it does highlight the fact that there are indeed serious risks in the services underpinning a company's operations.

3.29   Some of these risks were amusingly summarised in a 'nightmare' facilities management contract devised by a firm of solicitors specialising in the field. In their fictional example a company suffered the following series of disasters.

  •   Staff walked out after failing to receive their wages because of a technical problem with the payroll.
  •   Other staff left when the heating failed on an unexpectedly cold Autumn day.
  •   A subcontractor wiped out all the information on a customer database.
  •   Staff suffered food poisoning due to hygiene failures in the canteen.

3.30   The scale of these problems underlines the importance of quality assurance in all cases where services are outsourced.

Internal and external supply

3.31 So far we have looked at the outsourcing of services to an external supplier. However, an alternative is to set up an internal department to provide services such as finance, human resources, information technology etc. We looked briefly at this idea in the context of shared service units (Chapter 5).

3.32 Reasons for keeping shared services in-house include the following.

   • Costs may be cheaper if we do not pay a profit margin to an outside supplier.

   • There may be no suitable provider externally.

   • There may be reasons of confidentiality.

   • By keeping the activity in-house we retain control over quality.

3.33 Despite these reasons, organisations increasingly look to outsource non-core functions. This is in line with the arguments of Prahalad and Hamel (see earlier in this chapter), but also reflects certain disadvantages of using internally provided services.

   • Absence of competition can lead to complacency within the internal department providing the service.

   • Similarly, there may be a lack of efficiency, innovation and customer responsiveness.

   • There are no economies of scale, as the internal provider has only one customer.

3.34 These drawbacks must be weighed against the advantages of internal supply.

   • The transaction costs are low, because there is no process of supplier identification, supplier evaluation, tendering etc to go through.

   • The relationship between 'customer' and 'supplier' is likely to be long-term and stable, enabling the supplier to hone the service in line with customer requirements.

   • There is (usually) no profit motive within the internal supplier, which means that they can concentrate instead on the quality of service offered.

   • Customer and supplier are part of the same organisation, meaning that they should share the same culture and values.

Managing the outsource supplier

3.35 At all stages in the relationship, the buyer is concerned to ensure an appropriate level of performance from the supplier. It is helpful to consider how this concern is evidenced over the life of the relationship.

3.36 In the period leading up to award of contract, the buyer's objective is to agree terms that satisfactorily meet the objectives specified in the business case. He will focus on costs, service levels, and the minimisation of risk. Naturally, the supplier will be negotiating hard on all of these elements, and a satisfactory balance must be reached.

3.37 Once the contract has been awarded, the buyer will be concerned to ensure a smooth transition. Ideally, the supplier will immediately begin to perform to the levels of service specified in the contract, but it may be that 'teething problems' are experienced. If staff have transferred from the buying organisation to the supplier, the buyer will also be concerned about people issues: are the staff being treated according to the terms of the contract, which of course must reflect the legal provisions on transfer of undertakings?

3.38 With the transition phase over, it will be important to the buyer to see clear benefits arising. This is the justification of the entire exercise. Benefits may include reduced costs, improved service levels, and reduction in management effort within the buying organisation. To ensure that these objectives are being achieved, the buyer will need to focus on communication methods, such as reports and review meetings.

3.39 As the time approaches for renewal, the buyer should review the lessons learned at the time of initial contract award. If the relationship has not worked well, it may be necessary to consider a new supplier selection exercise. But if both sides have enjoyed benefits, a renewal of the contract may be appropriate. Even in this case, the buyer will want to incorporate changes arising from the experience gained over the life of the original contract. In particular, the buyer will want to discuss even further improvements in service levels and/or reductions in cost.

3.40 Clearly this cycle will repeat indefinitely. At all stages the buyer will be hoping to achieve continuous improvement in the supplier's performance, as measured by the service levels specified in the contract. At the same time, the supplier will legitimately be attempting to achieve economies of scale so as to make a fair profit for himself. If it appears that the benefits are not being shared with the buyer, this is a point to address at the time of contract renewal.

Identifying suitable performance measures

3.41 To ensure that the supplier is performing to the required standard, it is important to identify suitable performance measures. Often these will be specified in the contract.

3.42 Needless to say, the measures chosen will depend very much on the details of the particular agreement. But in all cases they will include measures relating to cost and measures relating to service quality. Some measures will be 'hard', in the sense that they can be assessed objectively (eg the time taken to deal with a complaint or difficulty); others will be 'soft', in the sense that they are to some extent subjective. For example, the buyer will be concerned with the politeness of the supplier's staff, but this is not something that can easily be measured.

3.43 To define suitable performance measures, the buyer must focus on the key objectives of the outsource contract. Clearly, the measures chosen must be related to these so that they provide a good indication of how well the relationship is working. It is also important to keep the measurement process simple: a small number of easily understood indicators is preferable to a proliferation of complicated measures.

3.44 Communication is also important. The supplier must be aware of the measures regarded as important by the buyer. This is an important guideline for him in planning his work so as to satisfy the contractual requirements. He must accept that the measures are reasonable in the light of the contract. And communication is of course a two-way process: if the supplier is already performing similar services for other clients he may be able to suggest suitable performance measures from previous experience.

Why does it go wrong?

3.45 Numerous surveys, together with anecdotal evidence, suggest that outsourcing projects often fail to deliver the expected benefits. Some of the possible reasons for this are listed below.

- The organisation fails to distinguish correctly between core and non-core activities.

- The organisation fails to identify and select a suitable supplier, leading to poor performance of the outsourced activity, or in the worst cases to supplier failure.

- The outsourcing contract contains inadequate or inappropriate terms and conditions.

- The contract does not contain well defined key performance indicators or service levels, which means that it is difficult to establish where things are going wrong.

- The organisation gradually surrenders control of performance to the contractor.

Much of this can be avoided if the outsourcing exercise is carefully planned within a defined strategic framework.

3.46 These reasons, along with others, lead to the phenomenon of insourcing. This is the opposite of outsourcing, and involves an organisation taking work in-house, having previously outsourced it.

3.47 An obvious reason why organisations might do this is that the outsource provider might not be doing a very good job. There may be problems with service quality, or the supplier may not be delivering the expected cost savings. In this case it will be appropriate to terminate the contract.

3.48 Even here, though, one might expect the organisation to find an alternative provider. Presumably the work will be insourced only if the organisation believes that no external organisation is able to perform satisfactorily and at an economic price. However, there are other possibilities. For example, the organisation may have re-thought its conclusions on what activities are core and non-core. If it now believes that the activity is core, it may take it in-house for general strategic reasons.

Chapter summary

- There are important differences between services and tangible products: impracticability of storage, lack of inspectability, uncertainties in contractual agreements, complexity.

- It is important to involve user departments in the specification of a service.

- Closely defined service level agreements are a crucial part of the specification process when purchasing a service.

- The outsourcing of services is an increasing part of the buyer's role in many organisations.

- Typical services that may be outsourced include logistics, information systems and facilities management.

Self-test questions

Numbers in brackets refer to the paragraphs where you can check your answers.

1 List the key differences between a service and a tangible product. (1.7ff)

2 Why should an external contractor 'audit' the service currently being carried out? (1.15)

3 List some of the quality characteristics of services identified by Parasuraman. (2.1)

4 What basic points should be covered in a service level agreement? (2.2)

5 Draw a matrix to illustrate whether an activity should be outsourced. (Figure 10.3)

6 What benefits may arise from outsourcing the logistics function? (3.17)

CHAPTER 11

Purchasing Capital Items

Chapter learning objectives

2.5 Analyse and explain purchasing and financing capital expenditure items.

- Key differences between operational and capital expenditure
- A range of capital expenditure (capex) items
- Financing considerations: benefit/cost analysis (BCA), investment, return on investment (ROI), breakeven, post project appraisal (PPA) and whole-life costing
- Public and private funding initiatives: private finance initiative (PFI), public private partnership (PPP), build-own-operate-transfer (BOOT)
- A simple budgeting cycle
- Economic factors of financing including inflation and interest rates

Chapter headings

1 Operational and capital expenditure

2 Financing considerations

3 Other factors in capital buying

Introduction

In this chapter, devoted to the purchase of capital items, we begin by examining the nature of capital expenditure (capex) as opposed to operational expenditure. We then move on to discuss a number of issues concerning the financing of capex.

1 Operational and capital expenditure

Distinguishing features in capital purchasing

1.1 What is meant by 'capital expenditure'? There are two main features that distinguish capital goods from other items purchased by an organisation.

- The first is the **length of their lifecycle**. Many goods are purchased for immediate use. This would be the case with a component used in a manufacturing process, or with an item purchased for onward sale by a retailer; these are not capital goods. A capital item is one which the purchasing organisation will be using for a long time, usually several years.
- The second characteristic is the **cost** of such goods. Capital goods are large-value items – items of small value are not regarded as capital goods even if their expected useful life is relatively long.

1.2   Typical examples of capital goods include buildings, manufacturing plant, computer hardware and software, and vehicles (eg delivery lorries). Other possibilities include certain internal 'projects', such as the design and installation of a new computer system. All of these assets have a reasonably long lifecycle (possibly very long in the case of buildings), and are expensive. They may be items which are peculiar to one industry, or even one firm, or alternatively they may be of a type that many firms purchase.

1.3   We will usually refer to capital equipment, as the purchase of manufacturing equipment is probably the most common type of capital purchase. 'Equipment' could include plant and machinery, motor vehicles, computers etc.

1.4   The purchase of capital goods differs in important ways from the purchase of other goods. The distinguishing features have often been discussed in the purchasing literature. They include the following main points, which will be discussed in more detail below.

   •   The basic purchase price of a capital asset is only one element, and sometimes not the most important element, in the total costs of acquisition. Other costs are also relevant and may arise at any time over the life of the asset. This problem has been tackled by the development of 'whole-life costing', discussed later in this chapter.

   •   The monetary value of the purchase is high, suggesting a need for specialised techniques of evaluation and control. This also raises questions relating to the financing of the purchase: outright purchase, leasing or some other means?

   •   The purchase of a capital item tends to be non-recurring. There is unlikely to have been a similar purchase in the recent past and specific experience is therefore lacking.

   •   The benefits to be obtained from the purchase are often somewhat intangible and difficult to evaluate. For example, a machine may be replaced by a superior model in order to secure quality improvements. How can the value of such improvements be measured in financial terms?

   •   Negotiations are usually more extended and complex than in other acquisitions.

   •   Specifications for capital equipment are usually more difficult to draft because of the technical complexity of the item to be purchased.

   •   A team approach is usually needed in which the contributions of other departments, and not just purchasing, must be effectively coordinated and managed.

   •   Buying a capital asset usually means buying a service too.

Other aspects of capital purchases

1.5   The non-recurring nature of capital purchases means that, unlike with most of a buyer's work, history provides little guidance. Purchasers must be alert to changes and developments in the relevant field.

1.6   The benefits of a capital purchase are often difficult to assess. Consider the example of a replacement machine purchased in place of an older model in order to improve quality. Exactly how is the improvement in quality to be measured? Exactly how much financial gain does this quality improvement translate to? Clearly, these questions would be difficult to answer even if all benefits were to be earned today. Add to this the difficulty that benefits are to arise over a lengthy period in the future and it is clear that financial evaluation is extremely complex.

1.7 There are many service elements associated with capital purchases. Purchasing services presents particular problems which do not affect the purchase of tangible products.

1.8 The service elements involved in purchase of capital equipment can include any or all of the following.

- Pre-purchase survey by the vendor – to establish the buyer's needs and whether the vendor can match them.

- Installation – either by the vendor, or by personnel of the buying organisation under supervision of the vendor.

- Training of operators – especially important if the vendor's warranty terms disclaim responsibility for damage caused by improper operation.

- After-sales service – both during a warranty period and beyond. The normal arrangement is for service to be provided free by the vendor during an agreed warranty period, whereas service work provided later is charged for.

1.9 Negotiations for capital purchases are very often more extended and complex than for other types of purchase. The sums of money involved make it essential to assess offerings from several potential suppliers. And the automatic repeat orders that take some of the strain from raw materials purchases are not usually an option with capital assets: each new acquisition must be evaluated afresh.

1.10 The specification for an item of capital equipment is likely to be difficult to draft. This is partly because the item itself may be a highly technical piece of equipment, often with a wide range of intended functional uses. In addition, to avoid restricting the list of potential suppliers, the specification must incorporate a reasonable degree of flexibility.

1.11 Finally, the importance of most capital purchases makes it important to obtain an input from different departments. Apart from the purchasing department, the potential users of the item will have a large say in proceedings. So too will top management and finance personnel.

2 *Financing considerations*

Benefit/cost analysis (BCA)

2.1 The purchase of a capital asset illustrates the difference between purchase price and total lifetime costs particularly clearly. In the nature of things, such an asset is expected to be used in the purchaser's business for a number of years. Over that time, it will give rise to many costs of maintenance and repair in addition to the original cost of purchase. There will also be costs associated with any inefficiency or actual failure in the machine. In choosing between one asset and another buyers must take into account the costs arising over the whole life of each.

2.2 These costs include any or all of the following elements in addition to the basic purchase price.

- Costs of delivery, installation and commissioning
- Costs of routine maintenance and periodic overhauls
- Costs of energy and labour involved in running the machine
- Costs of time lost during breakdowns

2.3 Another element in the total cost – in effect, a negative cost – is the disposal value of the asset, if any, when the time comes to replace it. An asset with a high disposal value has a lower total cost, other things being equal, than an asset with little resale value at the end of its life.

2.4 The relatively long time period involved, combined with the subjectivity of estimates for most of these elements of cost, make it difficult to assess the lifetime costs of a capital asset. One technical difficulty is that the relevant cashflows occur not immediately but in years to come; such cashflows are not easy to evaluate in today's terms even if they were known with certainty (which they never are). The process of evaluating future cashflows in today's terms is referred to as **discounted cashflow**. By applying this discounting technique to all the costs and benefits associated with the capital purchase we can calculate its **net present value**. This is an important indicator as to whether the asset should be purchased.

2.5 Another difficulty is that the purchase of most capital assets is of a non-recurring nature. That is to say, a similar asset is not likely to have been purchased in the very recent past and there is therefore no relevant experience to draw upon. Then too there is the fact that purchase of such an asset generally means purchase of a service too – installation, training of operators, after-sales maintenance and so on. This introduces a whole series of new problems.

2.6 As well as estimating the costs of ownership, it is also important to estimate the benefits. Otherwise, the comparison between different assets will be incomplete. However, this is even trickier than estimating the costs of ownership, partly because of the conceptual difficulties involved in valuing intangible benefits such as improvements in quality.

2.7 Benefits and costs should be analysed in advance of purchase. Often this will happen as part of a formal **feasibility study**. At this stage both tangible and intangible benefits should be assessed.

2.8 Self-evidently, if benefits exceed costs then the purchase is worthwhile; by contrast, the purchase will be rejected if costs exceed benefits. It is possible to express this in the form of a benefit/cost ratio.

- If the ratio is significantly less than 1, it means that benefits are less than costs. Conclusion: reject the project.
- If the ratio is significantly greater than 1, it means that benefits are greater than costs. Conclusion: proceed with the project.
- If the ratio is close to 1, it means that benefits and costs are approximately equal. Conclusion: further investigation is needed into the non-financial factors that might influence a decision. It would also be wise to check the figure work again – if the decision is this close, it would be nice if we could be sure of our figures.

Presenting the business case

2.9 Once the benefits and costs have been assessed it is often necessary to argue for adoption of the project by presenting the business case for it. To do this it will be important to prepare a structured justification of the proposal, which will often be presented by means of a personal delivery, eg to a group of senior managers.

2.10 The presentation will typically include the following elements.

- An executive summary
- A summary of the background to the proposal, including what has given rise to the need for analysing it
- The business objectives that we are attempting to achieve
- An outline of the various options that might be adopted to achieve those objectives
- Identification of the preferred option with a justification for its selection
- A plan of action, including appropriate 'milestones'
- A summary of the funds required and the likely financial outcomes
- A calculation of how and when the money will be paid back
- Details of all financing calculations, including discounted cashflows
- An overview of any risks, with details of contingency plans
- Measures of success that can be used to control outcomes
- A summary of the next steps required to get the project underway

Whole-life costing

2.11 The monetary value of capital asset purchases is often very significant. This means that, despite all the difficulties just mentioned, buyers must make a systematic attempt to assess costs and benefits. The technique of whole-life costing has been developed to cope with this problem. It is relatively simple in principle, though the calculations can appear complicated. In practice, these would always be carried out on a computer.

2.12 The buyer makes assumptions (inevitably subjective) about the level of costs that will arise in each year of the asset's useful life. Obviously a large element, namely the basic purchase price, will be paid at once (in year 0 as it is usually described). Other elements will arise as maintenance, repair and overhaul are required. These are all estimated in advance.

2.13 At the same time, the buyer attempts to quantify the benefits that will arise from ownership of the asset. This will be done in conjunction with personnel from other departments. The total benefits must be allocated to each year of the asset's useful life, exactly as was done in the case of costs.

2.14 At this point the calculations begin, usually on computer. Briefly, the idea is that costs and benefits arising in some future period are equivalent to a smaller amount in today's money. All costs and benefits are converted to today's values. Then an annual equivalent is computed. This is a single figure which measures the cost of ownership of the asset over a period of one year.

2.15 The point of computing the annual equivalent is that it enables buyers to compare assets with different useful lives. In principle, if the annual equivalent cost of owning Asset X is £10,000, while the figure for Asset Y is £11,000, then Asset X is chosen.

2.16 The procedure is described in more detail by Dobler and Burt (*Purchasing and Supply Management*). They identify the following stages.

- Determine the operating cycle for the equipment, including factors such as the interval at which servicing will be required.

- Identify and quantify the factors that affect costs, such as power consumption, average time between failures etc.

- Calculate all costs at current rates and prices.

- Project all costs and disposal value if any to the future dates at which they will be incurred.

- Express all amounts in today's values.

- Calculate the total cost in today's values.

2.17 The purchaser will also calculate the **payback period** of the investment (sometimes called its **recovery period**). This is a straightforward calculation: take the initial total outlay, and work out how many years it will take for the benefits to 'pay back' that outlay. For instance, suppose a machine is being bought for £1 million, and it is estimated that it will generate annual revenues (or cost savings) of £150,000 for 10 years, at which time it will be scrapped. The payback period is calculated as initial outlay divided by annual revenue, which is £1,000,000/£150,000, or 6.6 years. This might or might not be acceptable to the organisation. In general, an investment that pays back in a relatively short period is preferable to one that takes many years to pay back.

2.18 It is also possible to identify the **accounting rate of return** (ARR) of the purchase. In the above example, the asset generates revenue over 10 years of £1,500,000, which means a profit of £500,000 over 10 years, or £50,000 per annum. The accounting rate of return, in its simplest form, is therefore £50,000/£1,000,000 or 5 per cent. Again, the organisation has to judge whether this is an acceptable rate. (The accounting rate of return is often called the **return on investment** of the project.)

2.19 A final calculation that may be relevant is to do with the **breakeven point** of the investment. For example, suppose that the investment is the purchase of a machine designed to manufacture a new product. In evaluating the investment a key calculation would be the breakeven point: how many units of the product must we sell (at a given price) in order for our profits to pay back the initial investment over a defined period? Once this has been calculated we can examine it in detail and assess how likely it is that we can achieve the required level of sales.

Post-project appraisal

2.20 Once a new asset is installed and functional it may be appropriate to conduct a **post-project appraisal** (PPA). This is particularly the case when the asset itself is the specialised outcome of a project (eg the design and installation of a computer system) rather than the purchase of a tangible item.

2.21 The main purpose of the PPA is to learn lessons for the future. By studying what went well and what went badly it should be possible to improve future performance in similar exercises. Table 11.1 shows some of the dimensions along which this can be measured.

Table 11.1 *Areas of investigation in PPA*

Benefits achieved	*Performance of project manager*
Technical	Effectiveness
Operational	Relationships – stakeholders
Ecological	Communication
Economic	Tools and techniques used
Time	
Quality	
Risk	

Administrative performance	*Team performance*
Tools and techniques used	Relationships
Documentation	Effectiveness
Procedures evaluation	Communication

Public and private funding initiatives

2.22 Increasingly, UK governments (in common with many others across the world) have tried to involve private investors in works that traditionally would have been carried out by means of public funding. This kind of collaborative arrangement is referred to by the general term **public private partnership** (PPP).

2.23 The usual reason for involving the private sector in public works is to gain the benefit of increased efficiency, management skills and financial acumen – or so the government typically states! Critics of such schemes, most notably the trade unions, believe that a more important reason is a short-term financing advantage, which in the long term may lead to vital public assets being owned by private sector companies.

2.24 One way in which a PPP may be structured is by means of the **private finance initiative** (PFI). This was a creation of the Conservative government in the early 1990s, but was carried forward with enthusiasm by the Labour government that came to power in 1997. The basic idea of a PFI scheme is that the private partner pays for the construction cost (of a road, a hospital, a prison or whatever), and then rents the finished product back to the public sector. Ownership of the asset remains with the contractor. This kind of scheme is sometimes referred to as a DBFO scheme – the contractor **d**esigns, **b**uilds, **f**inances and **o**perates the project.

2.25 From the government's point of view, this reduces the need for unpopular measures (such as raising taxes). The contractor's payback comes in the form of the rental payments, and also from retaining any cash left over from the design and construction process.

2.26 Critics of PPP/PFI are inclined to exaggerate the extent of the problem: after all, it remains true that the majority of public projects are financed by government. Even so, the number of such projects is significant. Many new prisons and hospitals have been financed in this way, and major road schemes such as the Thames crossing and the Birmingham relief road are being financed through PFI.

2.27 The drawbacks of PPP/PFI are firstly, that in the long term taxpayers will pay more for the projects than if they were wholly financed by the government, and secondly, that some PFI projects appear to have been below acceptable standards. This, it is argued by some, is because the private sector contractors are motivated to maximise profits by cutting corners on quality and safety issues.

2.28 The fine details of a PPP/PFI financing deal will vary from one project to another. The possible financing structures have given rise to a number of acronyms.

- BOO (build own operate): ownership of the asset remains with the private contractor throughout its life.
- BOT (build operate transfer): the private contractor retains control for a time in order to receive profits from operational revenue, and then transfers ownership to the public sector.
- BOOT (build own operate transfer): similar to BOT except that ownership of the asset actually vests in the private company for a time.
- BOLT (build own lease transfer): the private company leases control to third parties before transferring ownership to the public sector.

2.29 Other variations of PPP schemes that you should know about are discussed briefly below.

2.30 In an **operation and maintenance contract** the private contractor is required to operate and maintain the public service for a defined period according to defined service standards. The contractor does not obtain ownership of the service.

2.31 In a **design-build joint venture** the government enters into partnership with one or more lead contractors. These join forces to deliver the project in the form of a joint venture. They are free to appoint specialist subcontractors.

2.32 A **turnkey contract** takes this one step further. Not only do the contractors design and build the project, they also operate it for a period during which any teething problems are overcome. At the end of the defined period the contractors hand over the completed project back into public ownership. This is similar to the BOOT contracts already mentioned.

The budgeting cycle

2.33 Authorisation for capital expenditure arises as part of the budgetary process. It is normal to prepare a separate budget for capex sitting alongside the operating budgets and contributing to the overall balance sheet budget.

2.34 Your syllabus requires you to know about the steps in a simple budgeting cycle. Although the syllabus caption sits in the context of capital expenditure it appears to refer more generally to the process of setting budgets. The stages in this process are described below.

2.35 The **budget period** is typically the same as the organisation's financial year. For control purposes, the annual budget will be broken down into smaller units, say months, but it is usual to begin by looking at annual figures.

2.36 It is normal to budget on an **incremental** basis. This means that the previous period's figures are taken as a starting point, and adjusted to take account of any known changes in circumstances (for example, if a supplier has announced a forthcoming increase in the cost of a material).

2.37 This takes place some time before the beginning of the budget period. Departmental managers then submit their budgets to the finance department, usually with a description of the key assumptions they have made and a justification of their figures.

2.38 It is the responsibility of the finance department to look at all departmental budgets and to review them in the light of overall organisational objectives. Often this will lead to a certain amount of iteration, with finance referring back to individual departments for possible amendments.

2.39 Eventually the overall organisational budget is settled, and the consequential departmental budgets are passed back to the managers concerned. The managers are thus aware of the limits on their authority to commit the organisation to expenditure.

2.40 Once the budget period is underway, there will be a process of regular review. Actual outcomes will be compared with budgeted figures and any significant variances will be investigated for control purposes. At defined periods (say quarterly) it may be necessary to take this one step further and produce a revised estimate of likely outcomes for the entire period.

2.41 As the next budget period approaches, the cycle begins again.

Economic factors of financing

2.42 Your syllabus specifies two particular economic factors that impact on the financing of capital assets: inflation and interest rates. These factors assume particular importance in view of the long-term nature of fixed assets.

2.43 With regard to **inflation**, the main impact is on projected cashflows arising from the acquisition. Even without inflation it is difficult to predict, for example, what sales volumes may be achieved for a new product, and what sales revenue may result from that. With unpredictable inflation rates in the future the problem becomes more acute. And the same consideration applies to costs.

2.44 The importance of this is that the capital acquisition is evaluated precisely in light of the estimated future cashflows to which it gives rise. Any factor that makes these estimates less reliable increases the risk of the acquisition.

2.45 Changes in **interest rates** are also unpredictable. This is a concern in the case where the capital asset is to be acquired by means of variable rate loan finance. If interest rates rise, the overall cost of the asset will be higher than expected because of additional interest payments.

2.46 All of this emphasises the need for caution in estimating cashflows expected to arise in the future.

Planning for capital expenditure and operating expenditure

2.47 The major sums invested in capital assets and projects call for specialised forms of investment appraisal, as discussed above. But before this, we need to decide whether the capital investment option is preferable; often, there are ways of avoiding capital expenditure if it seems convenient to do so.

2.48 As an example, we may be considering the purchase of a large item of capital equipment to be used in a project over the next 12 months. It may make sense to purchase the item right away, which will be capital expenditure (capex). However, alternatives could also be considered. We might, for example, decide that a better option is to rent the equipment for the period of the project only. This would be operating expenditure (opex).

2.49 Similarly, we might be considering an upgrade of internal IT systems. One possibility would be gradual change, increasing capacity and functionality by just a small amount, and dealing with one application after another over an extended period. This would be operating expenditure. Alternatively, we might decide that a more major upgrade is essential: we need to replace our existing systems with newly designed programmes perhaps residing on an altogether different software 'platform'. At the same time this will require major upgrading of hardware. All this would be capital expenditure.

2.50 In cases such as these, an important factor in the decision is the impact on cashflows. Often, the capex option will require a very large payment up front, with a potentially serious dent in cashflows. The opex option will typically protect cashflows: smaller amounts are paid out in total, and over an extended period. The opex option may prove more expensive in total, but if the organisation is not cash rich this may be a more acceptable method of raising the funds. For organisations who do not have immediate access to large liquid funds, the capex route may not even be an option.

2.51 Another factor influencing the decision might be the useful life of the capital asset. It would not make sense to purchase an expensive asset if we plan to use it for just a small fraction of its useful life (perhaps for the duration of a short project). In such a case it would be much more sensible to rent it, returning the asset to its owner after our need for it is over.

3   Other factors in capital buying

Leasing or buying the asset

3.1   The high value of capital equipment leads many buying organisations to favour leasing as a method of financing the deal. Under a leasing agreement, ownership of the asset remains with the manufacturer or, more likely, with the leasing company providing the finance. The 'buyer' pays regular installments which can be regarded as rental payments. Often, the buyer has the right to secure outright ownership once sufficient payments have been made under the agreement. (Broadly speaking, and with important differences of detail, this is similar to buying a personal item such as a washing machine on hire purchase.)

3.2   Apart from the advantage of avoiding high initial expenditure, leasing offers other advantages. For example, it may be appropriate if the equipment is needed for a particular project but will not be needed once the project is ended. If it is purchased outright the purchaser has the problem of disposing of it later.

3.3   Another advantage is that leasing offers some protection against technological obsolescence. To buy an expensive machine and then discover soon afterwards that a superior model is becoming available is bad news for a buyer. This is particularly relevant in a time when technological development is rapid.

3.4   Finally, there are tax considerations that affect the choice between outright purchase and leasing, but these are beyond the scope of the examination syllabus.

The buyer's role in the purchase of capital assets

3.5   There are many departments that deserve a voice in decisions about capital assets: purchasing, user departments, top management, finance staff and possibly others. To coordinate the various inputs so as to arrive at the best possible decisions requires careful management, usually under the leadership of purchasing staff. In many cases, it will be appropriate to adopt a formal team approach to the purchase decision.

3.6   What should be the contribution of purchasing staff in the work of such a team? This is a topic that has been very extensively discussed in the purchasing literature. Table 11.2 summarises the main tasks that are usually identified as the province of the purchasing function.

3.7   The importance of teamwork is particularly evident in the relationship between engineering and purchasing. When specifications are being drafted there is a potential conflict between engineering quality and commercial viability. Engineers quite reasonably have an interest in specifying equipment that will definitely perform what is required of it, but this may lead to over-specification, ie demanding a higher level of sophistication than is really required. Purchasing staff must have sufficient standing and sufficient technical knowledge to challenge this and to suggest alternatives.

Table 11.2 *The role of purchasing in the acquisition of capital equipment*

1.	Performing research to identify potential vendors and to obtain relevant data about them
2.	Consulting with referees – ie existing users of products manufactured by the potential suppliers
3.	Requesting quotations and evaluating bids, including consideration of price, lead time, operating characteristics, expected useful life, performance criteria, operating costs, recommended spares and maintenance schedules, warranty terms, payment terms and so on
4.	Organising and managing discussions and negotiations with suppliers, finalising agreed terms and conditions
5.	Awarding contract and placing order
6.	Checking supplier's compliance with agreed terms, eg in submission of drawings, meeting deadlines etc
7.	Monitoring installation and performance post installation

3.8 However, the concept of teamwork should not be taken to imply that all staff can take a hand in all aspects of the work. In particular, in dealings with potential suppliers it is vitally important that all communications move through purchasing staff. Otherwise there is a danger that non-purchasing staff will effectively give the supplier the authority to proceed before all necessary matters have been considered.

The terms of the purchase contract

3.9 The contract should include, as a minimum, the following terms.

- A detailed description of the asset to be supplied, with cross-reference to the specification
- The price
- The terms of payment
- The time and place of delivery and installation
- Provisions relating to warranty (ie guarantees relating to the machine's performance levels, durability of parts etc)
- General conditions of purchase, preferably the buyer's standard terms and conditions

3.10 The price of the contract will of course be a central feature of the negotiations. Ideally a fixed price should be agreed, but in the case of major equipment manufactured to the buyer's specification it may be that some variable element is required.

3.11 Terms of payment will usually be based on instalments. The supplier invoices the agreed proportion at the agreed date (or the agreed stage of completion), and the buyer makes payment, say, 30 days later. Clearly the supplier will want as much payment as possible up front, while the buyer will want to defer payment for as long as possible.

3.12 This provides good scope for negotiation, but whatever is agreed at this stage the buyer should certainly insist on a reasonable retention. For example, he might insist that 10 per cent of the contract price will become due for payment only after certain agreed performance criteria have been met during live running of the equipment.

Defects liability and after-sales support

3.13 A final important point: what happens when things go wrong?

3.14 Many capital purchases are extremely complex items, and there is always a possibility of defects in parts or failure in operation. Purchasing staff must address this possibility when evaluating the proposed acquisition. In general there are two aspects to consider.

- **Defects or failure during a warranty period**. Typically a supplier of capital equipment will give a warranty against such failures occurring during a stated period after installation (say a period of one year). Any defects arising during the warranty period will be rectified by the supplier at his expense.

- **Defects or failure arising after the warranty period has expired**. Practice in this area is partly a matter of custom within a particular industry, and partly concerned with the degree of goodwill the supplier wishes to afford to the buyer. In general, the purchaser will be obliged to pay for any rectification work carried out after the warranty period, often on the basis of an hourly rate for the work done.

3.15 From the buyer's point of view, the most important thing is to ensure that appropriately detailed terms are included in the purchase contract. While industry standards may provide guidance on this, more specific terms may be appropriate in cases where the equipment is particularly specialised.

Chapter summary

- The main distinguishing characteristics of a capital asset are its lengthy lifecycle and its high cost.

- There are many service elements associated with the purchase of a capital asset.

- Any capital purchase will be preceded by a detailed benefit/cost analysis.

- Whole-life costing is a technique for analysing all of the costs arising over the life of a capital asset.

- Once a capital purchase is complete it is normal to conduct a post-project appraisal.

- Increasingly, governments seek to encourage private sector investors to undertake public works on a partnership basis. These schemes are referred to as public private partnerships.

- Often a buyer will choose lease finance to fund a capital acquisition.

- Purchasing staff should play an important coordinating and leadership role in the purchase of capital assets.

- Terms of a purchase contract for a capital asset will typically be more comprehensive than for routine operating purchases.

Self-test questions

Numbers in brackets refer to the paragraphs where you can check your answers.

1   Give some examples of capital purchases. (1.2)

2   List the factors that distinguish a capital purchase from an operating purchase. (1.4)

3   List the service elements that may be included as part of a capital purchase. (1.8)

4   Explain the technique of whole-life costing. (2.11ff)

5   What is meant by a project's return on investment? (2.18)

6   What is the private finance initiative? (2.24)

7   Explain the impact of inflation on appraisal of a capital purchase. (2.43)

8   List the tasks that a purchasing function should undertake in dealing with a capital purchase. (Table 11.2)

9   List the key terms that should be included in the contract for purchase of a capital asset. (3.9)

10   How can a buyer guard against defects in a capital asset? (3.14)

CHAPTER 12

International Purchasing

Chapter learning objectives

2.6 Analyse and evaluate the drivers for international purchasing, factors and organisations that affect international trade and the impact on the purchasing function.

- Key drivers for globalisation and standardisation
- The organisations which affect international trade including the World Trade Organisation, World Bank, International Chamber of Commerce and European Union
- International trade zones, tariffs and international trading agreements
- Modes of transport and shipping regulations
- Incoterms
- Reasons for sourcing internationally, including market expansion and competitiveness
- Key considerations when sourcing from another country
- Impact of international standards
- Relative merits of off-shoring

Chapter headings

1   The growth of international purchasing

2   Considerations when sourcing from another country

3   Organisations affecting international trade

4   Incoterms

5   National and international standards

6   International transportation

Introduction

Particular problems will apply if a buyer chooses to buy from an overseas source, and in this chapter we examine how purchasers address the main issues relating to trading terms and costs. You should study the chapter with a view to obtaining a general understanding of problems peculiar to overseas trading, and not worry too much about very specialist applications.

1 The growth of international purchasing

Reasons for sourcing internationally

1.1 We can consider the growth of international trade from two viewpoints: the large-scale economic viewpoint and that of the individual purchasing department.

1.2 Countries partake in international trade for two underlying reasons, each of which contributes to their economic gain. First, countries trade because fundamentally they are different. They have different natural resources and have developed different areas of expertise. Not unlike people, countries can benefit from their differences by reaching agreement to do whatever each does best or can provide most efficiently.

1.3 Trade in raw materials demonstrates this principle most clearly: a country which does not have, say, oil is obliged to buy from a country where there is oil in abundance, sufficient for its own uses and for export. Similarly, over the years, for political or geographical reasons, some countries will have become expert at providing particular services. For example, the City of London is regarded as a world centre for the insurance market. International trade enables each country to undertake the manufacture of goods or provision of services it does particularly well.

1.4 The second reason countries trade is to maximise economies of scale in production. Each country can specialise in the production of a certain range of goods or the provision of a particular range of services and, by specialising, can produce the goods or services on a larger scale and so more cost efficiently than if it tried to produce a wider range of goods. International trade enables countries to take advantage of these economies of scale in a way that is mutually beneficial.

1.5 The theory that international trade is for the mutual benefit of the partners involved is known as the **theory of comparative advantage**. This theory states that a country will increase its national income and thereby potentially improve the standard of living of its population by specialising in the manufacture of those products or provision of those services in which it has the highest productivity or comparative advantage.

1.6 What this means is that Country A should concentrate on producing Good X for which it is particularly adapted (perhaps because of easy availability of natural resources). Even if Country B is able to produce Good X with greater efficiency, it may benefit from buying such goods from Country A in order to devote its own productive resources to Good Y, in which its comparative advantage (over Country A and perhaps all other countries) is even greater.

1.7 The net result is that the resources of Country A are added into the general sum of worldwide economic prosperity. If Country B decided to produce its own supplies of Good X it would have to divert resources from producing Good Y, and would also deter Country A from producing Good X (because of lack of demand). According to the theory of comparative advantage, the overall result of this would be to reduce total worldwide prosperity.

1.8 This analysis suggests that international trade is a stimulus to raising overall economic wellbeing.

The purchasing department's perspective

1.9   Certain obvious advantages of sourcing locally present themselves immediately. Communications are easier. Delivery costs should be lower. Delivery lead times should be faster and more reliable. Just in time techniques are more likely to be feasible. Rush orders are easier to cope with. No language problems arise. Given all this, why should buyers even consider sourcing from national or international suppliers?

1.10   The most obvious reason is availability of the required materials. There may simply be no local supplier who can meet the requirements. Even if there is, it may well be that a larger national or international supplier benefits from economies of scale that the local firm cannot match, leading to a price and/or quality advantage for the bigger firm.

1.11   Another factor applies in public sector contexts. There are European Union rules that regulate the activities of public sector buyers. Contracts with a value above a certain threshold must be advertised: it is not an option for a buyer to source locally without inquiring widely for potential suppliers.

1.12   International sourcing introduces special additional factors. Historically, sourcing from abroad has been attractive primarily because of the opportunity for cost savings. Certain overseas countries have been strongly competitive because of cheap wage rates and easy access to abundant supplies of local raw materials. Countries nearer home have been at a price disadvantage as a result.

1.13   Another reason has been the quality revolution which was pioneered in the Far East, and especially in Japan. Often, Western purchasers have found that reliability, quality and even cost considerations favoured suppliers from such countries, despite apparent disadvantages arising from physical distance.

1.14   Finally, an important feature of some markets has been the rise in countertrade. Under a countertrade agreement, a company exporting to a foreign country may be 'requested' (ie required) to purchase materials from organisations in that country. Typically, these agreements have taken place with countries that suffer from lack of hard currency, including many countries in Eastern Europe. The main problem is that in some cases the goods offered in return for securing export sales suffer from quality defects that discourage potential trading partners.

Globalisation and standardisation

1.15   Companies operating in international markets face a decision on the extent to which they should adapt their products and their marketing to the different countries in which they sell. One approach – referred to as globalisation and/or standardisation – is to provide the same offering worldwide. The alternative – referred to as adaptation – is to change the products and the marketing mix in order to suit local needs.

1.16   Although marketing considerations suggest that adaptation is preferable, because of being more customer orientated, there are many advantages of standardisation. For example, there are cost benefits in production and research and development because of concentration on standardised products. And a company can build international recognition for its brands. This is the approach favoured by companies such as McDonald's – though even in this case there are minor variations in the product ranges to suit local tastes.

1.17   G Yip in *Total Global Strategy* (1992) suggested that there are four groups of factors which together form the drivers for an industry to become global.

- Market
- Cost
- Government
- Competition

1.18   **Market factors** include a convergence of market requirements from across many parts of the world, as lifestyles and tastes converge. Organisations which look for competitive advantage and seek to delight customers – who are themselves global in outlook – increasingly expect their suppliers to offer a global service.

1.19   Another factor is that as more people are exposed to world travel there grows a demand for uniform products or services to be available on a worldwide basis.

1.20   We also know that demand is related to price, which in turn is related to cost. The nature of many markets is that market size is achieved by satisfying global demand from just a few production facilities. This allows costs to drop, given the benefit of economies of scale and the learning-curve experience. When costs fall, so do prices.

1.21   Finally, the explosion in information technology has meant that data about markets and overseas business environments are quickly known and assessed, enabling any given marketplace to respond quickly to any interest shown.

1.22   **Cost factors** are also relevant. In addition to the volume effect on costs that can be achieved by taking a global approach, such an approach is also driven quite dramatically by technological change and the trend for shorter product lifecycles.

1.23   Equally, information technology has helped to reduce costs. Computer-aided design (CAD) and computer-aided manufacture (CAM) allow products to be designed in any country, and quickly be made available in any other location in the world. This makes it simpler for manufacture to be located in areas of lowest overhead cost, leaving design and development in areas where there are high degrees of talent and experience. It also makes it easier for engineering teams in different parts of the world to collaborate in the design of new products.

1.24   **Government factors** include the amalgamation of separate countries into vast trading blocks, the best example being the EU. In addition to creating a larger accessible market (the Single European Market), EU regulations have removed many non-tariff barriers to trade through the setting of common standards for many products. Many of the difficulties in producing a standardised product, so very necessary for true global operations, have thus disappeared.

1.25   Overall, barriers to trade have been steadily eroded by the work of the World Trade Organisation. There has also been a growing trend to privatise industries whose control previously lay in public hands. In the UK this has especially helped globalisation, with one industry in particular – telecommunications – taking full advantage. The timing for British Telecom could not have been better: not only was there an upsurge of technological advances, but this coincided with freedom from government control, thus allowing BT to be a major global enterprise.

1.26 **Competitive factors** are a key influence on global strategies. The pressure to think global stems from what we can see emerging today in the major economies, as well as the rising economies.

1.27 As a result of the technological advances made in the last two decades in particular, the real costs of information processing and communication have dropped dramatically. This has made it possible for a company to manage a globally dispersed production system. Indeed, a worldwide communications network has become essential for many international businesses.

1.28 The trend towards globalisation of production and markets has important implications for the manager of a business being of an international dimension or about to embark on becoming one. The manager of today's business operates in an environment that offers a great deal more opportunity but one that is more complex and competitive than the one his predecessor faced a generation ago.

1.29 Opportunities are far greater because the movement towards free trade has opened up many formerly protected national markets and because new technologies such as the World Wide Web are helping to create global electronic marketplaces.

1.30 As a result, the potential for export, for making direct investments overseas, and for dispersing production facilities to optimal locations around the world are now greater than ever. This makes the environment in which managers and specifically buyers operate more complex given that more professional buyers are now choosing to undertake business in countries with radically different cultures.

Offshoring

1.31 The term 'offshoring' refers to the relocation of business processes to a lower cost location, usually overseas. In recent years this has become a familiar practice – most readers will have had the experience of telephoning a large organisation and finding themselves talking to a call centre in, say, India. Although the term is particularly familiar in the context of services, some companies have also relocated their production facilities.

1.32 This practice is in essence a form of outsourcing (refer back to Chapter 10 for discussion of this.) However, the overseas element gives rise to additional considerations.

1.33 In relation to production offshoring, there is an important issue relating to patent law. Companies will hesitate to offshore research and development work to countries where patent protection is weak, because of the danger that overseas workers could steal the ideas. Moreover, it is often difficult to find the required skill sets for difficult research and development work in regions with cheap labour. For these reasons, it is more common to find companies retaining R & D in the home country, and offshoring only the actual manufacturing.

1.34 Services offshoring has become possible through the growth in communications infrastructure. It is now common to find services such as call centres and data processing carried out in low-cost countries such as India, the Philippines and Eastern European countries.

1.35   Clearly a major attraction for companies in the West is the cost advantage that this policy offers. However, it is easy to exaggerate this. During 2005, an outsourcing consultancy (Ventoro LLC) carried out a major survey of organisations who have adopted offshoring, and found that cost savings actually achieved (approximately 19% on average) fell far short of what had been expected (40% or more). Even so, this is a significant saving.

1.36   Apart from the possible cost savings, supporters of offshoring point to the benefits of free trade, providing jobs to the poorer country and lower costs to the origin country. Though jobs may be lost in the origin country, the workers are (in principle) able to move to higher-value jobs in which their country has a comparative advantage.

1.37   Naturally, this last point is disputed by those workers in developed countries who have lost their jobs. And from the buyer's point of view there must also be a concern that the quality of the service provided may decline. Many large companies have met with hostility from customers who have received poor customer service and technical support from overseas centres. Often the complaints have focused on an inadequate level of skill in spoken English, together with the resentment that some people feel at the general principle of 'exporting jobs overseas'.

1.38   A further criticism of offshoring is that workers in less developed countries are subject to exploitation. Some critics even go so far as to say that the very reason why companies are adopting this approach is so that they can avoid the higher standards of worker protection that prevail in the West.

1.39   Offshoring also, arguably, increases the level of risk in the supply chain. It is more difficult for a buyer to exercise control over a service provider who is geographically distant.

2   Considerations when sourcing from another country

Introduction

2.1   There are particular problems in dealing with suppliers abroad. Perhaps the most awkward issue to deal with is that of quality. As already mentioned, one reason for the increase in international sourcing has been the desire of Western firms to benefit from the quality advances pioneered in the Far East. However, not all overseas countries operate to the same quality levels as have become accepted in developed economies. The problem is exacerbated by the difficulty of making specifications unambiguous when a foreign language is involved. Absence of agreed international standards may also be a problem in some cases.

2.2   Price too is a more difficult issue than when dealing in home markets. The specific difficulties of dealing with foreign currencies come to the fore.

2.3   Delivery is likely to be slower and more uncertain. Political instability can wreck even the most tightly controlled schedules, but even without this complication sheer distance must be reckoned with. To compensate for longer lead times importers may order in large quantities, but this leads to high stock levels and associated costs.

2.4   Finally, the complications of international shipping procedures and documentation place additional burdens on purchasing staff. This is also the case in relation to payment methods.

Culture and communications

2.5   One of the more obvious problems in dealing with overseas suppliers is that they are not British! This remark is not intended in any racist or xenophobic sense. It is merely intended to make the obvious point that the residents of a particular country, such as the United Kingdom, share a common culture and a common language, both of which influence their business dealings with each other. When dealing with overseas suppliers it is necessary to adjust to a different culture and language.

2.6   The difficulties here are both technical and behavioural. Technical difficulties concern the simple issue of understanding what is being offered and accepted, and what has eventually been agreed. Behavioural difficulties are related to how people interact with each other and form pleasant and rewarding business relations.

2.7   To deal first with the technical difficulty of communication, it is clearly vital that agreements once concluded are expressed in language that both parties understand. But before that stage is reached oral discussions will take place during which offers and commitments will be expressed that have a great influence on the course of negotiations. Buyers must make every effort to ensure that such discussions are unambiguous.

2.8   It is an essential element in a binding contract that the parties reach agreement. That element is absent if there is misunderstanding: one party believes he understands what the other has said, but in fact has not done so. Even leaving aside the legal niceties, it is clear that successful business relations are endangered if the two parties have different ideas as to what has been agreed.

2.9   Native speakers of English are in a fortunate position in that their first language is widely recognised as the standard language of international trade. However, that should not lead buyers to think that they can ignore communication difficulties. Even if negotiations are conducted in English, it is important to ensure that the supplier understands technical terms and idioms in the same way as the buyer.

2.10   An effort to acquire some understanding of the relevant foreign language can be a great help in this respect. It is also a major step in improving business relations. It is a positive sign that the buyer has made efforts to adapt to the supplier's position and will usually be welcomed even if the level of proficiency is not great.

2.11   This leads on naturally to the less technical and more behavioural problems of dealing with overseas suppliers. As in all negotiations, it is important to make a positive impression on one's business partners. This is more difficult in the case of overseas partners because of cultural differences.

2.12   Many of these differences have been described in the purchasing literature. For example, it is common to refer to Japanese patterns of business behaviour which can cause confusion to British and American buyers.

2.13 One instance of this is the much greater link between social and business relations in Japan; social communication forms a larger part of the negotiation process than is common in Britain or America. Buyers doing business in Japan should not assume that extensive entertaining by their hosts is an unimportant prelude to the main talks.

2.14 Another instance sometimes cited is the Japanese practice of avoiding a direct 'no', so as not to cause embarrassment to their guests. This can sometimes leave a British or American buyer believing that something is still up for debate, when the truth is that the supplier regards it as unacceptable.

2.15 Instances such as this could be multiplied by reference to other countries where business practices differ from those of Britain and America. However, the best practical measure is to benefit from the experience of others. Buyers doing business with overseas suppliers should brief themselves by discussing such points with colleagues who have previous experience. Some of Dobler and Burt's suggestions for dealing with overseas suppliers are listed in Table 12.1 below.

Table 12.1 *Suggestions for negotiating with overseas suppliers*

1.	Speak slowly and ask questions to check understanding.
2.	Print business cards in both English and the foreign language.
3.	Study the culture in advance.
4.	Be prepared for negotiations to be drawn out over a longer period than usual.
5.	Become familiar with local regulations, tax laws etc.
6.	Prepare in advance on technical issues, financing arrangements, cost and price analyses etc.
7.	If possible, ensure that the person recording the discussions is drawn from your team
8.	Arrange discussions so that the other team can 'win' their share of the issues.

Documentation, Customs procedures, payment and legal issues

2.16 The documentation associated with international trade is extensive and often bewildering. This includes documents of title, shipping documents and many types of certificate relating to the goods (insurance, health, quality etc). Of course, not every one of these will apply to every transaction, but the buyer who sources from overseas must certainly reckon on a substantial increase in form-filling.

2.17 Goods imported will have to proceed through UK Customs. This leads to more paperwork, possible delays and a need to master fairly complex compliance procedures.

2.18 The supplier will also be concerned about the method of payment. The buyer would prefer payment to follow delivery and inspection; the supplier may prefer the reassurance of advance payment at least in respect of part of the total. Buyer and supplier must agree on whether open account trading is acceptable (as would be normal between businesses in the same country), or whether more elaborate payment mechanisms must be used. For example, it is common for suppliers to insist on a **letter of credit** issued by the buyer's bank to guarantee payment once the appropriate documents are received.

2.19   There are various ways of arranging international payments.

- **Payment in advance**: simple and low risk for the seller – but high risk for the buyer (and therefore not great 'marketing'...)
- **Letters of credit:** the buyer's bank guarantees payment to the supplier/exporter, once the terms and conditions of the sales contract have been shown to be satisfied (eg by presentation of the bill of lading or other documentation).
- **Bills of exchange:** similar to a post-dated cheque, payable at a defined future date (eg 90 days from the date of creation).
- **Open account trading**: ordinary credit terms, where the seller bears the risk of non-payment. This is only used where there is a good level of trust between buyer and supplier.

2.20   It may be worth explaining letters of credit in a little more detail. The seller's aim in such a measure is to ensure that he will get paid, without the need for litigation (particularly in a foreign jurisdiction). The buyer's aim is to ensure that payment is *not* made until he is sure that the goods have been safely transferred to him. How does this work?

2.21   Two local banks are used as intermediaries. The buyer instructs the *issuing bank* (in the buyer's country) to open credit with the *advising bank* (in the seller's country) in favour of the seller. The seller can draw on that credit (ie obtain payment) at the advising bank, once it has delivered to the advising bank any documents specified by the buyer (eg a clean bill of lading). The advising bank then forwards the documents to the issuing bank, and is re-imbursed for the credit sum it advanced. Finally, the issuing bank presents the documents to the buyer, in return for settlement.

2.22   From the supplier/exporter's point of view, a letter of credit is the most secure method of payment in international trade, as it offers a legal guarantee of payment.

2.23   Finally, the legal systems in the buyer's and the supplier's countries will be different. The parties to an agreement must agree on two important matters.

- Which country's law should apply in the event of a dispute under the contract?
- In which country's courts should any dispute be conducted?

3   Organisations affecting international trade

Tariffs and non-tariff barriers to trade

3.1   International trade is often subject to impediments in the form of taxes and duties (tariffs). There are also non-financial barriers to international trade. The usual reason for such barriers is to protect domestic industry from the effects of overseas competition – a policy called **protectionism**.

3.2   Non-tariff barriers to international trade include the following.

- Quotas – limits on the quantities of specified products that are allowed to be imported
- Complex customs procedures

- The need to comply with different health and safety regulations in different countries

- Government subsidies to domestic producers (which make it more difficult for overseas firms to compete on price)

- Exchange controls – limits on the ability of a domestic importer to obtain the foreign currency needed to pay his overseas supplier

3.3 In recent years there have been efforts to reduce protectionism, and to foster free trade between nations. This is because of the following objections to protectionism.

- It inhibits economic growth.

- It leads to political ill will between nations.

- Protectionism by one country leads to retaliation from other countries. The spiral of retaliation stifles international trade.

The World Trade Organisation

3.4 The WTO (formerly the General Agreement on Tariffs and Trade, or GATT) is dedicated to promoting free trade between nations. Its stated objectives are as follows.

- To eliminate quota restrictions

- To reduce tariff barriers progressively

- To remove restrictive non-tariff barriers to trade

- To ensure that measures applied to one are applied equally to all

- To ensure that any remaining protectionist measures are transparent to all

3.5 A cornerstone of WTO's goals and aspirations is the notion of the most-favoured nation (MFN). This is the principle that whatever advantage, privilege or immunity is granted or restriction applied by one member to another member it shall be granted or applied immediately and unconditionally to all other members.

3.6 For trade agreements with fellow WTO members a non-discriminatory reduction in tariff rates is now possible under the MFN principle. For example, the USA agrees with Germany to lower its tariff on imported machine tools; the new tariff rate then applies to any machine tools from any nation. So, under the MFN rule, we see that a guarantee is given that exporters in such nations will pay tariffs no higher than that of the nation that pays the lowest. In other words, **all** members/countries granted MFN status pay the same tariff rates.

3.7 The work of the WTO influences people's daily life in all sorts of ways. Areas included are quality and choice, the manner in which employment is offered or lost, economic and social policy, distribution of income and the gap that exists between rich and poor countries. Membership stands at around 150 countries.

3.8 The WTO has as a major task to implement trade agreements negotiated under GATT (the so-called Uruguay round of talks). These agreements primarily serve to open markets for:

- agricultural produce

- industrial products

- industrial services, especially banking, communications and tourism

- protection of intellectual property rights, ie designs and copyrights of traded goods.

3.9 The WTO operates as follows.

- At least once every two years a ministerial conference is convened to ensure that the participating countries' trade ministers take responsibility for the organisation's operations and future direction.

- This ministerial conference represents the official body which has overall control of the WTO and is serviced by the General Council, which in turn oversees the functions of the WTO throughout the year. Further, the General Council has a responsibility to offer guidance and take high-level decisions on the activities of three other allied councils: those on Trade in Goods, Trade in Services and Trade-related Intellectual Property Rights, plus their selected subcommittees.

- It is also the responsibility of the General Council to finalise rulings on the other important activity of the WTO: its Disputes Settlement Body, which ensures the functioning of the judicial system of the WTO for trade disputes and breaches of rules; and the Trade Policy Review Body which, among other matters, discusses and publishes regular country reports about trade policies and trade liberalisation. Here there is a significant advancement from when this organisation was GATT in that it can now, in its newly constituted form, impose binding arbitration in trade disputes.

3.10 As with many organisations of this complexity the WTO has certain weaknesses. For many commentators its main weakness is that in overall terms it benefits the rich countries more than the poor developing countries. This situation is further exacerbated because many of the developing countries cannot afford to have a representative in Geneva, where its headquarters is situated, and as a result are at a disadvantage, being unable to participate directly in what is a fairly complex system.

3.11 Another area which comes up for adverse comment is the WTO's actions on trade disputes. Here again, many of the developing countries, which have the most to benefit from such a system, find themselves precluded because they do not have the necessary legal expertise.

The World Bank

3.12 The World Bank is a body including five agencies, the best known of which is the International Bank for Reconstruction and Development. Its aim is to promote long-term economic development, especially in the world's poorest countries. In particular, it helps to finance key infrastructure in developing nations, such as roads and water supplies, and projects to relieve suffering, such as programmes to do with HIV/AIDS.

3.13 The Bank provides grants, technical assistance and loans at preferential rates to member countries who are in difficulty. In return, it requires action to promote democratic ideals, to limit corruption, and in general to modernise and Westernise the political environment within the beneficiary country.

3.14 Voting rights for member countries depend partly on the level of financial contributions to the Bank, which means in practice that the work of the Bank is controlled by developed countries. Critics argue that this leads to insufficient recognition of the needs of developing countries. Despite this, there is no doubt that the Bank is an important contributor to the infrastructure needs of such countries.

The International Chamber of Commerce

3.15 The ICC was founded in 1920 to serve world business by promoting trade and investment, open markets for goods and services, and the free flow of capital. Its activities include the following.

- Assisting in trade disputes by means of arbitration, conciliation and other forms of dispute resolution
- Advocating open trade and market economy systems
- Combating corruption and commercial crime
- Publication of incoterms (see next section of this chapter)

3.16 The organisation's headquarters are in Paris. The permanent staff are headed by a Secretary General, who works with national committees to carry out ICC's work programmes. These committees represent the ICC in their respective countries. They recommend to the ICC their respective national business concerns.

Trade zones and international trading agreements

3.17 A trading bloc is a professional economic arrangement created amongst a group of countries. There are more than 30 trading organisations and blocs across the globe. It is noticeable that trade **within** each of the three major trading blocs (European, Asian and North American) is expanding on a vast scale. However, trading **between** these blocs or indeed with other nations has been on the decline.

3.18 It is convenient to introduce some terminology.

- A **free-trade area** is the least restrictive economic integration between nations. Essentially in a free-trade area all barriers to trade among members are removed. Further, no discriminatory taxes, tariffs or quotas will be imposed. Free-trade areas can also be created by industry sector; a prime example is agriculture. The most well known free-trade area is EFTA (the European Free Trade Agreement).
- A **customs union** is one further step along the chain of economic integration. Like members of a free-trade area, members of a customs union take down barriers to trade in both goods and services among themselves. Additionally however, the customs union establishes a common trade policy with respect to non-members. This generally takes the form of a common external tariff, whereby imports from non-member nations are subject to the same tariff when sold to any member country. Then the tariffs collected by the customs union are shared among members according to a prescribed formula.

3.19 There are numerous trading blocs throughout the world. Here are some examples.

- ANCOM (The Andean Community, in South America)
- ASEAN (The Association of Southeast Asian Nations)
- CACM (The Central American Common Market)
- EFTA (The European Free Trade Agreement)
- NAFTA (The North American Free Trade Agreement)

The European Union

3.20 The main West European trading bloc was originally referred to as the Common Market. A **common market** is a trading group which sets up tariff-free trade among its member nations while at the same time applying a common external tariff to imports from outside the signatory countries.

3.21 Another feature of a common market is that quotas and other similar non-tariff barriers are determined by and for the whole common market. This differs from a customs union, for example, in which individual members regulate to suit their own individual ends.

3.22 Another unique feature of a common market is that commercial law is drafted centrally, which then overrides domestic national laws of member states.

3.23 In Europe, the Common Market was set up in 1957 by the Treaty of Rome. The main provisions of the treaty are as follows.

  • Formation of a free-trade area: the gradual elimination of tariffs, quotas, and other barriers to trade among members.

  • Formation of a customs union: the creation of a uniform tariff schedule applicable to imports from the rest of the world.

  • Formation of a common market: the removal of barriers to the movement of labour, capital and business enterprises.

  • The adoption of common agricultural policies.

  • The creation of an investment fund to channel capital from the more advanced to the less developed regions of the community.

3.24 Much of the co-operative spirit engendered at this time came from the acceptance of what were known as the **four freedoms**. This was seen as being of paramount importance for the overall economic prosperity of the region.

  • Free mobility of goods
  • Free mobility of services
  • Free mobility of labour
  • Free mobility of capital

3.25 In the mid-1980s European integration took rapid advances. After many years of ponderous debate and institutional immobility, the member states concluded the signing of the Single European Act, which was a major revision of the founding Treaty of Rome. It was this enactment that cemented the foundations of the Single European Market, which eventually came into being in 1992. These advances have culminated in much closer integration, signalled by the current title of European Union (EU).

3.26 The most tangible obstructions to a single market evolving within Europe were the physical barriers, namely, customs and immigration posts at border crossings between member states. So the European Commission sought to eliminate internal frontier barriers and controls by 1992. This meant freedom in both the movement of goods and the movement of people. For the purposes of this course we concentrate on the movement of goods.

3.27 Customs formalities, paperwork and physical inspections are commonplace at frontier or border posts. The European Commission took a two-pronged approach to this, which has resulted in the virtual eradication of paperwork at community frontiers.

3.28 First, member states consolidated all paperwork into a standard format called the **single administrative document** (SAD). This paperwork was phased in at the beginning of 1985.

3.29 Second, they virtually got rid of the SAD on 1 January 1993, which resulted in the elimination of some 60 million documents per year, a staggering number of transactions. It was important to have this two-stage approach because to change from what was in existence to practically nothing would have been impossible to achieve in one go.

3.30 The Single Market philosophy applies to services just as much as to goods. Banking and transport are among the markets that have been opened up by European directives.

3.31 Table 12.2 shows some of the important features of the EU.

Table 12.2 *Key features of the European Union*

Feature	Description
Three pillars	The 'three pillars' of the Union are the European Community (covering issues of economics, law and trade), the common foreign and security policy, and the common approach to justice and home affairs.
Economic union	Goods and capital can flow from one member state to another without hindrance. A common currency (the euro) has been adopted by many of the member states (though not yet by the UK). There are no exchange controls or customs barriers.
Mobility	There is a unified transport system with no impediment to movement across national borders. EU members may take up employment in any of the member states (mobility of labour).
Product protection	A single patent office covers all member states. Once a patent is registered it is protected throughout the EU. Common standards of specification exist.
Procurement	Decisions on public procurement in the EU for contracts above a certain value must be based on value for money which is ensured by competition. This particularly applies to tenders, which must be advertised widely. The tendering process must ensure that all tenderers are treated equally, regardless of nationality, by being transparent at all times. In particular, EU directives on this need have focused on public contracts for utilities, non-discrimination in specifications, and objective decision criteria.

3.32 The European Commission negotiates on behalf of the EU within the World Trade Organisation (WTO). Further, it participates in the work of the Organisation for Economic Cooperation and Development (OECD) and coordinates western assistance to the countries of Central and Eastern Europe including the former Soviet Union. To that end it has more than 100 diplomatic missions around the globe.

4 Incoterms

The nature of Incoterms

4.1   When buying from abroad, a purchaser may find himself involved in up to four separate contracts: the actual purchase contract, a contract of carriage, a contract of insurance, and a contract of finance (perhaps involving a letter of credit). The buyer must be able to cope with all of these, despite the language differences that may exist.

4.2   The communication difficulties involved in international trade have long been recognised as a problem. In particular, the interpretation of certain commonly used technical terms is of key importance to both buyers and suppliers, and must be absolutely free from ambiguity. A step in this direction was taken in 1936 when the International Chamber of Trade (nowadays the International Chamber of Commerce) published the first edition of incoterms.

4.3   This publication, which has been updated several times since then, sets out agreed explanations of many of the terms used in international trade to define obligations of seller and buyer. The incoterms were fully revised in line with developments in commercial practice, and republished in September 1999. The current revision is effective from 1 January 2000 and consists of 13 standard commercial terms. Many of these have been used for centuries in international trade and different interpretations had become possible, which are now standardised by Incoterms.

4.4   Buyers and suppliers may contract with each other on whatever terms they think most suitable. They are not obliged to use incoterms. However, by doing so they remove many of the ambiguities that could otherwise be introduced into their agreement. If the agreement specifically refers to an incoterm, both parties understand immediately what their rights and obligations are in that respect. There is minimal danger of subsequent misunderstanding or dispute.

4.5   Parties may negotiate to determine which type of incoterm agreement is most suitable. In doing so the buyer should observe the need to develop a good business relationship on a long-term basis.

Applying incoterms to a contract

4.6   For convenience incoterms are referred to using three letter designators that should be linked with the relevant point where risk and responsibility pass.

Incoterm	Name	Risk and responsibility pass at:
EXW	Ex works ...	named place
FCA	Free carrier ...	named place
FAS	Free alongside ship ...	named port of shipment
FOB	Free on board ...	named port of shipment
CFR	Cost and freight ...	named port of destination
CIF	Cost, insurance and freight ...	named port of destination
CPT	Carriage paid to ...	named place of destination
CIP	Carriage and insurance paid to ...	named place of destination
DAF	Delivered at frontier ...	Named place
DES	Delivered ex ship ...	named port of destination
DEQ	Delivered ex quay ...	named port of destination
DDU	Delivered duty unpaid ...	named place of destination
DDP	Delivered duty paid ...	named place of destination

4.7   The detail that follows is a brief overview of all thirteen incoterms. The International Chamber of Commerce publishes full details.

EXW (ex works) ... named place

4.8   This is the easiest form of export that can be used by the seller. EXW is the price of goods when collected by the buyer. It is free of any delivery charges.

4.9   The obligations of the seller are to place the goods under the contract at the factory gate or other area in the factory vicinity that will enable the buyer to uplift the goods. The buyer must then make all arrangements to uplift the goods from the premises and ship them to the destination at his own risk and expense.

4.10   This term requires the least effort by the seller, but should not be used where the buyer cannot carry out export formalities, when FCA may prove more appropriate.

FCA (free carrier) ... named place

4.11   This term is replacing FOB in areas such as multi-modal, container and through transport ('roll on, roll off' or ro-ro), and for delivery to airports. It is recommended for all modes of transport to a specific carrier or specific destination.

4.12   FCA means that the seller fulfils his obligation to deliver when he has handed the goods over, cleared for export, into the charge of the carrier named by the buyer at the named place. The place stipulated by the buyer could be an inland clearance depot (ICD), rail terminal, berth or freight agent's warehouse.

4.13 The seller retains responsibility and risk until the goods have been handed over to the nominated carrier. This term, introduced in the 1990 revision, is suitable for all transport modes but is particularly relevant for airfreight or sea freight containerised transport (FCL or LCL).

4.14 A further clarification was introduced in incoterms 2000 to enable 'FCA ... seller's premises' where the risk transfers when the goods are loaded. This change was to address a weakness in EXW where the goods are made available but without being loaded. This use of EXW proved impractical in many situations.

FAS (free alongside ship) ... named place

4.15 This term is similar to FCA except that the goods must be delivered to the berth or quay alongside a vessel nominated by the buyer or his agent. FAS leaves the buyer with responsibility for getting the goods from the quayside to the vessel, plus costs after that point. It is often suitable where FOB has previously applied.

4.16 FAS cannot be used where the buyer cannot carry out export formalities, and it can only be used for sea or inland waterway traffic.

FOB (free on board) ... named port of shipment

4.17 FOB is one of the most common incoterms quoted and is suitable for conventional cargo, eg break-bulk. Incoterms 1990 introduced new classifications that are more suitable for container movements, multimodal shipments and specific transport modes.

4.18 Under FOB the seller has responsibility for delivering to the port/vessel nominated by the buyer. The responsibility and risk remain with the seller until the goods have actually passed the ship's rail at the port of shipment. When the 'ship's rail' serves no practical purpose (ie ro-ro traffic or containers) the term FCA is more appropriate.

4.19 FOB can only be used for sea and inland waterway traffic.

CFR (cost and freight) ... named port of destination

4.20 With CFR the seller undertakes and bears the expense of delivering goods from his premises to the port of destination, However, the risk of loss or damage to the goods, and other costs relating to events after the goods are delivered on the vessel, are transferred to the buyer when the goods pass over the ship's rail at the port of shipment, so the cost of marine insurance is borne by the buyer.

4.21 The term is suitable for sea and inland waterway traffic, as CPT could prove more accurate for container or through transport. The seller is required to provide all export documents, ie certificate of origin, export licence, pre-shipment inspection certificates, etc, if required.

CIF (cost, insurance and freight) ... named port of destination

4.22 This term is similar to CFR with the addition that the seller arranges marine insurance to protect the goods for the benefit of the buyer against loss or damage to the goods during carriage. Since it is the seller who enters into the contract of insurance he may choose the minimum level of insurance. The buyer may require a higher level and this should be clarified when drawing up the sales contract.

CPT (carriage paid to) ... named place of destination

4.23 CPT was one of the 'new' terms introduced in the 1990 revision of incoterms and, as such, has been designed to suit the needs of modern business. The term is used primarily for traffic moved by container (including airfreight containers) or any multi-modal method.

4.24 CPT specifies a named place; the relevant risks are transferred to the buyer on delivery to the designated place. The precise place should be considered when drawing up the sales contract. With CPT the seller is responsible for arranging and paying for the transit to the named destination.

CIP (carriage and insurance paid to) ... named place of destination

4.25 This term is similar to CPT with the addition that the seller arranges marine insurance.

DAF (delivered at frontier) ... named place

4.26 DAF is often used for goods being exported to European customers by road or rail but could also be used for other means of transport. The seller reaches agreement with the buyer that the price the buyer pays is for all charges to a specified border point in the buyer's country. The risks remain with the seller until delivery has been effected.

4.27 'Frontier' can be used for any relevant frontier, including the frontier of the country of export, not just the frontier of the country where the goods are destined. In consequence it is vital to determine the 'frontier' for the particular contract.

4.28 The buyer will pay all import costs into his country.

DES (delivered ex ship) ... named port of destination

4.29 With this term the seller delivers by sea or inland waterway to the named port of destination but the goods are not cleared for import – they are simply available to the buyer on board the vessel at the port of destination. The seller pays all costs of taking the goods to the port of destination and is responsible for the goods until that time.

4.30 The buyer needs to arrange unloading, customs clearance and onwards transport, etc. The seller remains liable for all damage and risks until the goods are ready for the buyer on board the vessel at the port of destination.

4.31 DES should only be used where goods are transported by ship or inland waterway.

DEQ (delivered ex quay) ... named port of destination

4.32 DEQ means that the seller fulfils his obligation to deliver when he has made the goods available on the quay at the port of destination, cleared for import. The seller pays all the costs of transport and taxes and delivery charges to this point.

4.33 DEQ is often used with additional qualification such as 'duty paid' or 'VAT paid', making the goods available cleared for importation into the buyer's country. The buyer has to arrange collection.

4.34 DEQ should only be used where the seller is able to obtain relevant import licences (directly or indirectly) and is suitable for sea or inland waterway traffic.

DDU (delivered duty unpaid) ... named place

4.35 The seller agrees to deliver the goods to the final destination (ie the buyer's premises) but not to pay for import clearance, customs duty, VAT, etc. The buyer is responsible for these charges. The buyer carries out customs formalities unless the contract states otherwise. DDU is suitable for all transport modes

DDP (delivered duty paid) ... named place

4.36 DDP represents the ultimate extension of responsibility as a supplier. The seller arranges for the entire undertaking from despatch to final delivery, bearing all the main costs. The advantage to the buyer is that they know exactly what they are paying, particularly if quoted in local currency. The main disadvantage to the seller is that capital costs are tied up until payment is received.

4.37 DDP is the opposite of EXW as it represents the maximum obligation that can be imposed under incoterms on the seller. If the seller cannot obtain an import licence this term should not be used.

4.38 DDP is suitable for all transport modes.

Examples of Incoterms

4.39 Some of the more common expressions defined in incoterms are illustrated below. We use the example of goods produced in Lyons by a French supplier and shipped from Rotterdam to Southampton.

4.40 Goods sold on ex works terms (EXW) are the supplier's responsibility only as far as the factory gate. In other words, the supplier's obligation is merely to make the goods available at his factory or warehouse by the agreed date. 'Ex works Lyons' represents the least possible obligation for the supplier, and the largest possible involvement for the buyer. The price paid covers the goods only, as the buyer must arrange and pay for carriage and insurance. It would be usual for the British buyer to appoint an agent in France to handle this.

4.41 The supplier takes more responsibility under FOB (ie free on board) terms. His obligation is to place the goods in the ship at the agreed port of shipment. He must therefore pay for the cost of transporting the goods to that point, and for their insurance in transit. (Of course, he will pass on such costs in the price he charges the customer.) Once the goods have been placed on board ship, responsibility passes to the buyer. He pays for shipment and for insurance during the voyage.

4.42 The term 'FOB Rotterdam' would be used to describe this in our example. A similar term is 'FAS Rotterdam', which means free alongside ship. The difference is that the seller's obligations end slightly earlier, when the goods are placed alongside the ship at the named port of shipment.

4.43 Even greater obligations attach to the seller under CIF (ie cost, insurance and freight) terms. He must arrange and pay for transport and insurance to cover the goods right to the port of destination, including any unloading charges once they arrive. Again the price charged to the buyer would obviously reflect the additional obligations assumed by the seller. The term 'CIF Southampton' would be used to describe this in our example.

4.44 The above terms, together with the others described in Incoterms 2000, are briefly summarised in Table 12.3.

Table 12.3 *A summary of Incoterms 2000*

Group		Terms of category	Duties of seller/buyer
E	Departure – all carriage paid by buyer	Ex works or EXW	The seller's only duty is to make the goods available at own premises. May assist with transit but not a requirement.
F	Main carriage paid by buyer	FCA, FAS, FOB	Seller will undertake all pre-carriage duties but main carriage arrangements are the responsibility of buyer.
C	Main carriage paid by seller	CFR, CIF, CPT, CIP	Seller arranges for carriage of goods, but once despatched has fulfilled obligations
D	Arrival – main carriage unpaid by seller	DAF, DES, DEQ, DDU, DDP	Seller's obligations extend to delivery of goods at the specified destination; eg seller is liable for damage in transit.

4.45 From the buyer's point of view a very important consideration is the **true delivered cost**, ie the actual amount he has to pay inclusive of all 'add-ons' such as freight, insurance, customs duties etc. Careful study of the applicable incoterms will enable him to calculate this in any particular case.

5 *National and international standards*

National standards

5.1 The content of a specification will be influenced to some measure by national and international norms and standards. These help to ensure that specifications will meet certain accepted criteria of technical or managerial performance.

5.2 Many developed countries have organisations that establish and monitor technical and safety standards. Examples include the BSI in the UK, DIN from Germany, AFNOR from France and NSAI from Ireland.

5.3 Alongside these national organisations, there are similar European bodies. For example, CEN is the European standards committee and CENELEC is the European electrotechnical standards committee. Both these organisations incorporate national standard setting bodies; CENELEC incorporates BEC from the UK, DKE from Germany and ETCI from Ireland.

5.4 CEN and CENELEC in turn form a joint European standards institute, looking at common matters within a single European body, independent from national governments and providing European technical standards (called EN) for publication as harmonised national standards within each member state. Since 1987, CEN and CENELEC have adopted the international standard ISO 9000 as the appropriate European standard, known as EN 29000. This move had a tremendous impact upon industry worldwide as well as for the creation of the European single market in 1992.

International standards

5.5 Another body responsible for harmonising standards on the international front is the International Organisation for Standardisation (ISO). This is a non-governmental organisation whose development began in 1947. Today the work of the ISO in publishing technical agreements in the form of international standards covers over 95 per cent of the world's industrial production.

5.6 The role of the ISO cannot be overestimated given that its work encompasses areas of potential conflict for the buyer trading internationally. Its work at a basic level is concerned with tolerances, technical drawings, recognised symbols and so on, areas which can cause confusion when one country trades with another. Its output is quite staggering; on average it produces some 650 new standards per year and to date has produced in excess of 5,500 standards.

5.7 In addition to its role in the development of global standards, the ISO aims to promote the smooth and equitable growth of international trade. It does this by improving international communications and collaboration amongst its representatives, which now number in excess of one hundred countries. It also operates an information service, known as ISONET.

The ISO 9000 series of quality standards

5.8 The objective of the ISO 9000 standard is to assure buyers that their suppliers are meeting quality requirements. ISO 9000 lays down general principles of control that suppliers must adhere to. A supplier that meets the standards may request certification, which demonstrates to his customers and potential customers that his control systems are satisfactory. However, buyers must still beware: this is not the same as certifying that the outputs from the suppliers' production systems are of a satisfactory quality. This is sometimes expressed by saying that ISO 9000 is a process standard, not a product standard.

5.9 ISO 9000 now appears in its year 2000 version. (You may see references in some textbooks to the previous version, ISO 9000: 1994. The latest version is ISO 9000: 2000.) The series now comprises three quality standards: ISO 9001: 2000 (which lays down **requirements**), ISO 9000: 2000 and ISO 9004: 2000 (both of which lay down **guidelines**).

5.10 What this means is that an organisation wishing to follow ISO 9000 must develop a quality management system that meets the requirements of ISO 9001. In doing so, the organisation may choose to follow the guidelines of ISO 9000 and 9004, but is not obliged to do so.

5.11 An organisation may meet ISO 9000 standards without actually being certified. In practice, though, customers and potential customers are likely to want to see evidence of independent certification. In this case the main stages are as follows.

- Start with a gap analysis to identify where current systems fall short.
- Take appropriate steps to close the gaps.
- Carry out an internal audit to ensure that all ISO 9001 requirements are satisfied.
- Seek certification from an independent registrar.

5.12 ISO 9000 is based on eight quality management principles.

- Focus on your customers.
- Provide leadership.
- Involve your people.
- Use a process approach.
- Take a systems approach.
- Encourage continual improvement.
- Get the facts before you decide.
- Work with your suppliers.

6 *International transportation*

Total costs of transport

6.1 The costs associated with the transport of goods can be high. Their impact may be a significant factor in determining the prices of finished goods for sale to customers. That in turn is important in maintaining and improving the organisation's competitiveness. Purchasing staff can play an important role in controlling transport costs while maintaining service quality, and this makes a contribution to the organisation's profitability.

6.2 One influence on costs is the nature of the goods being shipped. In the case of items which are relatively bulky in relation to their value (such as steel or cement) the cost of transport is often a very significant proportion of the overall price. On the other hand, where items are relatively light in comparison to their value transport costs may be only a small proportion of the total price. This is the case for example in industries such as electronics or pharmaceuticals.

6.3 An even more obvious influence on transport costs is distance: it costs more to move goods 200 miles than it does to move them 20 miles. This is obviously an important issue when sourcing from overseas.

6.4 An important guideline is to focus on the total costs of transport, recognising that there are many elements involved and that to some extent there is a need to balance conflicting objectives. For example, high levels of customer service tend to conflict with low levels of costs. Similarly, if purchasers are content with lengthy transit times in order to keep down direct purchase prices, there may well be consequences in terms of stockholding costs. This is because if lead times are long, order sizes must be large in order to compensate.

6.5   A focus on total costs implies a level of cooperation between different functions such as production and marketing. Purchasing staff must become accustomed to dealing with colleagues from other departments, in effect negotiating with them so as to secure arrangements which serve overall corporate objectives.

Characteristics of transport modes

6.6   The main types of transport mode used by industrial concerns are air freight, rail freight, road haulage, carriage by water (inland or overseas), and pipeline. In addition, certain specialised methods may be used for particular (usually small) consignments: an example is private courier services for delivery of small items where the demand is urgent.

6.7   The design of an overall transport strategy must take account of the particular features and benefits of all of these possibilities. In practice, it is likely that a combination of some or all will be used. In this section we look at each mode in turn and outline the features of each.

6.8   The prices charged by a haulier (whether by road, air, rail or sea) will depend on a number of factors such as the value of the product, the costs incurred by the haulier, the level of competition in the market and a number of less direct factors such as the extent of government regulation.

Air freight

6.9   Air freight has become an increasingly common mode of transport. This is a result of an increase in the number of airports and the number of high capacity jet freighters, combined with improvements in transport links between airports and onward destinations. The vast majority of air freight is still carried in the bellies of passenger jets, in the form of unit load devices (ULDs) which are containers of different customers' goods, put together by freight forwarders. The advent of barcoded 'track and trace' systems means that each item can be monitored and progressed quickly through Customs on arrival at its destination.

6.10   Over large distances air transport usually offers big advantages in terms of speed (important for perishable goods, and also for firms practising just in time principles), but these may be outweighed by high costs. Another advantage of air freight is that it provides a relatively smooth passage for goods. Provided that ground handling is not too rough this gives benefits for transporters of delicate materials. It also means that packaging requirements are minimised, leading to cost savings. This may help to offset the high basic rates charged for air transport. Even so, it is likely that air freight will be confined to urgent requirements and high-value items where the freight cost is a less significant part of overall costs.

Rail freight

6.11   The use of rail freight has declined in the UK over recent decades but it remains a significant option, especially over long intercity routes. This is because of the cost structure of a rail operator. While fixed investment costs are very high, operating costs are low. In other words, once the operator has paid what is needed to get the system in place (rolling stock, rail track etc), the cost of actually running a freight train over a 300 mile journey is relatively low. This makes rail charges competitive with road haulage over longer distances.

6.12 Getting the best value from rail services depends on being able to maximise use of space. Small consignments tend to cost relatively large sums of money; consignments that use the train's capacity effectively are cheaper. This is especially true in the case of heavy, low-grade bulk materials. Containerisation, which we shall look at a little later, has increased the usage of rail freight.

Road haulage

6.13 Over short distances, road haulage usually scores over rail freight in terms of cost. This is especially so if a load is large enough to qualify as a full truck load (benefiting from lower rates) but would not be large enough to qualify for discounted rates by rail.

6.14 Another important advantage of road transport is its flexibility. A lorry is normally easier to load. It can proceed across the country with a minimum of regulation to cope with on the way. It delivers 'from door to door', whereas with rail transport it is often necessary to unload from the train and reload to truck in order to complete the journey. Although it may be delayed by traffic congestion, a lorry will still usually beat the train for speed of delivery.

6.15 Finally, with air and rail freight there is the problem of transport to and from the terminal. This increases the amount of handling involved, which has an impact both on costs and on the safety and security of the materials being carried. Road transport scores well in this respect. Usually, the goods will be loaded at source and then left untouched until unloaded at their destination.

6.16 Road and rail haulage have both benefited from the vast increase in containerised transport, whereby goods are loaded into standard-sized containers at container depots. These are then transported by sea, and they can be attached straight away to road 'tractors' or to trains which pull the container, still unloaded, to the recipient container depot or to the customer.

6.17 Container transport offers:

  • a higher degree of security than previous 'break-bulk' movements;
  • standardised unit load sizes; and
  • the ability to move goods door to door.

6.18 Full container loads (FCL) give the international purchaser the ability to maximise container content by efficient packing design, and they ensure delivery to a nominated place. Less container loads (LCL) can be handled via a freight forwarder or groupage operator who will 'break down' the consignment for on-delivery.

Sea freight

6.19 Carriage by water is by far the slowest means of transportation, whether inland or on international routes. This is partly because of slow speeds, but also because of infrequent sailings. The method does have the compensation of being cheaper than road, rail or air transport. However, the price advantage is not always as great as it seems, because shipping rates do not cover transport to and from dockside. The price element in the equation is most favourable in the case of heavy, low-value materials.

6.20   Since delivery lead times are long, it is normal to use carriage by water only for items where advance planning of requirements is possible. Even then the inflexibility of the method may rule it out. This is because relatively few organisations are close enough to navigable water to make the method attractive.

6.21   As mentioned above, however, transport has undergone a quiet revolution over the past 40 years. The late 1970s and early 1980s saw the introduction of container vessels in international trade. Some major ports (such as Rotterdam, Singapore, and Baltimore) were developed or expanded, while others (such as the Port of London) suffered if they were not readily accessible to the larger container vessels. The major seafreight trading routes between industrialised countries are now dominated by container transport.

6.22   Container vessels operate to regular sailing schedules and this allows the international purchaser to plan deliveries ahead of time. Many organisations, particularly major US multinationals, have now adopted a just-in-time approach to international deliveries allowing for sailing, clearance times and on-delivery.

Pipelines

6.23   Pipelines are of course a fairly specialised means of transport with application to only a few types of goods. Oil, chemicals and water are the main examples. From the purchasing viewpoint this transport medium is in a sense the simplest, since there are rarely any difficult choices to be made.

Choosing a transport mode

6.24   In choosing a transport mode, the buyer must be guided by the general features described above. He must also take into account the need to integrate transport strategy. It is inefficient to be making the decision on transport mode each time a new delivery is in prospect. Better is to lay down general principles, and to incorporate them into deals with a small number of regular transport suppliers.

6.25   To put the basic framework in place the buyer must consider a wide variety of factors, and must relate them to the particular needs of his organisation. Some of the relevant factors are discussed below.

6.26   Perhaps the most obvious factors are cost and speed of delivery. These have already been mentioned. Another obvious point is the buyer's past experience with particular modes of transport for particular goods. Clearly if things have gone badly in the past there is a need to make changes for the future, while good results in the past may suggest that existing methods should be retained.

6.27   The nature of the goods to be carried is also important. Variables include the physical state of the goods (solid, liquid or gaseous), volume, weight, shape, type of packaging, value, perishability, fragility, whether hazardous or not, special storage requirements and special handling requirements.

6.28   The risk of loss or damage is another factor to be considered. Some transport modes are less risky than others, and this may be particularly relevant in the case of fragile goods. If goods are damaged, the buyer's concern will be to obtain prompt compensation, so a record of good claims processing is also a factor that can favour one transport mode above another.

6.29 Convenience and flexibility are also important. If the need is to service a particular destination then the buyer must be sure that the chosen transport mode can reach that destination. In addition, he must be sure that transport schedules enable him to reach the destination in good time. Infrequent sailing or flight schedules may be an obstacle. This is an area where road transport scores heavily for obvious reasons.

Modes of transport in international freight movement

6.30 Basic principles of selecting transport modes apply as much to the importer (or exporter) as to inland traders. However, it is clear that the overseas element adds an additional layer of complexity to what is already a complicated picture.

6.31 To some extent these difficulties can be passed on to someone else's shoulders, at least where imports are concerned. This is because the buyer can opt to purchase on CIF terms and place the responsibility for transport on the supplier. This may indeed happen in many cases, but it is not really a sensible option for purchasers simply to leave transport matters entirely in the hands of their suppliers.

6.32 In cases where an ex works or FOB contract is signed the buyer must take responsibility for at least some of the transport arrangements. Often he will do so by appointing a freight forwarder in the overseas country. The seller then hands over the goods to the freight forwarder and the forwarder arranges transport to the importer.

6.33 In international trading it is common to find that a multi-modal transport choice is appropriate. In other words, rather than completing all the transport by means of road, or water, or air, the firm chooses a combined approach that maximises speed and cost efficiency at each stage of the journey. For example, a load might leave the seller's premises by lorry, be loaded on ship at a departure port, be unloaded onto a train at the port of destination and so transported to the buyer's premises.

6.34 The transport systems actually available in the overseas country (or countries) may impose a constraint on the choice of mode. Both rail and road networks may be limited in less developed countries. Security and work practices can be outmoded and slow.

6.35 The time factor is particularly important in overseas trade, where long distances typically mean slower transit times. Often the only solution is to use air freight, despite its high cost.

6.36 Finally, insurance premiums differ depending on the mode of transport chosen (as well as in relation to other factors of course). Air freight, despite its generally high cost profile, scores well in this respect because damage and pilferage are uncommon.

Shipping regulations

6.37 Each type of transportation is regulated by an international convention.

6.38 In relation to sea transport, the Hague Rules require the carrier to exercise due diligence to provide a seaworthy vessel at the beginning of the voyage. They also require the carrier to care for the goods properly during transit. The carrier's liability is limited to a financial amount specified separately by each of the nations adopting the rules. The Hague Visby Rules (a later development of the Hague Rules) made technical changes to the limit on liability. Further changes in this area were introduced by the Hamburg Rules.

6.39   In relation to air transport, the regulations of the Warsaw Convention apply. This defines a carrier's liability in respect of passenger luggage and cargo. In due course this will be replaced by the Montreal Convention.

6.40   In relation to road transport, the rules are contained in the CMR Convention (don't worry about the full French title!) The carrier is liable for loss or damage unless he can prove that it occurred through certain specified causes for which carriers are not held liable. The carrier may also be liable for delay in delivery.

6.41   In relation to rail transport, the rules are contained in the COTIF/CIM Convention. Like the CMR Convention, this applies only to international carriage (not to domestic traffic). It contains rules similar to those in CMR, though there is a higher monetary limit on the amount of the carrier's liability.

Chapter summary

- Countries engage in international trade because of the comparative advantage they enjoy in producing particular items.

- Local sourcing has some obvious advantages, but these may be outweighed in particular cases by reasons for sourcing from overseas.

- Companies operating internationally must decide between globalisation/standardisation and adaptation to local markets.

- Offshoring refers to the relocation of business processes to a lower cost location, usually overseas.

- Trading internationally gives rise to particular problems for buyers: quality, price, delivery lead time, shipping procedures and documentation, culture and communications, customs procedures, and legal issues.

- Some nations attempt to discourage imports by means of tariffs and non-tariff barriers. The World Trade Organisation has the aim of promoting free trade and eliminating such barriers.

- Other organisations with a role in international trade are the World Bank and the International Chamber of Commerce

- Many nations are grouped into free trade areas and customs unions. For the UK, the most important of these is the European Union.

- Incoterms are standard contractual terms applying in international trade.

- There are a number of standard setting bodies, both national and international, whose work can aid buyers in preparing specifications in international trade.

- Modes of international transport include air freight, rail freight, road haulage, sea freight and pipelines. Often it will be appropriate to use multi-modal transport, ie a combination of different modes.

Self-test questions

Numbers in brackets refer to the paragraphs where you can check your answers.

1   What is meant by countertrade? (1.14)

2   Distinguish between the policies of globalisation and adaptation. (1.15)

3   Define offshoring. (1.31)

4   List suggested techniques for improving negotiating with overseas suppliers. (Table 12.1)

5   What two legal points must be agreed by buyer and seller when they are operating in different countries? (2.23)

6   What non-tariff barriers may impede international trade? (3.2)

7   What is the aim of the World Bank? (3.12)

8   List activities undertaken by the International Chamber of Commerce. (3.15)

9   Distinguish between a free-trade area and a customs union. (3.18)

10   What are the four freedoms accepted within the European Union? (3.24)

11   What is meant by the following incoterms: EXW; FOB; CIF? (4.8ff)

12   What are the eight quality management principles on which ISO 9000 is based? (5.12)

13   What are the advantages of air freight? (6.10)

14   What are the pros and cons of sea freight? (6.19)

15   What convention provides the regulations relating to air transport? (6.39)

CHAPTER 13

Mock Exam

THE EXEMPLAR PAPER

The exam paper below was published by CIPS in 2006 as an illustration of what might be expected under the new syllabus. If you are able to make a good attempt at the paper you should be very well prepared for the live examination.

The examination is in FOUR compulsory questions worth 25 marks each. (*Note that with effect from the November 2009 exam this format will change: see page vii.*)

SECTION A

You are strongly advised to carefully read and analyse the information in the case study before attempting to answer the questions.

The Betterman Hospital Trust

The Betterman Hospital Trust (BHT) is located on five different sites in the Midlands of the United Kingdom. The trust, while being part of the National Health Service (NHS), has considerable autonomy over its own administration, but it has to operate within the budget allocated to it by central government and adhere to public sector guidelines.

Purchasing is conducted independently at each of the BHT's five sites by the senior administrator at that site. The total spend for the trust is £12.5 million per year, hence purchasing is clearly one of the most important parts of the trust's activities, particularly with budgets in the public sector being so tight. It is becoming clear, however, that purchasing needs a much more professional approach than has been the case up to now, and the trust's board of management have decided to appoint a qualified purchasing professional. After following a careful recruitment procedure, the board appointed a professional purchasing manager, Rebecca Lopez. Rebecca has had considerable experience of purchasing in various sectors of manufacturing industry but has no experience of public sector purchasing. However, she hopes to apply some of her expertise from working in a profit focused environment.

Rebecca's first task has been to undertake an initial survey of purchasing activities across the five sites. Her main findings are as follows.

*   Approximately 80% of purchase orders are low-value, consisting of stationery, cleaning equipment, paint, furnishings, and consumables such as syringes and gloves.

*   A substantial percentage of the annual spend is on materials used for the in-house provision of services, in particular cleaning and catering. These two services require a major input of management time.

*   There are about 3,000 product lines, which are purchased from a large number of suppliers. Maintenance, repair and operating (MRO) supplies constitute 90% of the items purchased, but account for only 10% of the value.

*   The supplier base is extremely wide, and in some cases the same item is being supplied by different suppliers across the five sites.

- Much of the 20% of high-value expenditure is on capital items such as x-ray equipment, MRI scanners and computer systems. However, purchasing staff have little choice but to spend the majority of their time on the low-value items.

- Records are maintained manually and procedure manuals are in paper format, as are all supplier catalogues, making it time-consuming and laborious to search for information.

- One of the problems that arises with the more expensive surgical items and equipment is the total lack of standardisation of products. This often reflects the personal preference of surgeons.

- Much of the purchasing is carried out by supplier representatives going directly to users and getting them to place the purchase order without following the official procedures.

- Competitive tendering procedures are widely used in the public sector and where the value of the purchase exceeds a threshold value; the EU tendering procedures should be followed; however, these tendering requirements are frequently ignored.

The by-passing of the purchasing department is a particular problem, for example in the procurement of capital items such as computer hardware and associated software, where several contracts have been placed by a user department for computer systems. In some instances there have been serious compatibility problems as similar equipment has been ordered from various suppliers but with widely different specifications. A further problem has been that the machines were bought against the supplier's quotation with no reference to BHT's terms and conditions, and in several cases no competitive quotations had been obtained. Although Rebecca has only a basic knowledge of public sector procurement practices, she realises that what has happened may not be compatible with public sector purchasing procedures.

Rebecca's initial survey has revealed to her a number of areas where action could be taken to produce greater efficiency and savings, but she has also had some difficulty in understanding the reasons behind some of the practices utilised in this public sector organisation. She also feels that the procurement function should be centralised in one department. There could be an extensive programme to standardise all specifications for goods and services purchased, and some of the services provided in-house could be outsourced. Rebecca now needs to prepare her report to senior management about what she considers to be the way forward for the procurement function within BHT.

The information in this case study is purely fictitious and has been prepared for assessment purposes only.

Any resemblance to any organisation or person is purely coincidental.

QUESTIONS

Answer all questions.

All the following questions relate to the case study and should be answered in the context of the information provided.

Question 1

Appraise Rebecca's ideas for the centralisation of the procurement function and the standardisation of purchasing procedures and specifications across BHT, and make suggestions for a possible structure for the function. (25 marks)

Question 2

(a)   Compose a set of briefing notes for Rebecca that will explain to her how competitive tendering operates in public sector purchasing.   **(15 marks)**

(b)   Discuss the reasons for the widespread use of competitive tendering in the public sector and in particular the use of the EU tendering procedures, and the possible consequences of ignoring them.   **(10 marks)**

Question 3

(a)   Evaluate Rebecca's proposal for the outsourcing of cleaning services for the hospital, indicating clearly the advantages and disadvantages.   **(15 marks)**

(b)   Develop procedures for maintaining performance with potential service providers.
                    (10 marks)

Question 4

Discuss the extent to which Rebecca's skills are transferable from manufacturing to the public sector.   **(25 marks)**

CHAPTER 14

Mock Exam:
Suggested Solutions

Solution 1

Tutorial note: A starting point for a solution to this question is the general discussion of centralisation and decentralisation in Section 2 of Chapter 4 of the Course Book. The solution below aims to adapt that discussion to the particular circumstances of BHT, which is an essential part of your exam technique in dealing with scenario-based questions. Similar remarks apply to the discussion of organisational structure, which are based on Section 1 of Chapter 4, but with adaptation to the particular case.

An important organisational issue is the extent to which purchasing responsibilities should be centralised, ie placed in the hands of a single department reporting to a single executive, in the present case Rebecca.

An organisation such as BHT, operating from five separate sites, may consider a single purchasing function (centralisation) or separate functions at each site (decentralisation). In the case of BHT, centralisation is certainly a feasible option in that all five sites are likely to have very similar purchasing requirements.

A major advantage of centralisation is the greater specialisation that is possible among purchasing staff. If numerous purchasing staff are scattered around five sites, each of them must have general responsibility for a wide range of the site's requirements. General responsibilities lead to general knowledge, and highly specialised knowledge may be absent. By contrast if all the purchasing staff are based at a single centralised location, there is opportunity to divide tasks among them on the basis of specialised skills. Each buyer can focus on a particular area and develop his knowledge to greater depth. This has great benefits when a wide range of complex materials are required by the organisation, as is certainly the case with BHT.

A further advantage is that the requirements of different sites can be consolidated. This reduces the frequency of very small orders for a particular material and enables buyers to obtain better prices and service. The number of suppliers is likely to be smaller, and order administration and processing is more streamlined.

Greater coordination of purchasing activities may result from a centralised structure. For example, uniform purchasing policies and procedures can be introduced and standardisation is facilitated. Staff training and development can be undertaken systematically.

Centralisation generally enables greater standardisation of procedures and specifications, avoiding 'maverick' buying and requirements.

- Standardisation of procedures should enable greater consistency of action and better performance monitoring and management (against consistent measures), while providing better control and improved compliance.

- Standardisation of specifications should enhance quality and efficiency in a number of ways: facilitating the consolidation of orders; larger (but fewer) orders, for economies of scale and reduced transaction costs; a reduced supplier base (with fewer 'specialist' requirements); reduced inventory and handling costs (less variety and greater utilisation); improved quality management (ease of inspection etc); simpler and more accurate ordering; and simpler internal and supply chain communication.

Centralised purchasing suffers from the disadvantage that communication is difficult. However, this can to some extent be countered by developing detailed purchasing manuals, arranging regular visits to sites by central purchasing personnel, and by training courses emphasising group policies. Electronic links are also extremely important in overcoming this difficulty.

There are also some disadvantages of centralising. Buyers are no longer close to users and it is more difficult to develop a close understanding of their needs and problems. Face-to-face discussions may be difficult to organise, and buyers may be slower to respond to local needs. There may be a loss of motivation at local level. Overall, though, the benefits of centralisation appear to be compelling in the case of BHT.

However, it is worth pointing out that the choice is not necessarily between two extreme possibilities. There is a spectrum of organisational arrangements bounded at one end by full centralisation and at the other by full decentralisation. In between, there are arrangements in which some activities are centralised while other matters are decided at local level.

As an example of this, a modern trend in the organisation of a purchasing function is the centre-led action network (CLAN). This is a relatively decentralised model that has become popular in many large organisations. The CLAN model is based on procurement staff located in each of the five sites, reporting primarily to the local management, but with a responsibility to a small centralised procurement centre.

The procurement centre leads the network, sets standards, encourages the spread of best practice and persuades the different elements of the network to cooperate. Often this is achieved by the concept of a **lead buyer**. The lead buyer approach involves delegating defined purchasing responsibilities onto a designated individual within a user department.

Over the long term, BHT might find it beneficial to adopt such a structure, but the currently disorganised state of purchasing suggests an immediate need for full centralisation until procedures are improved to a professional level.

The way in which purchasing tasks are divided among members of staff obviously depends mainly on the size of the department. BHT's purchasing department would be fairly large, and might be organised somewhat as follows.

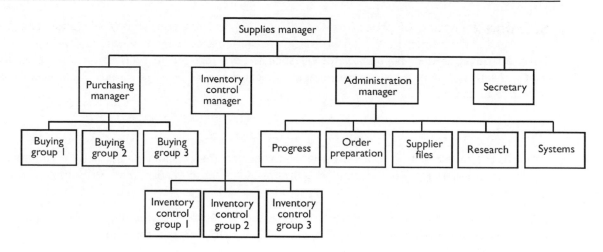

Solution 2

Tutorial note: In the first part of the question we are required to prepare briefing notes. In the solution below we adopt a bullet point format, but note that each bullet point must be fully explained in order to earn the marks.

Part (a)

- In the public sector, once a buyer has specified the product or service he requires, and has decided to use the tendering method, he must ensure that he complies with EU Regulations.

- The Regulations do not apply to private sector purchasing but they do cover purchasing by public bodies, unless their financial value is below certain thresholds.

- Subject to certain exceptions, the Regulations require public bodies to use open tendering procedures.

- They must **advertise** the invitation to tender according to certain rules designed to secure maximum publicity across member states.

- The contract notice advertising the requirement must be published in the Supplement to the European Journal before it may be published in any other media.

- Contracting authorities have the choice of four contract award procedures: open, restricted, negotiated and competitive dialogue.

- For the **open procedure** there is no requirement for pre-qualification of suppliers. Tenders must be issued within six days of request by a prospective bidder. The contracting authority must set the closing date for receipt of tenders no less than 52 days from the publication of the contract notice.

- For the **restricted procedure**, pre-qualification of suppliers is permitted but the contracting authority must indicate in the contract notice a pre-determined range of suppliers to whom tenders will be sent. This must be not less than 5 and no more than 20. The contract notice must allow a minimum of 37 days for prospective bidders to register an interest and submit the required information for pre-qualification.

- Under the **negotiated procedure** where a contract notice is required, prospective bidders must be given a minimum of 37 days to register their interest to negotiate. Where there is a sufficient number of persons who are suitable to be selected to negotiate, the number selected must not be less than three.

- The **competitive dialogue** complements the existing open, restricted and negotiated procedures. It is intended to be used for large complex projects in circumstances where, currently, the use of the negotiated procedure might be considered.

- In general, buyers are obliged to award the contract on the basis of the lowest quoted price, or on the basis of the economically most advantageous tender. If they choose the latter alternative, they must make the fact known to candidates, and must explain by what criteria, and their relative importance, they mean to assess 'economically advantageous'.

- The results of the tendering procedure must be notified to the Office of Official Publications of the European Communities, and these are then published.

- Unsuccessful bidders have the right to a **debrief**, if they so request. This must be undertaken within 48 days of the unsuccessful bidder's request.

Part (b)

The public sector buyer is subject to a high level of accountability. He must ensure that appropriate processes have been followed to acquire best value for the taxpayers' money he is responsible for, and must equally ensure that a full 'audit trail' exists so that his actions and decisions can be vetted. The public sector buyer must ensure that appropriate service levels are achieved in the provision of services to members of the public. These objectives are thought to be best achieved by an insistence on competitive tendering (unless the contracts are very small).

Other objectives of the directives include the following.

- To open up the choice of potential suppliers to public sector bodies, so reducing costs

- To open up new, non-discriminatory and competitive markets for suppliers

- To ensure free movement of goods and services within the EU

- To ensure that public sector bodies award contracts efficiently and without discrimination

The main means by which a breach of the directives may be remedied are by an action by an aggrieved supplier or contractor against a purchaser, or an action against them by a member state in the European Court of Justice.

The remedies include the following possibilities.

- Suspension of an incomplete contract award procedure

- Setting aside of a decision in an incomplete contract award procedure

- An award of damages (in cases where a contract has already been entered)

Solution 3

Tutorial note: You may well be confused by Part (a) of this question and its reference to 'Rebecca's proposal'. No such proposal is even mentioned in the scenario, and we therefore have absolutely no idea what specific ideas Rebecca has in mind (eg what suppliers she has in mind to approach, or even whether suitable suppliers are thought to exist). For this reason it is difficult to relate an answer closely to the circumstances of the scenario, and mostly we must stick to general considerations relating to the pros and cons of outsourcing.

Part (a)

Outsourcing is the ultimate expression of a buyer's attitude to a supplier as an extension of in-house resources. Facilities or functions that were produced in-house – such as the cleaning function in BHT – are instead performed by external contractors working very closely with the buying organisation.

There are many advantages of outsourcing.

- Cost – Rebecca will hope that an external supplier will be able to provide the service more cheaply. The overall cost quoted by the supplier must be compared with alternative suppliers, and also with the cost of in-house provision.

- Increased effectiveness – Rebecca will hope that an external supplier will be able to carry out the function more effectively. It will be important to establish performance indicators so that this point can be reliably assessed.

- Reduction in administrative hassle – we are told that 'a substantial percentage of the annual spend is on materials for the in-house provision of services, in particular cleaning and catering'. The administrative time spent on this could be passed on to an outside supplier.

- Greater focus on core competencies – with more time available, purchasing staff could devote greater effort to the more strategic requirements of the hospital operation.

This last issue gives rise to an important consideration: is cleaning a core competence of a hospital? Research suggests that functions suitable for outsourcing are those that are non-core, and for which suitable external contractors are available. We are told nothing about the availability of suitable contractors, but the issue of core competence has been a hot topic in UK hospitals in recent years. Press reports suggest that some 60,000 patients in UK hospitals will be infected by the superbug *clostridium difficile* (C diff as it is known in the trade). This has been attributed to inadequate cleaning procedures within hospitals, and in many cases the root cause has been identified as the outsourcing of cleaning services.

Clearly Rebecca must give careful thought to the 'core competence' issue before she proceeds further. Even if she satisfies herself that cleaning is non-core, and therefore a candidate for outsourcing, she must still reckon with general problems associated with any outsourcing decision.

- The difficulty of finding a suitable supplier. Eventually, outsourcing will lead to a significant saving in time, but the initial exercise of finding suitable suppliers and 'educating' them in what is required will be a drain on time. And a wrong choice of supplier could lead to severe problems in terms of operations and costs.

- The difficulty of specifying service standards. Drawing up a detailed specification is always tricky, and service specifications are notoriously more difficult than specifications for tangible products.

- Reduced control. A decision to outsource means that internal staff no longer have total control over the operation. Rebecca must satisfy herself that the proposed supplier is a suitable organisation to hand control over to.

- The difficulty of ensuring consistent standards once the outsource contract is up and running. This is the subject of Part (b) below.

Part (b)

At all stages in the relationship, Rebecca will be concerned to ensure an appropriate level of performance from the supplier.

In the period leading up to award of contract, Rebecca's objective is to agree terms that satisfactorily meet the objectives specified in the business case. She will focus on costs, service levels, and the minimisation of risk. Naturally, the supplier will be negotiating hard on all of these elements, and a satisfactory balance must be reached.

Once the contract has been awarded, Rebecca will be concerned to ensure a smooth transition. Ideally, the supplier will immediately begin to perform to the levels of service specified in the contract, but it may be that 'teething problems' are experienced.

With the transition phase over, it will be important that Rebecca sees clear benefits arising. This is the justification of the entire exercise. Benefits may include reduced costs, improved service levels, and reduction in management effort within the buying organisation. To ensure that these objectives are being achieved, Rebecca will need to focus on communication methods, such as reports and review meetings.

As the time approaches for renewal, Rebecca should review the lessons learned at the time of initial contract award. If the relationship has not worked well, it may be necessary to consider a new supplier selection exercise. But if both sides have enjoyed benefits, a renewal of the contract may be appropriate. Even in this case, Rebecca will want to incorporate changes arising from the experience gained over the life of the original contract. In particular, she will want to discuss even further improvements in service levels and/or reductions in cost.

At all stages Rebecca will be hoping to achieve continuous improvement in the supplier's performance, as measured by the service levels specified in the contract. At the same time, the supplier will legitimately be attempting to achieve economies of scale so as to make a fair profit for himself. If it appears that the benefits are not being shared with BHT, this is a point to address at the time of contract renewal.

To ensure that the supplier is performing to the required standard, it is important to identify suitable performance measures. Often these will be specified in the contract.

Needless to say, the measures chosen will depend very much on the details of the particular agreement. But in all cases they will include measures relating to cost and measures relating to service quality.

To define suitable performance measures, Rebecca must focus on the key objectives of the outsource contract. Clearly, the measures chosen must be related to these so that they provide a good indication of how well the relationship is working. It is also important to keep the measurement process simple: a small number of easily understood indicators is preferable to a proliferation of complicated measures.

Communication is also important. The supplier must be aware of the measures regarded as important by BHT. This is an important guideline for him in planning his work so as to satisfy the contractual requirements. He must accept that the measures are reasonable in the light of the contract. And communication is of course a two-way process: if the supplier is already performing similar services for other clients he may be able to suggest suitable performance measures from previous experience.

Solution 4

Tutorial note*: The examiner's answer guidance for this question suggests that a solution should begin with a general discussion of differences between the objectives of public and private sector organisations. This is pure bookwork and can be taken directly from Chapter 1 of the Course Book. We can then go on to identify some of the specific skills that Rebecca will be able to transfer from her private sector background to her new public sector role.*

A major classification of buying environment distinguishes between private sector and public sector organisations. The main influence on strategic decisions in a private sector firm is the achievement of commercial objectives. In most cases, this can be simplified further: private sector firms are profit-maximisers, and managerial decisions are assessed on the extent to which they contribute to organisational profit.

Related to this is the very strong influence of competition. In nearly all cases, a private sector firm will be one of several, or many, firms offering goods or services of a particular type. Consumers are free to choose between the offerings of different firms, and their choices of course have a dramatic impact on the revenue and profits earned by the firms concerned. Securing competitive advantage is a large step towards realising the objective of profit maximisation.

The 'constituency' served by a private sector firm is limited in number – shareholders, customers, employees, all referred to collectively as 'stakeholders' in the modern phrase. This helps the firm to be focused in its strategy: it is usually clear which outcomes will benefit the stakeholders. Moreover, all members of the constituency are there by choice. They could have invested their money elsewhere, or in the case of employees they could have offered their labour and talents elsewhere.

In all these respects, and others, public sector organisations differ from their counterparts in the private sector. The implication appears to be that purchasing in the private and public sectors are two completely different disciplines. However, this is far from the truth and the differences cited above should not mask many essential similarities between the work of the public sector buyer and his private sector counterpart.

One reason for this is that differences in objectives, organisational constraints and so on may not necessarily lead to differences in procedure. For example, public sector buyers may not be seeking to maximise profit, but their concern to achieve value for money is stimulated by other influences, equally strong; in particular, the public sector buyer must achieve a defined level of service within a defined budget.

Similarly, the private sector buyer faced with a profit objective will identify customer satisfaction as a key criterion in meeting the objective. But equally, the public sector buyer will work in an environment where providing a quality service so as to delight 'customers' is an essential part of the organisational ethos. Buyers in both environments will be concerned to a large extent with ensuring quality of output by influencing the quality of inputs. In addition, improving customer service and reducing cost inefficiencies to maximise value for money are now priorities in both sectors!

It is easy to see that many skills used by purchasing staff are as valuable in the public sector as in the private sector. Here are some examples relevant to Rebecca.

- Knowledge of purchasing systems
- Methods of efficiently handling low-value orders
- IT skills
- Inventory management skills
- Knowledge of procurement management and structures
- Ability to negotiate on cost
- Experience of electronic trading
- Experience in drafting contracts
- Knowledge of risk management techniques
- Experience in competitive tendering
- Experience in supplier rationalisation
- Knowledge of ethical sourcing and corporate social responsibility

Subject Index